The Economics of Transaction Costs

Also by P. K. Rao

DEVELOPMENT FINANCE
ENVIRONMENTAL TRADE DISPUTES AND THE WTO
INTERNATIONAL ENVIRONMENTAL LAW AND ECONOMICS
SUSTAINABLE DEVELOPMENT: Economics and Policy
THE ECONOMICS OF GLOBAL CLIMATIC CHANGE
THE WORLD TRADE ORGANIZATION AND THE ENVIRONMENT

The Economics of Transaction Costs

Theory, Methods and Applications

P. K. Rao
Director, Global Development Institute
New Jersey, USA

First published 2003 by
PALGRAVE MACMILLAN
Houndmills, Basingstoke, Hampshire RG21 6XS and
175 Fifth Avenue, New York, N. Y. 10010
Companies and representatives throughout the world

PALGRAVE MACMILLAN is the global academic imprint of the Palgrave Macmillan division of St. Martin's Press, LLC and of Palgrave Macmillan Ltd. Macmillan® is a registered trademark in the United States, United Kingdom and other countries. Palgrave is a registered trademark in the European Union and other countries.

ISBN 0–333–80268–3

This book is printed on paper suitable for recycling and made from fully managed and sustained forest sources.

A catalogue record for this book is available from the British Library.

Library of Congress Cataloging-in-Publication Data
Rao, P. K.
    The economics of transaction costs: theory, methods, and applications /
    P. K. Rao.
        p. cm.
    Includes bibliographical references and index.
    ISBN 0-333-80268-3
        1. Transaction costs. 2. Costs, Industrial. 3. Contracts–Economic aspects.
        I. Title.
HB846.3 .R36 2002
338.5'142–dc21   2002026952

10   9   8   7   6   5   4   3   2   1
12   11   10   09   08   07   06   05   04   03

Printed and bound in Great Britain by
Antony Rowe Ltd, Chippenham and Eastbourne

To my parents

Contents

Preface

Progress in the utilization of the key approach to economic analyses depends largely on the expansion and enrichment of the concept and methodology of transaction cost economics (TCE). This requires strengthening at the analytical and applied levels. A well-defined formulation of the concept provides significant improvements in the usefulness of modern economic theory. The concept and interpretation of 'transaction costs' (TC) currently varies from simplistic to arbitrary in several cases. It goes to the credit of the promoters of the analysis of that, in a span of about four decades, the field has demonstrated itself as an ever-increasing explanatory power for various economic phenomena. The current literature addresses only partially some of the requirements of relevant theory and applications. This book is intended to enhance the usefulness of the theme. It is expected to improve the analytical bases of the role of TC in varied economic phenomena and extend the areas of application. Some of the limitations of the mainstream economic analyses arise from their lack of appreciation of the role of TC in various situations. In fact, there may not even exist relevant data for the purpose of empirical TCE, but that is no excuse for ignoring the important dimension that affects economic behaviour and performance. Various chapters in this book seek to address the need to devise pragmatic economic methods and applications for improving the real world economic systems at different levels of operation.

The comprehensive development of this area of economic science draws upon the existing knowledge base in neoclassical economics and institutional economics, and applied areas of economic analyses such as industrial organization, behavioural economics and environmental economics. The proposed TCE does not conflict with the usage of much of existing economic analysis; rather, TCE complements the latter. This book provides a unique comprehensive analytical as well as applied treatment of the topic of TCE. The relevance and significance of the theme is elucidated with enriched theoretical developments and a wide-ranging spectrum of economic applications.

Some of the 'down to the earth' applications include the choice of alternative forms of economic and managerial (or administrative) governance (including specification of rules of operation and simplification of rules, wherever necessary) of day-to-day activities of life, economic or other. Is it prudent (or pragmatic) to levy income tax starting from the bottom 5 per cent of the population, or to devise the threshold at the 20 per cent level? Is it sensible to seek sales tax returns from all entrepreneurs, or from those who sell at least a critical minimum below which collection of sales tax may be uneconomical? Do we need a dozen standard forms or a couple of proforma to be filled by an applicant to establish his/her eligibility for a loan for an economic activity? Do we design screening criteria based on pre-processed information, or start as if the world has been launched into action today? These are some of the operational questions that TCE is capable of answering better than most other well developed schools of economic thought. A meaningful interface between the ingredients of law, economics and organization is the essence of TCE. There are many more steps to be advanced in this interface, and this book is one more step in that direction, building on some of the infrastructure already developed by a rare collection of thinkers.

Readership of this book is expected to include a wide range of economics professionals, with primary readership comprising economists, graduate students and researchers in economics departments, law schools, business schools and government institutions, from the fields of general economics, industrial organization, law and economics, economic theory and political economy, as well as practising professionals in law, industry and public policy.

I wish to gratefully acknowledge the review comment by Professor Stéphane Saussier of University of Paris I. I am grateful to Palgrave Macmillan for supporting this book project, and I owe special thanks to Ms Nicola Viinikka and Ms Amanda Watkins, Senior Commissioning Editors, for their constant support and patience with my repeated delays in the completion of the project. Mr Keith Povey provided an excellent editorial review. My family remain important contributors to facilitating this endeavour.

P. K. RAO

Glossary

Adverse selection   Whenever there is informational asymmetry between parties, the agents may take advantage of this feature with private information and avail pre-contractual opportunism.

Agency maximand   The internal goal-oriented objective for serving an agency's interest rather than that of the system the agency serves.

Asset specificity   Human, physical, financial or other specific assets that tend to be relevant only for pre-specified applications, and may not be redeployed to alternative applications at any reasonable cost. This feature involves dependencies in contractual or other relations among parties, and implies costs of rigidity of resource allocation.

Asymmetric information   Lack of symmetry or equivalence of the information contents in the decision-making context among parties to a common issue.

Bargaining costs   The transaction costs involved in negotiation between and/or among parties to a settlement or bargain. These include costs of search and collation of information, communicating with other interacting parties, drawing up and revising agreements or contracts, and reaching a transaction settlement. They include the opportunity costs of bargainer's time, the costs of monitoring and enforcing the agreement, and any costly delays and failures to reach agreement when efficiency requires that parties co-operate.

Bounded rationality   Behavioural feature that is 'intendedly rational but only limitedly so'. This arises out of limitations on cognitive ability of humans as well as their interactions with all types of machinery. This feature limits comprehensive foreseeing and handling of some of the complex problems, and suggests that all decision-makers are subject to imperfect information and limited cognition or calculation of optimality in every situation.

Certainty equivalent   The perceived equivalence between a specific fixed sum and an uncertain specified random sum.

Coase theorem   If there are no wealth effects and no significant transaction costs, then the outcome of bargaining or negotiated contract is efficient (apart from distributional considerations), and is independent of initial assignment of property rights or ownership.

Competitive equilibrium A composition of prices, demand quantities and production patterns such that (a) every individual consumes according to his/her own preferences in accordance with utility maximization, subject to the applicable budget constraint; (b) every firm produces goods and services so as to maximize its profits; and (c) the total supply of goods and services equals total demand for the same in any given time period.

Complete markets A set of (idealized) markets for every possible commodity or factor under all states of uncertainty.

Contracts A set of agreements, written or otherwise, that stipulates specific actions of compliance by the parties to that contract.

Implicit contracts Stipulations unwritten but often implied as rules of expected performance among parties to an agreement or transaction.

Relational contracts Incomplete long-term agreements between parties that take into account the features of imperfect and incomplete information, establish provisions for unforeseen contingencies and problem resolution. Private ordering remains a relevant feature governing the existence of these contracts.

Contestable market The market characterized by free entry and exit for potential entrants using the same or similar technologies as in the case of the incumbent firms or economic entities, and having access to the demand and market functions as in the case of the incumbents.

Economies of scope The reduction in total cost that can be attained when a set of products and services are all performed by a single firm rather than by different independent firms.

Efficiency The criterion of maximizing performance with respect to a pre-specified objective such as wealth maximization or utility maximization.

Expected value The weighted average value of all possible realizations of a random or stochastic characteristic, where the weights are the corresponding values of each state of realization (using probabilities that are subjectively or objectively assessed).

Externality Unintended effect of action/inaction of one set of entities on another set of entities, based on direct and indirect interdependencies.

General equilibrium (economy) All markets in an economy are in equilibrium simultaneously, with balanced demand and supply; prices do not vary.

Incentive compatibility The feature in which the provision of incentives to the agents or sub-units enables, *ceteris paribus*, maximization of the objective function of the provider unit/principal.

Institutional arrangement The governance structure between decision-making entities that specifies the nature of interactions at the operational or micro levels.

Institutional environment The rules of interaction and their constraints specified by broader institutions and their governance structures at the macro levels that influence micro level interactions and institutional arrangements.

Institutional reform A rearrangement of institutions and their environment to meet specific objectives of reform.

Institutions A set of formal or informal rules of interaction and governance of resources of all types; these are stipulations that structure political, social and economic interactions, and consist of both formal rules (as in the laws and regulations) and informal constraints (such as customs and traditions). Formal and informal institutions may also be described as two partly distinct categories.

Internalities The goals that apply within non-market organizations to guide, regulate and evaluate agency performance or its human capital.

Market An institution with its rules governing buying and selling of goods and services as a forum of organized exchange.

Market failure Failure to achieve efficient allocation of resources, because of one or more of the problems such as externalities, missing markets and increasing returns.

Moral hazard The process of post contractual opportunism in the presence of informational asymmetries between parties.

Nash equilibrium A strategic situation in which a specific strategy in a set of strategies corresponding to each player of a game is the best for each participant, in light of others' strategies; these later elements are based on available information – complete or incomplete. This characterizes desirable features for an equilibrium, since no player may have an incentive to deviate from such a situation.

Network externality The feature that the effects of the existence of a network (physical or other) itself influences the nature of interactions between members of the network and those outside the network. Network membership need not be formal for the purpose of this phenomenon.

Optimality Maximization or minimization of an objective function subject to a set of constraints over a defined time horizon.

Organization An operational arrangement involving staff and functionaries within an institutional setting. Thus an organization is a part of an institution but not vice versa.

Pareto optimal A situation from which any deviation could not increase the welfare of any party without decreasing that of one or more other parties.

Pecuniary externality The externality that focuses on the effects through the functioning markets and the price mechanisms.

Price dispersion The simultaneous existence of multiple prices for a given commodity in a competitive market.

Private ordering The mechanisms created among decision-making entities in response to adaptive and sequential decision-making between relatively autonomous parties (belonging to a contractual arrangement or otherwise) for information sharing, co-operation, dispute resolution or other interactions not formally dictated by the law.

Relational contracts These are agreements between parties that take into account the features of imperfect and incomplete information, and establish provisions for unforeseen contingencies and dispute resolution. Private ordering remains a pertinent governing feature for the existence of these contracts.

Risk-neutral The feature that a decision-maker is indifferent between a fixed sum of payment or a risky prospect which has its expected value equal to the fixed sum.

Technological externality The effects of the process in which the production function of a firm has in its influences the inputs and outputs of other firms; that is, the technological possibility of one firm affected by another's activities.

Transaction   A transaction describes one or more of the following: (a) exchange of commodity or service, through market or other institutional arrangement; (b) transfer of rights and/or duties among parties; (c) activity undertaken or chosen to be not undertaken by an entity, whether legal or otherwise; and (d) the largest unit of economic activity that cannot be subdivided for the purpose of transacting between two or more economic agents/entities.

Transaction costs   (a) costs of undertaking a transaction, including search and information costs, bargaining costs and monitoring-enforcement costs of implementing a transaction; and (b) the opportunity costs of non-fulfilment of an efficient transaction.

Wealth effect   The variation in the amount an economic agent is willing to pay for an object at a particular price as a consequence of change in the wealth of the economic agent.

Part I
Theory and Methods

Theory and Methods: Introduction

The economics of transaction costs (or transaction cost economics – TCE) remains a largely unexplored area of economics. This results from a number of factors including, but not limited to, the following: limited contributions currently using mathematically fashionable and precise characterizations of economic insights (in a world where it is more impressive to know if one is precisely wrong than approximately right); lack of an all-purpose computable technical methodology leading to quantitative prescriptions of economic parameters; and considerable focus of TCE on the relative roles of institutions and organizations that may generally be less than flexible to the design of an institution or organization as a matter of choice. Clearly, some of these constraints in the advancement of the science of TCE are not founded on potential weakness of the approach itself. Rather, a less than perfect world where some 'rational' choices are beyond the purview of any analysis imposes limitations on the application of TCE. However, this is not to claim that the state of TCE is such that it is ready to prescribe a panacea for all shortcomings of economic systems, if an opportunity for the application of TCE arises. On balance, both the foundations of TCE and its usage in appropriate economic problems have to make further advances; this will create benefits of knowledge and its productive use in economic systems.

Part I of the book lays the foundations for a variety of practical applications of TCE, and seeks to reinforce the roles of TCE and neoclassical economics (NE) in the context of economic problem-solving. This provides a comprehensive approach that is more realistic for real-world economic configurations and their governance. A wide-ranging set of issues will be examined in this book. After a review of different concepts and assumptions related to the approach of TCE, a comprehensive

3

analytical framework for formal economic analysis is advanced in Chapter 1. Later chapters of the book address key issues such as the role and limitations of the widely known Coase theorem; relationships between economic externalities and transaction costs; the roles of uncertainty and asymmetric information in the size-distribution of transaction costs; recognition of the complementary roles of new institutional economics (NIE) and neoclassical economics (NE); the relevant modifications in some of the standard approaches and results derived from NE; and an integration of the latter with TCE to provide new neoclassical economics (NNE).

The main elements of industrial organization, one of the pillars that motivated the development of TCE, are presented briefly in Chapter 2. After summarizing the fundamentals of Coasean economics, the widely deliberated Coasean propositions are reviewed critically in Chapter 3. The interlinks between economic externalities and transaction costs, and between information economics and TCE are also examined in this chapter.

Chapter 4 deals with some of the aspects of new neoclassical economics that integrates standard neoclassical economics with TCE and, more generally, with NIE. The classical principles of economic efficiency based on marginality conditions or of economic optimality based on simplified assumptions are reviewed, and new perspectives offered. The distinctions in the analysis and policy prescriptions of traditional NE and of the new integrated approaches are examined in the broad areas of economic growth and development, economics of free trade, cost–benefit analysis, and the economics of international credit lending with conditionalities for reforms. Chapter 5 provides an overview of NIE, an area of increasing significance for application in the design and analysis of institutions. Besides the fundamental issues of economic and institutional governance with markets and government apparatus, the issues of behavioural economics such as trust and co-operation are also examined in this chapter.

1
Background

1.1 Introduction

The economics of transaction costs is often seen as a specialized area confined to application in some cases. However, it is a misnomer that this theme is confined only to cases where some costs are to be considered explicitly or weighed in for decision-making. The general approach of this area is one of comparative economic analysis, where there is economic efficiency enhancement with due consideration of comprehensive and practically significant costs; these transaction costs (TC) and their behavioural implications are added dimensions relative to traditional and simplified economic analysis. Clearly, any real-life economic problem includes complex factors and interlinks. To offer an overly simplified solution is sometimes counter-productive. Broader comprehension than is done in much of traditional economic analysis is called for, and this is feasible with the application of transaction cost economics (TCE). The approaches of new institutional economics (NIE) tend to subsume those of TCE, but the latter by itself is potentially capable of providing relevant insights. TCE should be used in conjunction with, but not to the exclusion of, other relevant economic approaches, as Williamson (1985) suggested.

The fundamental premise of TCE is that transaction is the basic unit of analysis, and that economic governance is a prerequisite for economic resource optimization and enhancing economic efficiency. TCE, even its most vociferous critics seem to agree, contributed to an important aspect of economic reasoning and thinking: recognizing that transactions entail exchange costs and that these matter at all levels, in both the short and the long run. TCE has been an important contributor to the development of the economics of organizations, industrial

5

economics and the study of modern political economy. Various TCE approaches provide insights into aspects of economic governance, including *ex ante* provision of incentives for performance and *ex post* arrangements for institutional governance. These, in addition to several other important areas of application, are explained in later chapters.

Much of the economic debate treats, rather simplistically, alternative choices of economic governance in terms of markets and government institutions. This can lead to misleading diagnosis and policy prescriptions if we ignore the fundamental role of TC in alternative forms of institutional and organizational design. Dogmatic ideology paves the way for pragmatic methodology in resource management with proper understanding of the role of TC in each economic configuration, and for rational economic decision-making that allows for adaptive and flexible approaches in tune with realistic features of the economic system.

The primary concern of this chapter is to lay down various concepts and assumptions underlying TC, main approaches and their interpretations, a comprehensive framework, and analytical methods for TCE with an eye to applications in practical economic governance issues. In this coverage, a few important aspects of TCE that are complementary to the presentation are also included. Among these are analytical issues such as the existence or otherwise of a Paretian welfare function under uncertainty, problems of bounded rationality and behavioural roles of incentives and asymmetric information, and the operational problems of measurement and information.

1.2   Transaction costs: concepts and assumptions

TCE is an approach to the study of economic systems and organizations, the comparative merits of alternative forms of economic organization (often called assessment of discrete structural alternatives) with its focus on microanalytic and behavioural assumptions governing the statics or dynamics of economic agents and institutions, and based on an integrated perspective of institutions, the law and economics. Perhaps this sounds ambitious. The spectrum of dimensions that are sought to be addressed provide potential for robustness of analysis, sometimes at the expense of the precision of analytical models and empirical solutions. The emphasis is on seeking economic solutions to less than hypothetical and more real-world problems, involving comparative assessment of potential and actual choices.

The classic contribution of Coase (1937) marked the beginning of the recognition of the role of TC in the theory of the firm as well as its extensions to other forms of economic institutional governance. In the TCE framework, firms are viewed as governance structures rather than as mere production–distribution entities. A similar approach extends to all institutions. Coase's (1937) foundation provided an insight into the emergence of firms and markets, with a clear focus on the role of exchange costs in the related interface. Coasean insights have engaged a stream of continuous investigation ever since. Firm-level decisions, especially those regarding internal production and contracting out (or outsourcing of goods and services), business decisions in terms of choice of activities under vertical and horizontal integration of business activities (including economies of scope and economies of scale – which will be explained later) have been assessed in terms of incidence of their relative TC in addition to traditional direct costs. Thus, make or buy decisions at the firm level have been influenced to a large extent by the role of perceived TC. Several empirical studies (see some examples later in this chapter) also confirmed these aspects, and thus the influence of TCE is verified.

Almost all areas of economic activity are governed by the influence of TCE, although some are not documented as such. It must also be noted at this stage that economic activities are not expected to be designed with the intention of minimizing TC, but rather to be optimized with due consideration of relevant and legitimate constraints. Misapplication of TCE in terms of seeking to minimize the TC of a set of transactions could be a major contributor in enhancing TC when the system as a whole is considered. Partial analyses that do not consider the interlinking systems can lead to lopsided TC minimization.

What are transaction costs

Among the modern origins of the appreciation of the role of TC is the contribution of Arrow (1969, p. 48): 'market failure is not absolute; it is better to consider a broad category, that of transaction costs, which in general impede and in particular cases block the formation of markets'; such costs are the 'costs of running the economic system'. The main approach of TCE is, as Williamson (1989) suggested: assign attribute-differentiated transactions to governance structures (which depict differing competencies and other potentials, and associated costs) in a transaction-cost-minimizing manner. TC were interpreted broadly (ibid., p. 142) as the 'comparative costs of planning, adapting, and monitoring task completion under alternative governance structures'.

In another perspective, North (1990, p. 27) described these as 'the costs of measuring the valuable attributes of what is being exchanged and the costs of protecting rights and policing and enforcing agreements'. These definitions indicate the priority of the focus of TCE on the institutions and evolution of governance structures in relation to the role of TC. Furubotn and Richter (2000) suggested that TC include the costs of resources utilized for the creation, maintenance, use and so on of institutions and organizations. Mere focus on the costs of information and related organization are sometimes insufficient to comprehend the totality of costs. This book adds a new dimension to the concept and includes opportunity costs of alternative costs of organization of a policy, programme or activity. Relevant details are given in section 1.5 below.

In one of the classifications (Milgrom and Roberts, 1992), there at least two categories of TC. The first type of TC arise from informational asymmetries and incompleteness of contracts among parties. One of the best examples for this is the government in relation to the public. The second type of TC arise from imperfect commitments or the opportunistic behaviour of parties. This is related partly to legal and social norms as well as the provision of verifiable commitments (see Chapter 6 for a more detailed discussion).

TC bring to the surface the issue of economic (and political) organization as a problem of formal and informal (or explicit and implicit) contracting. TC include: *ex ante* costs of negotiating and forming a contract or agreement, *ex post* costs of monitoring and enforcing a contract or agreement, and search and information costs. It is important to recognize that the two sets of cost elements are usually interdependent, and hence an attempt to minimize one set of TC should also consider the corresponding implications for the entire vector of cost elements. It is not uncommon that lopsided approaches to these cost-reducing problems result in net additions to costs, direct and indirect. For example, in order to reduce the costs of violations by individuals or other entities, one might conceive of greater 'powers' for the law enforcement machinery, but this could imply greater liability costs (at the administrative unit level) or victimization costs (at the society level, based on social costs) later when the enlarged scope for exercise of power is accidentally or intentionally misused.

Among the major categories of transaction costs are: market-based, administrative and/or managerial, and political. Market TC consist mainly of costs of information, bargaining/negotiation over transactions, contracting (formal or informal), monitoring and enforcement of agreements, and search and information costs. In order to carry out a market transaction, it is relevant to discover the corresponding participants in the transaction, to conduct negotiations or communications leading up to an agreement or contract, to draw up the contract (formal or otherwise), undertake relevant monitoring and enforcement activities and so on (Coase, 1988). Managerial TC comprise the costs of setting up or establishment and/or adaptation of organizational features, costs of operating an organizational entity, including those of information gathering and processing as well as alternative modes of resource deployment. Political TC are quite general, and need to be specified in terms of system characteristics for specific assessment. In general, these could also be conceived as a set of costs of broader institutional configurations within which other institutions and organizations exist (or are allowed to operate).

An important perspective of TC assessment arises from the role of *ex ante* versus *ex post* cost considerations in the TC components. The former set of costs includes costs of information gathering, negotiation and decision-making, and the latter set includes the costs of monitoring and enforcement, including those of remedial measures for deviations from pre-specified agreements and contractual provisions (explicit and implicit), costs of misalignments and maladaptation of transactions that drift out of agreed specifications or alignment, and costs of dispute resolution. The agreements and contractual provisions are not confined to designed contracts as per one or more contract laws; rather, these include the role of the government as an institution under an explicit and implicit contract with the public in terms of its expected role and functions. It must be noted that the two sets of costs are usually interdependent and therefore must be addressed simultaneously rather than sequentially or separably (Williamson, 1985). An important complex issue here must be noted: in many scenarios, economic agents cannot a priori assess the cost differentials accruing to alternative economic arrangements' *ex ante* costs, much less the *ex post* costs.

TC involve the use of real resources that could be deployed alternatively (more or less productively) elsewhere in the economy or the socioeconomic system. TC are pervasive at all levels and types of activity (and inactivity) or transaction: costs of establishing, maintaining, adapting, regulating, monitoring, devising enforcing rules, and executing transactions (Furubotn and Richter, 2000). In a broader generalization, opportunity costs of specific misallocative activities or transactions can also fit into the category of TC.

Measurement costs, administration and TC

Dahlman (1979, p. 161) argued that, in a rational economic decision-making sense, the Coasean approach to TCE leads to the position that 'institutions fulfill an economic function by reducing transaction costs and therefore ought to be treated as variables determined inside the economic scheme of things'. While the latter part of this assertion holds good, the former must be interpreted carefully. Institutions can be designed to reduce TC, but often they are not. Regulatory administration is often an outstanding example of the public system that seems to require the application of TCE principles for economic reform in many countries.

One of the major components of TC is measurement costs in a non-standardized measurement system. These are sometimes called 'costs of exchange'. Attempts to assess these costs empirically in any specific situation and corresponding specific transaction are illustrative of the critical role of this component of TC in the processes of economic governance in public systems. In many public systems, the archaic bureaucracy, its inertia and private motivations are only part of the explanation for the existence of high TC to the detriment of economic growth and prosperity of societies. Benham and Benham (2000) summarized a few studies and illustrative examples. Three cases are described below:

(i) In Egypt in 1996, the official published price for a new telephone connection was $295, and the official published 'urgent response' price was $885. The proxy for the opportunity costs was estimated as the difference in the apartment costs of identical nature with and without pre-existing telephone service. This ranged from $1180 to $1770, reflecting the existence of significant TC.

(ii) In Lima, Peru in 1983 a team of researchers examined the costs of obtaining a business licence to start a garment factory. The study showed that an average person would need to spend 289 days sifting through and complying with complex procedures to set up a factory legally, yet the outcome might not always be assured without corrupt practices.

(iii) Regarding the average waiting time (in 1989) to clear shipped items already in port, it took 15 minutes in Singapore, and 7–14 days in Tanzania.

Published data seldom offer clues to the true costs of goods and services in many countries and several public systems. In many developing countries, the price for the provision of a service has several components, both documented and undocumented. The costs of bribes include, for example, not only the amount of money changing hands, but also the additional costs of arriving at that particular transaction-specific equilibrium: the time and resources required to negotiate and implement the illegitimate compensation.

Besides this, there are the additional costs of paying for the services or goods themselves: time and resources also need to be deployed to pay the official billing for services such as public utility electricity – this is not as simple as receiving a bill and paying it through the postal system. Several million days are lost in attending to the latter activity in many developing countries. Accordingly, the opportunity cost of measuring opportunity is likely to to be high, as suggested by Benham and Benham (2000).

Information costs and TC

The role of information costs (which may be deemed to be extremely high in situations of substantial incompleteness of information) in TCE is important both in direct cost terms as well in their impact on the economic behaviour of economic actors or entities comprising a combination of heterogeneously placed decision-makers. Dahlman (1979) suggested that the Coasean definition of TC in terms of search and information costs could possibly be dubbed simply as costs of imperfect information. This suggestion falls short of the recognition of the entire span of elements of TC, especially the differential costs and behavioural implications of each of the elements of TC. Thus it is not accurate to simplify TC merely in terms of information costs.

In another notable contribution, North (1990) implicitly assumed TC to tend to zero as information is perfect and symmetrical among parties. He stated: 'The costliness of information is the key to the costs of transacting, which consist of the costs of measuring the valuable attributes of what is being exchanged and the costs of protecting rights and policing and enforcing agreements' (p. 27).

However, in a later assertion, he concluded: 'Transaction costs arise because of the costs of measuring the multiple valuable dimensions involved in exchange (broadly, information costs) and because of the costs of enforcing agreements. Information is not only costly but incomplete, and enforcement is not only costly but imperfect' (North, 1995, p. 68).

Measurement of various relevant features and the acquisition of information is often as difficult as the task of economizing on these. This is because the costs of measurement and acquiring information are often unknown in advance. This another problem of incomplete information and decision-making with bounded rationality (see below for more details).

Major features of TC

The most important dimensions of transactions may be identified; these include complexity, frequency of occurrence, duration or continuity, uncertainty, measurement and monitoring features, and implications on interlinked transactions.

Among these, some features run in parallel: asymmetric information and incomplete specifications of transactions and their commitment implications, and imperfect commitment or strategic behaviour at different stages of transaction implementation (*ex ante*, *ex post*, and during the negotiation of an agreement on a transaction).

Bounded rationality, opportunism and asset specificity are identified as three main factors that lead to the existence of TC (Williamson, 1985). This assertion is not established in the form of rigorous economic analysis, but is largely supported in the logic of further developments in TCE. A detailed explanation of the bounded rationality feature is given in section 1.4.

Opportunism refers to the behavioural aspect: 'self-interest seeking with guile' (ibid., p. 47). Williamson's (1985) specifications are rather vague in this context: 'opportunism refers to the incomplete or distorted disclosure of information, especially to calculated efforts to mislead, distort, disguise, obfuscate, or otherwise confuse'. Contractual specifications are often inevitably incomplete in relating to specific performance requirements of parties to the contract under various known and unknown contingencies. The incomplete contracts perspective lays the ground for the prevalence of opportunism, both pre-contractual and post-contractual, in most situations. Accordingly, strategic incompleteness of contracts is also an action one or more parties indulge in at the stage of contract formation *ab initio*. The prospect of *ex post* negotiation tends to influence choices at that stage as well.

The economics of information uses the concepts of moral hazard and adverse selection to describe the behavioural traits in the presence of asymmetric information among parties to an agreement or other transaction. Moral hazard is a problem of post-contractual opportunism in the presence of unobservable asymmetric information, and adverse selection is the phenomenon of misdirecting other parties based on a party's private information that is not shared with other parties in the transaction – thus constituting an aspect of pre-contractual opportunism. In general, opportunistic behaviour contributes to loss of efficiency and leads to enhanced TC.

Asset specificity refers to the extent to which non-fungible assets are tied to particular transactions specified by contracts or other commitments. Assets are specific to a particular use if the 'returns' they provide are much more highly valuable only in that use, relative any other alternative uses. As an illustration, when copper wiring used for energy transmission is stolen for its melted copper value, the asset specificity is lost – even if the entire metal is restored. The degree of specificity of an asset may be assessed in terms of the investment value that is lost when the asset is switched from its intended use to an alternative use (usually a less efficient and/or less valuable use).

Dietrich (1994) suggested that some of these definitional aspects may not be entirely consistent with the assumption of bounded rationality, and traces the confusion to the distinction between parametric uncertainty (a technical and non-strategic element) and behavioural uncertainty (a strategic element). A major assumption invoked in TCE is that of the risk-neutral attitude of economic agents, as explained below.

A number of transactions fit into the category of intermediary product groups. Williamson (1985) argued that entrepreneurs (owners) in this class diversify risks to a fairly high degree to arrive at risk-neutral positioning. Where this assumption both facilitates and captures features of most transactions, non-compliance or exceptions can be handled separately.

The critical issue is of the differential risk acceptance attitudes of economic agents and their implications for TC. Averages in many cases may not provide the relevant insight into the tasks of economizing on TC.

Empirical studies in TCE

Over the years, and especially since the 1980s, several empirical studies have been carried out that tested the predictive nature of results and insights of TCE. As a result, this stands on a firm footing relative to several other areas of economics. The centrality of TCE for the purpose of empirical studies is to assess the merits of alternative organizational arrangements, and TC cannot be observed for organizational forms that are not in vogue. In the absence of valid bases for comparison, claims regarding the efficiency of one or other of the forms of existing organizations as TC minimizers are often easy to make and difficult to refute. The issue then is one of approximating observable and unobservable features that distinguish alternative forms of organization, and verify them using testable hypotheses. Masten (1996) also pointed to econometric estimation problems such as simultaneity and selection biases, but these are not confined only to issues of TCE. A number of studies have been cited in Masten (1996); several of these focus on vertical integration in industry.

Monteverde and Teece (1982) were among the first to test systematically contractual interpretations of vertical integration. Asset specificity was seen as an important determinant of vertical integration. This finding was upheld consistently in a number of studies that followed in the automobile, electricity and other engineering industries; see, for example, Joskow (1988). In an empirical study of the mainframe computer industry for the period 1950–70, the period covering the industry's formative and growing stages, Krickx (1995) found that TC played an important role in contributing to the process of enhanced vertical integration for integrated circuits in the industry.

The choice among alternative quantity and price-adjustment processes, efficiency of incomplete contracts, the choice between lump sum and variable pricing, licensing versus sale of patented technology, choice of long-term contractual terms, franchising and employment contracts are some of the many functional areas of application using empirical studies. Klein and Shelanski (1995) and Masten (1996) provide good lists of empirical studies in various areas of application. In the marketing area, applications are surveyed in Rindfleisch and Heide (1997).

Critical view of TCE

Among the critics of TC, Fischer (1977) believed that TC have a 'well deserved bad name as theoretical device', and the reason advanced is worse than the allegation: '—because there is a suspicion that almost anything can be rationalized by invoking suitably specified transaction costs'. Suspicion does not constitute reason enough for a judgement. Besides, it was not the theory but the measurement of TC that posed significant problems in forging ahead. Given the complexity of the issues to be handled, TCE cannot offer elegantly simple formulae, nor do much of the data exist in standard accounting practices. The situation has changed during recent years, however, with greater advancements in both theory and empiricism, and more progress seems attainable with a reasonable combination of different economic approaches to real-world issues of economic governance and resource allocation. TCE attempts to integrate more fields from other social sciences than traditional economics ever recognized. A comprehensive approach to TCE, explained later in this chapter, and in Chapters 3 and 4, provides some of these directions.

Among recent critical reviews of TCE is Slater and Spencer (2000) who suggested:

(i) Internal organization for TC economizing can be of short-term significance only, and, in the longer term, as TC become negligible, 'all transactions could be carried out through the market, and the need for complex governance structures would be eliminated' (p. 80);

(ii) TCE adopts a 'closed-system approach', sidesteps radical uncertainty, and 'opts instead for a form of conservative certitude wherein there exists no possibility for fundamental change under existing (capitalist) institutions' (p. 82);

(iii) Lack of explicit time-dependency, or in effect static description, is considered to be another limitation of much of TCE; and

(iv) There cannot be a persistent role for TC if the fundamental role of uncertainty is not properly recognized and reflected in the analysis.

These criticisms and concerns may be addressed briefly. TC are not negligible either in the shortrun or the long run, hence the role of adaptation is considered within the framework of TCE. It is usually not within the realm of TCE to address major political reforms and corresponding institutions. No branch of economics can possibly accomplish a prescriptive analysis in this regard as it overlaps several aspects of political and social life. Explicit time-dependency is very much within the TCE framework (as this chapter later clarifies). Similarly, the role of uncertainty is one of the important considerations within the TCE formulations, though some do not use formal models explicitly for this purpose.

The dynamic multi-period economic system differs from a static system not only in terms of the number of time periods but also in terms of what happens in between those time periods: the roles of adaptation of agents and economic entities, smoothing the effect of random shocks and other disturbances in different intervals caused by system uncertainties, and changes of strategy from one time period to another in a strategic setting. Formal models of TCE do not seem to have arisen to incorporate these features so far, but these can be developed and tested empirically when an optimization approach similar to that suggested later in this chapter is developed further.

1.3   Fixed costs, variable costs and transaction costs

Fixed costs are specific investments deployed, including for the creation of organizational or other infrastructure, in order to facilitate transactions – usually dependent of the volume of the transactions only in certain ranges (and not as a continuous variable). Variable costs depend directly on the number and type of transactions. These notions apply to traditional cost components as well as those of TC. TC specified as a fixed known proportion of costs of transactions is a trivial specification and does not warrant the special role of TCE. Since TC are not always independent of production costs, the estimation of the former warrants the estimation of the latter in most cases.

Economizing on costs is taken to include economizing on production costs in a given mode of production and institutional setting, and economizing on TC with respect to pragmatic potential alternative organizing relations of the production economy. Here production need not imply a typical physical resource-based system; it includes a wide variety of input–output relations, including those of governance of an economic or related entity.

Are TC also classified in terms of fixed costs and variable costs? The answer is in the affirmative, and these cost elements are not to be confused with the traditional counterparts that usually figure in production cost economics and other economic systems. When we refer to cost minimization it is usually with reference to all the components of costs, traditional as well as TC. The following section illustrates the role of monetary as well as non-monetary approaches to the assessment of TC.

Money as medium of exchange and TC

TC concepts are in general in relation to market-based cost considerations, but nothing in the approach and methodology of TC relies on the existence of a functioning market system for deploying the relevant rationale of decision-making in terms of TC considerations. Thus TC could also be formulated in terms of costs based on non-market factors. The common numeraire for potential ranking of alternatives need not be based on monetary metrics. The comparison of multidimensional 'costs' can pose problems of vector ranking and agreements on potential trade-offs among competing performance criteria, however.

An economy has a monetary pattern of trade if the exchanges taking place possess the characteristics (Jones, 1976): (i) there is one good that enters into every exchange; and (ii) any other good entering is not resold if purchased and not repurchased if sold. The one unique good is called the 'medium of exchange'. According to this concept, ultimate exchanges involve two-stage trades or transactions. Monetary exchange effects a given reallocation of goods with minimum aggregate TC with reference to a specific structure of trading and transaction costs (Niehans, 1969). Jones (1976) concluded that the use of search costs to guide individuals through a market with neither trading posts nor clearing houses has lead to the emergence of the pattern of exchange.

Among the major features contributing to the existence of TC is that of bounded rationality, explained below.

1.4 Bounded rationality, uncertainty and irrationality

One of the underlying principles of TC is the principle of bounded rationality. TCE assumes that, as Williamson (1985, p. 30) stated: 'human agents are subject to bounded rationality, whence behavior is "intendedly rational, but only limitedly so" '. It was also suggested that bounded rationality is 'the cognitive assumption on which transaction cost economics relies' (ibid., p. 45). Let us state the principle, originally given by Simon (1957, p. 198):

> The capacity of the human mind for formulating and solving complex problems is very small compared with the size of the problems whose solution is required for objectively rational behavior in the real world – or even for a reasonable approximation to such objective rationality.

Among the reasons for bounded rationality are informational uncertainties and informational complexities. In addition to the uncertainty that arises from 'states of nature' or changes in the external environment affecting a system, behavioural uncertainties (including strategic behavioural uncertainties) contribute to compounded uncertainty effects and pose impediments supporting bounded rationality. Recognition of the role of a longer-term strategy or far-sightedness in a decision-making context emerged over the years. Williamson (1996, p. 9) modified some of his previous assertions (stated above), insisting on the bounded rationality requirement to read 'limited but intended rationality is translated into incomplete but farsighted contracting'. It was also suggested that far-sightedness bestows on economic agents the ability to 'devise responsive institutions' (Ibid). This prescription remains largely qualitative, and formal models for quantification have been rather limited.

Uncertainties and unforeseen contingencies may not allow the existence and operational usefulness of a 'complete ordering' of alternatives for decision-making, as argued by Simon (1957, pp. 241–60). This assertion has serious implications for TCE. In this scenario of impossibility of complete ordering, there may not exist a metric or norm for comparison of alternatives, since we are left with potential partial orderings only, and this form of indeterminacy does not enable provision of a common denominator or numeraire. In a recent paper, Simon (2000) suggested that new insights in barriers and bounds to rationality suggest the role of evolutionary dynamics with reference to historical conditions and localized patterns of interaction. The latter are better examined with refined applications of TCE.

Non-existence of Paretian welfare

Under uncertainty, expected utility theorems of economic analysis apply under specific conditions. Expected utility theory shows that a person's preferences may be represented by a utility function defined in the domain of alternatives. These functions are expectational in the sense that, if an alternative has uncertain results, its utility is the expected value of the utility of its possible states.

We need two more definitions for further analysis here.

Coherent preferences.   Preferences are stated to be coherent if they satisfy the axioms of expected utility theory, to allow representation of preferences by an expectational utility function.

Paretian social preferences.   These allow preferences represented by a composite utility function U as a function of individual utility function, with A representing state of nature or event:

$$U = W\{[U_1(A), \ \ldots, \ U_h(A)]\} \text{ for all } A$$

with the provision that the marginal utility of W increases with U_i for any $i = 1, \ \ldots, \ h$.

In general, economic agents do not have preferences that are based on unanimity about probability of occurrences of stochastic events. The following theorem establishes the impossibility of the existence of coherent Paretian social preferences.

Probability Agreement Theorem: Suppose that each person has coherent preferences. Then if social preferences are coherent and Paretian, the individual and social preferences must all agree about the probabilities they assign to every event. (Broome, 1990, p. 479).

Uncertainties, bounded rationality and asymmetric information contribute to the non-existence of a Paretian social welfare function under uncertainty. This result should not be very surprising. Earlier, Arrow (1979) found the following in the context of incomplete information-based bargaining between parties: (i) the parties tend to reveal information when there are no income effects (that is, the utility function is linear in income and remains risk-neutral with respect to income); and (ii) the probabilistic distributions of parties are known and remain independent of each other.

Analogous results on the impossibility of joint utility maximization in decentralized regimes in a multi-period setting were derived by Hurwicz and Majumdar (1988) for resource allocation mechanisms. Similarly, Laffont (1985) derived results based on rational expectations models and showed that joint expected utility maximization solution does not exist if the events and their probability values are not shared truthfully among participating economic agents.

Finally, the role of irrationality is also relevant in this context. Is irrationality an economic commodity? Caplan (2001, p. 22) stated that the existence of irrationality merely suggests that it is yet another economic good for which economic actors have preferences; some decision-makers are 'rationally irrational'. The cost of such irrationality may also be considered a component of TC, although this assessment has not engaged much attention in the literature so far. Section 1.5 provides a framework, and analytical approaches to the issue of optimizing TC in cases where choices exist for devising governance relations and adapting institutions. The formal model is akin to the familiar models of optimal resource allocation for efficiency or utility maximization. The deviation is to seek enrichment of such models with the formal role of TC in various stages of analysis and policy derivation.

1.5 The comprehensive definition and framework

Positive definitions of TC focus on the magnitudes of various cost elements categorized as the relevant components of TC, explained in section 1.1 above. The normative aspect of the interpretation of TC emphasizes the extent of deviation of a solution or operative economic feature relative to the optimal (but not necessarily ideal) configuration. In simplified models of optimization, this simply measures the extent of sub-optimization, and is sometimes described in terms of the solution under the classifications 'second-best', 'third-best' and so on. These higher-order solutions merely refer to added constraints on the decision system underlying the solution structure, and constrained optimal solutions tend to be placed lower in maximization problems (as in utility or revenue maximization) than the first-order optimal solutions, and these are higher in minimization problems (as in cost minimization). What constitute legitimate constraints determine the benchmark for distinguishing optimal and sub-optimal solutions as well as assessing the relative costs of sub-optimization. If we examine formally the role of TC within the analysis of neoclassical economics we may apply the well-known LeChatelier Principle (see Samuelson, 1948). The recognition of the role of TC as an additional constraint would, for example, imply a lesser elasticity of consumer demand functions relative to those without such recognition.

In one of the related notions, the gap between the Pareto-optimal level of performance efficiency and any given sub-optimality is referred to as 'deadweight loss'. Using this concept, Samuelson (1995, p. 6) tried to relate TC to this concept and suggested: 'To try to capture all that which contributes to deadweight loss under the verbal rubric of "transaction costs" weakens a useful concept without gaining understanding of incompleteness of markets, asymmetries of information, and insusceptibilities of various technologies to decentralized pricing algorithms.'

Among the developers of TC definitions is Dahlman (1979, p. 148): '— they represent resource losses due to lack of information'. Warneryd (1994) argued that this is equivalent to treating TC that arise where an economic decision-maker faces uncertainties about the activities of other actors in the economic system. Formally, this is stated as follows: the expected value of perfect strategy information to a strategy g user is called the TC associated with strategy g.

There is a clear need for integrating positive economics and normative economics in the context of developing formal economic models for TCE. Integrated transaction cost economics (ITCE) comprises the following:

(i) Positive/behavioural-based TCE; and
(ii) Normative/efficiency-based TCE.

An important extension of TC is to include opportunity costs of alternative forms of organization. This does not necessarily refer to organizational structures, but rather to the mechanisms and activities

that are relevant in the assessment of the comparative costs of organization. Although the focus of TCE has been on the latter, due attention
seems to be lacking from some of its applications. This book provides
relevant extensions and applications in various chapters (see, for
example, the economics of structural lending in Chapter 4).

Formal optimization methods of economic analysis often used
in neoclassical economics suggest the equivalence of first-best and
second-best models of ITCE if we could rearrange the plausible sets of
constraints and their costs without changing the TC minimizing objective itself.

It is necessary to distinguish between efficiency maximization and TC
minimization, although part of the literature seems to ignore this distinction. In the latter case, institutions evolving towards TC minimization are treated as though this automatically implies efficiency
maximization. In some cases, the two criteria coincide, but this does
not hold in a general scenario.

We need to introduce the concept of convexity, since it plays an
important role in formal TCE. Briefly, a convex function possesses a
minimum, and the function can be subjected to minimization via
changes in the argument, under regularity conditions of the function;
a function f is called convex on a domain set C if the following property
holds:

$$f[(1 - v)x + vy] < \text{or} = (1 - v)f(x) + vf(y)$$

where $0 > v > 1$, and and x and y are in C.

TC are dominated by set-up costs associated with each exchange or
significant transaction, and by their nature such costs are disproportion-
ate to the economic activity itself. This brings in an important non-
linearity in the form of a non-convex cost structure, as Dahlman (1979)
pointed out. In all such cases, there may not exist a unique minimum
for TC minimization. Technically, convexification of the cost function is
feasible, possibly leading to a unique minimum. However, in terms of
economic interpretation, such convexification requires changes in the
bundle of commodities and/or activities in the form of augmentation.
But this may not always be a practicable approach. Besides, trading an
externality requires specification of corresponding demand and supply
equilibria and integrating with the rest of the applicable economic
system. Most important, limitation in this effort could possibly be in
terms of achieving the competitive market features (especially large
number of buyers and sellers of such augmented 'commodities and
services').

For the purpose of quantitative analysis, only some cases admit the common dimensionality and a measure of TC and a simple addition to other costs using the same monetary framework (whether or not the same currency is used). Therefore, it is generally desirable that TC are formulated to form a separate dynamical relation in the form of augmented cost functions on their own, in addition to the dynamics of cost functions, production functions, and other economic relations known in standard neoclassical economic literature.

The TC minimizing problem is formulated as a dynamic optimization problem, stated below. Let us use the notation:

T =   time horizon;
c =   policy variable (for example, consumption);
d =   specifications of institutional features;
D ( ) =   discount function for valuing future costs;
I ( )   =   institutional specifications;
s ( ) =   switching costs or transition costs in the adoption of new policies;
y =   state or response variable, for example, capital; and
f =   TC function relating the above.

The problem is to minimize J where:

$$J = \int_0^T D(t)f[c, \ l(d), \ s(c, \ e), \ y]dt$$

This objective function is subject to a set of constraints, including the specification of initial conditions, dynamics of y, specifications of s and l.

Alternatively, one could also formulate the objective function in terms of other desired formulations such as utility maximization, welfare maximization or profit maximization. Each of these formulations will include appropriate reformulated constraints and dynamical relations governing state variables and other relevant factors. Typically, these problems, in principle, admit solutions using dynamic optimization methods, including optimal control theory (see, for example, Seierstat and Sydsaeter, 1987; Takayama, 1993). Such applications of techniques led to the formulation of the Hamiltonian H, which combines the interactive effects of the objective function and constraints; this H represents the present or current value (depending on the formulation) of the total system under consideration. Variations in the sets of constraints (for example, alternative institutional features) will depict appropriate sensitivity in the solution and interpretation of various parameters. It must be noted that it is not the techniques of analysis that are the limiting factors for widespread application of TCE, but rather the severe problem of data (or more generally, information) that constrains many applications of TCE methods. This feature necessarily brings us back to descriptive yet logical approaches to the application of TCE in the real world; usage of TCE itself involves TC in such a world.

It is important to note that TC minimization is a means of achieving some other, broader, objective specific to an economic system (profit or revenue maximization for a firm, utility maximization for an individual, and social welfare maximization for a society or national economy), and not an end in itself. If the role of TCE is seen simply as one of minimizing TC, it is then only a minor part of the total set of analyses relevant under the TCE framework. The assessment of alternate forms of governance is a critical issue, and this governance is not necessarily evaluated in terms of optimization methods. These methods enable some quantified results, given a broader framework that provides the institutional configuration for resource optimization. Also, TC exist in some cases for a reason; these are irreducible in some cases where legal and other stipulations require some provisions to be complied with even if the absence of the stipulations reduces TC. It is often meaningless, for example, to expedite legal adjudication with incomplete evidence, or to avoid safeguards in customers, bank transactions to reduce attendant TC. The roles of the law, TCE and organization are to be viewed in an integrated manner, and analytical methodologies assist only some of the sub-systems of this process. To seek a comprehensive analytical method for TCE is thus contradictory of the premise of TCE.

In somewhat related methods of analysis, Dorward (1999) formulated the optimization problem in terms of maximization of a fairly comprehensive firm-level utility function (an extended version of the consumer utility function) which has in it the arguments: gross revenues, transformation costs (comprising the costs of forming contracts, screening, negotiation, and contract monitoring and enforcement), contract-specific transactions by volume and type (different contracts are assumed to remain independent of each other), associated risks of losses under alternative contractual arrangements, and a risk-preference specification. While this is a desirable approach, analytically, its demands on data are rather prohibitive, and could enhance the TC of carrying out the exercise. Yet, it may be desirable in some cases where the expected benefits outweigh the costs of carrying out the methodology.

Without going into technical details, we can now discuss salient features such as the role of the consideration of switching costs (to accommodate irreversibility, or other costs of adjustment – even with potential reversibility), economic behavioural implications of the role of different TC components (in this case, TC are specified as a vector rather than a lumped sum of all components), and other structural modifications that have an effect on the optimal solutions. Although it is not possible to provide many interpretations based on an implicit optimization model such as the one stated above, suffice it to state that the way forward in the development of analytical methods (and comprehensive approaches) to the TC issue is in terms of the above, thus enriching the erstwhile neoclassical economic formulations rather than conflicting with them.

Does the above suggested framework recognize and take into account the salient features that TCE emphasizes relative to mainstream neoclassical economics? What is the role of bounded rationality, of asset specificity, and *ex post* opportunistic behaviour of economic actors? Are these main features reflected in any version of the above optimization framework? The answer is yes, if we resort to different alternative formulations such as those under dynamic game-theoretic formulations (which can also be transformed into equivalent optimal control models). Does this assertion merely emphasize technicalities and effectively trivialize the contributions under TCE? No, because this only augments the existing literature and understanding of TCE, and suggests analytical directions for further development of TCE allowing for a set of quantifiable prescriptive solutions.

The common allegation that much of TCE is 'verbose' is not well founded, and analytical methods that augment TCE analyses bridge the perceptional gaps between neoclassical economics and TCE. Let us also note that every economic problem involves the role of TC (albeit in varying degrees), but every problem does not require analytical optimization methods to seek a solution incorporating TC elements, in addition to other economic ingredients. Some of the operational aspects of policy or implementation are often founded on burdensome archaic procedures (especially in many public systems) and these require a major simplification of the rules and procedures that reduce various elements of the TC vector. An explicit and complex optimization model is not needed to fulfil TC-reducing or performance-maximizing tasks. Less than transparent procedures often generate private 'rentals' for the enforcing agents in public systems; TC reduction in this case involves the reduction of avenues for corrupt practices and the role of the rule of law. An integrated perspective of a law, economics and organization approach is more rewarding than separate exercises of law, of economics, and of organization (see also Williamson, 1989). Again, in dealing with economic approaches, it is useful to apply TCE in conjunction with neoclassical economics to assessing the comprehensive economic dimensions.

1.6 Conclusions

Much of the emphasis of the application of TCE is in the sense of qualitative comparison of alternative institutions. According to Williamson (1985), the absolute magnitudes of differences in TC do not matter as much. This claim may not always be tenable, however.

The basic insight of TCE is that transactions must be governed as well as designed and carried out, and that some institutional arrangements are better suited than others for achieving economic and other desired efficiency criteria.

TCE treats the business firm as a governance structure; standard neoclassical economics describes the firm as a production unit or function.

Is TCE an element of positive economics or does it constitute another route to normative economics? Perhaps it is a combination of both – it begins with an appreciation of the working features of the real economic entities and then seeks to examine the normative features of a desirable 'efficient' system by providing the efficiency properties of alternative institutional configurations.

As Groenewegan (1996, p. 1) suggested, the general 'strategy' that lays the foundation for TCE is: after obtaining the characteristics of a transaction, the potential governance structures are examined in terms of TC minimizing capabilities. In this context, the comparative analysis of organizations and the assessment of TC needs to include the full complement of opportunity costs; only an approach such as this is capable of combining the roles of positive economics and normative economics, and enriching the contribution of TCE.

TC minimization is not always a desirable approach. Instead, a balance of positive and normative considerations should enable a formulation of the TC optimization problem to recognize the legitimate constraints and objectives with reference to which TC minimization is sought. Unconstrained TC minimization is neither a necessary nor sufficient condition for social welfare maximization in a general economy, and profit maximization in a business entity. We are still concerned with the role of TC because these are not usually reflected in direct financial cost accounting and need to be aligned properly in order to achieve desirable efficiency criteria.

2
Elements of Industrial Organization

2.1 Introduction

There is always the issue of organization of industry (rather, the issue of *efficient* organization), whether or not there exists a formal subject called 'industrial organization' (Stigler, 1968). According to a later assessment of the subject (Phillips and Stevenson, 1974, p. 324), the principal concerns of industrial organization relate to the application of micro-economics 'to the problem of monopoly, restraints of trade, and the public regulation and ownership of enterprise'. However, as the theme lends itself to multiple ramifications, there have been several additions to the issues (such as firm hierarchies and decentralization) and analytical methods or approaches (such as incomplete contracts theory, and applications of the economics of asymmetric information; see Chapters 3 and 4 for some of the details) for their analyses. The theory and practice of industrial organization forms a significant foundation for the development of the economics of transaction costs (TC). Historically, some of the foundations were laid during the pre-Second World War era to explain the economics of organization of markets and firms, and the determinants of firm boundaries. It took a few decades for the economics profession to appreciate the arguments of some of the early foundations. Coase (1937) raised and provided an explanation for the simple question: Why do firms exist? Because it is costly (TC exist) to rely exclusively on the market-based price system to organize economic activities, firms have to be formed. The determinants of firm boundaries include the profitability implications of organizing specific additional or new transactions within the firm or the market, or across firms.

This chapter does not intend to review all the relevant developments (some are included under overlapping areas of analysis in different chapters of this book). Only some of the important foundations of these economic thoughts that are still relevant for current economics of modern industrial organization are summarized here. Efficient industrial organization warrants efficient organization of the firm and its enabling environment. The latter includes the complementary roles of the market and the government, both taking into consideration the role of TC in alternative institutional and organizational arrangements. In summary, economic governance is the general economic problem, and firm governance is a relatively microscopic problem; both these aspects are interdependent, however. Spulber (1999) provides one of the modern treatments of the microstructure of the market, viewed in terms of the causes and effects of intermediaries in the market system (the role served to some extent by the firms).

The essence of the theory of the firm, and the major alternative interpretations of this are examined in order to elucidate the relationship of the theories with the role of TC. In fact, much of the theory of the firm can be seen as a theory of TC applied to a segment of industrial organization. The managerial and resource-based theories of the firm are also related, in addition to the neoclassical profit-maximizing theories of normative economics, to the underlying role of TC. These features are stated briefly, and later the focus of principal–agent theory is also related to the role of TC, especially with regard to the asymmetric information and bounded rationality features; agency costs are but a component of TC.

Technical innovation remains the engine of industrial dynamism, the economics of innovation is explained in terms of the influences of varying types and magnitudes of innovations, and the influences include a set of factors, each of which separately and jointly operates within the realm of transaction cost economics (TCE). Adaptation efficiency, in contrast to production efficiency, is among the critical features required for enterprise sustainability. Here, again, the salient characteristics of the analysis of economics and organization of the 'efficient enterprise' lead toward the recognition of the role of TC in achieving requisite sustainability of the enterprise. The issue of trade-offs between irreversibility and adaptability is better resolved when the cost elements include TC as well. This chapter also raises questions for further analysis.

2.2 Economics of the firm

The fact that market economies have generally performed better around the world suggests that the roles of the firm and the market function better in conjunction with an institutional setting of the polity, and a government which is supportive of the former. The role for rent setting and rent seeking (see Chapter 5) is kept to a minimum. None the less, there exists a high likelihood that the rent-seeking phenomenon operates vigorously during the transition from a centralized or bureaucratically controlled command economy to a market economy if there are insufficient safeguards of the law and its enforcement. In command economies, TC are all-pervasive, in contrast to market prices in a market economy. The drag on the economy perpetuates a cycle of inefficiency and preservation of rent-creating activities. The critical roles of firms and markets as the main infrastructure of functioning (rather, performing) economies is to be seen in terms of the TC minimization process underlying the economy and its dynamic structures.

As Machlup (1978, p. 414) stated, the firm as a theoretical construct has neither less nor more than the kind of information the theorist chooses to endow it with 'in order to design a good, useful theory'. The usefulness of the theory lies in its practical application and verification. In terms of historical foundations, Coase (1937) is generally considered to be the first economist to raise the issue as to which economic activities are carried out efficiently within the firm, and which outside the firm. The cost differentials in carrying out these activities give rise to a set of applicable TC, which typically include the following: costs of measurement, information, negotiation and contract agreement, enforcement of agreement and/or dispute resolution, and monitoring/supervision. In Coase's (1937) approach, the firm emerges in order to economize on TC: 'the most obvious cost of "organising" production through the price mechanism is discovering what the relevant prices are' (ibid., p. 390).

Based on Coasean insights, firm-level decisions regarding internal production and contracting out, business decisions in terms of choice of activities under vertical and horizontal integration have been seen in terms of the relative costs of attendant transactions (details were discussed in Chapter 1).

The firm's boundaries include the market, its organization and the interacting institutional environment. What are the corresponding costs of organizing some of the activities through the market? The costs of bargaining and settling on price agreements are among the TC of operating a market-based system. According to Coase (1937, p. 394–5): 'a firm will tend to expand until the costs of organising an extra transaction within the firm become equal to the costs of carrying out the same transaction by means of an exchange on the open market or the costs of organising another firm'. This description bypasses the practical issues of the role of uncertainties and limitations of some markets in their price formation mechanisms. Application of this marginality condition requires considerable additional information, however. Firm boundaries are generally guided by the efficiency (profit) implications of organizing specific additional or new transactions within the firm or the market or across firms. This principle of marginality or marginal efficiency, a standard for analysis in the application of neoclassical economics (see Chapter 3 and 4), is easier to state than to apply realistically in most cases. Most of the imperfectness of application arises from inaccurate assessment of corresponding TC, along with direct costs.

In an important contribution, Hayek (1945) argued that the market economizes on the information and communication costs of economic entities and leads to economic efficiency; there is little explanation for the role of the firm in this perspective. Besides, this view does not hold good in all cases, despite the generally positive role of markets and efficiency-enhancing features relative to some of the non-market organizations. The limitations arise especially in the presence of externalities and/or whenever the TC of some of the thin-market-based economic activities do not possess the competitive market efficiency properties (see Chapter 3 for details).

Among significant contributions to the theory of the firm is Penrose (1959), with a perspective on the stakeholder theory of the firm. The firm is viewed as a bundle of human and non-human resources under one administrative structure. This structure offers the cohesive and efficiency-enhancing infrastructure for the firm (including leading to new knowledge), a role not envisaged for the market organization. In a social welfare context, Penrose also recognized that vertical integration in firms can contribute to detrimental effects on society through the role of the incumbent firm in posing entry barriers for new firms. The complementarities of the Coasean approach and Penrosean approach are noteworthy. After a critical review of some of the assumptions of TCE, Pitelis (1998) concluded that reduced transaction costs and enhanced resource endowments could further enhance profits, through cost saving and/or teamwork and knowledge enhancement benefits (*à la* Penrose), and these further support Coase-type predictions of firm behaviour and performance.

One of the implicit assumptions of TCE (see also Klein and Shelanski, 1995) is that market forces work to bring about an efficient sort between transactions and governance structures, so that observed relationships and actions can be explained in terms of TC minimization. The conventional TCE perspective that firms and markets are distinct entities is subject to some challenges. Voluntary exchange is typical in the market, and a hierarchical management and authority is typical of the firm. If firms exceed a certain threshold in size and operations, most attributes of governance begin to resemble those of a central authority in a bureaucracy or a command economy. Milgrom and Roberts (1988) raised the issue that greater vertical integration and firm size can also lead to costs similar to centralized authority in bureaucratic organizations. The problem of opportunistic behaviour by the central authority cannot be ruled out, however.

Vertical integration

It is widely known that efficiency considerations are often the motives for vertical integration and corresponding ownership structures of firms in an industry, but it is also useful to recognize the roles of achieving the objectives of integration by means of internal production, outsourcing and contract formations. Let us also note that the complexity of contracts and their enforcement can also be an incentive for internalization of production if the TC of contracting exceed those of internalization.

Let us use the following definition:

> *Transaction-specific asset*: an asset whose value is substantially higher when used in a specific transaction between two parties or different identified entities.

When transaction-specific investments are substantial, they lead to vertical integration as a measure of risk minimization. Specific assets and economies of scope offer general explanations for the existence of firms (Wiggins, 1991). Thus vertical integration rests on the relative TC of asset-specific transactions, and of the complexity and cost of contracting or outsourcing. Specific assets and economies of scope, both being ingredients of TC, are stated as the factors contributing to the existence of the firms (ibid.).

The savings in costs (production and TC included) which result from the scope of a firm's activities are referred to as the economies of scope (Teece, 1980). Panzar and Willig (1981) stated that an application of this concept is relevant for explaining the emergence of multi-product firms in a competitive environment, since production costs alone do not explain the economic forces influencing the scope of firms.

Economies of scope exist when the total cost of delivery to the final destination of two or more goods (or services) within an enterprise or economic entity is less than the cost of producing the same in separate entities. Scope economies need not be exploited within a given entity; different entities can combine to exploit the resource-saving potential and enhance efficiency (Teece, 1982).

According to Jensen and Meckling (1976), the behaviour of the firm is similar to the behaviour of a market and represents the outcome of a complex equilibrium process. But this position does not obviate the role of TC in alternate forms of governance. It is the nature and magnitude of comparative TC that should enable decisions regarding the choice of a firm and the market in directing specific activities.

Vertical integration is the result of combination of balances that suggest internal production, outsourcing and corresponding risk factors, specific investment costs, and the efficacy of contracts for goods and services in all linkages of the firm. A firm can also be seen as an entity that exists with an incomplete contract (Tirole, 1988), with the implication that some of the costs of non-contractable activities (and contingencies) must be recognized in the comprehensive assessment of activities of the firm.

The general concept that firms exist to minimize TC is a well-known standard in TCE. But firms exist for a number of other reasons as well. Analytically, the question is whether some or any of these constitute necessary and/or sufficient conditions for the existence of the firm as an economic entity. Concise answers have not yet been found. The stand of the TCE literature needs to be stated explicitly: TC minimization is a means but not always an end in itself for achieving broader economic objectives. Subject to the provision that TC minimization does not lead to inefficiencies as a result of such actions, the criterion becomes relevant. In other words, an intertemporal and system-wide assessment of the implications of plausible alternative interventions for TC minimization may be called for. In industrial organizations, the role of TC minimizing criteria often coincides with profit maximization and to that extent there exists congruence of objectives of economic governance. However, whenever the adjustment costs (as in case of significant human costs of labour lay-offs) are very significant, the issue is then one of assessing the category-specific TC of all stakeholders. A potential Pareto welfare-enhancing scenario may be called for in such complex scenarios, where TC minimization provides just one of the relevant criteria.

Resource-based view of the firm (RBVF)

This view suggests that the firm is a collection of some non-fungible and imperfectly imitable assets that enable it to compete successfully with other firms, and is primarily based on Penrose (1959). The role of asset specificity is evident in this description, and thus remains close to the TCE formulations. Flexibility in asset shifting and resource allocation is one of the determinants of the firm's adaptive efficiency. This approach brings into focus the role of both normative and adaptive efficiency.

The motives for industry diversification include both demand and supply factors. Risk-based diversification for minimizing risks across asset allocation is one of the approaches. The main approach suggested here is that of the role of the existing endowment of resources, and their quality in terms of shiftability and adaptation. Excessive asset specificity may not enable adaptive efficiency, and the sustainability of the erstwhile efficiency may be lost over time. A firm that has developed an advantageous resource position (including technological positioning) derives profits similar to 'first-mover' advantage. However, the asset specificity aspect of such resource endowment constrains the firm's ability to transfer these resources to new and desirable applications, in the absence of binding long-term contracts. Silverman (1999) argued that there exist complementarities between TCE and RBVF. One of the hypotheses advanced by Silverman (1999, p. 1112) states, in part: 'Ceteris paribus, a firm is more likely to diversify into a business the more likely that contracting out its technological resources in that business is subject to high contractual hazards.' The role of contractual hazards, viewed in conjunction with asset specificity, has also been tested empirically in a few significant case studies (see Chapter 6 for more details).

The traditional RBVF sought to explain the competitive advantage within and across firms, and how that might be sustained over time. RBVF assumes that firms can be viewed as bundles of resources that are distributed heterogeneously across firms, and that resource differences persist over time (Eisenhardt and Martin, 2000; Wernerfelt, 1984). Firm capability or organizational capability has been incorporated among resources in a relatively static sense. Two definitions are relevant here:

Organizational capability:
An organizational capability is a high-level routine (or collection of routines) that, together with its implementing input flows, confers upon an organization's management a set of decision options for

producing significant outputs of a particular type. (Winter, 2000, p. 983)

Dynamic capabilities:
The firm's processes that use resources – specifically the processes to integrate, reconfigure, gain and release resources – to match and even create market change. Dynamic capabilities thus are the organizational and strategic routines by which firms achieve new resource configurations as markets emerge, collide, split, evolve, and die. (Eisenhardt and Martin, 2000, p. 1107)

The definition of organizational capability does not refer explicitly to time-dependent changes, but the definition of dynamic capabilities does address this issue. The role of TC is prominent in the latter.

Teece *et al.* (1997) extended RBVF to dynamic markets involving rapid and unpredictable changes. The concept of dynamic capabilities was defined in a context where the competitive landscape is shifting; dynamic capabilities involved features by which firm managers 'integrate, build, and reconfigure internal and external competencies to address rapidly changing environments' (ibid., p. 516). This assertion brings us to the formal role of adaptation.

Adaptation

Adaptation is one of the central concepts of TCE. This aspect needs continued further focus in future studies, however. Among the early economists and management experts, Hayek (1945) and Barnard (1938) emphasized the role of adaptation in ensuring efficiency enhancement, in social and economic systems. Under Hayekian perspectives, adaptation occurs spontaneously through market institutions and the price formation processes. From the organization theoretic perspective, Barnard focused on co-operative and intentional adaptation designed by economic and managerial actors.

Adaptation and costs of adaptation in the process of achieving a desired economic objective have historically been considered important aspects of economic systems, and their potential to follow 'efficient' paths of economic progress. In this context, the role of market and price systems in enabling cost minimizing adjustment or adaptation to new information and other changes has been a major area of focus of several studies over the twentieth century, and before. Hayek (1945, p. 524) argued: 'the economic problem of society is mainly one of rapid adaptation in the particular circumstances of time and place'.

The price system, when allowed to function properly, was given the key role in this adjustment and adaptation process. In the context of economic organizations, Barnard (1938, p. 6) suggested: 'the survival of an organization depends upon the maintenance of an equilibrium of complex character... calls for readjustment of processes internal to the organization... the center of our interest is the process by which (adaptation) is accomplished'. Thus, adaptation, in the sense either of spontaneous markets or of hierarchical co-operative actions, remains critical for the required adjustment process for an economy or an economic organization. The costs of achieving these adjustments and adaptations need to be considered in a TC minimizing sense. This is the role of TCE. Recognition of the underlying behavioural assumptions and *ex post* features of any organizational or institutional rearrangement are among the major features of TCE application.

Williamson (1996) clarified that the TCE possesses and/or subscribes to the following features: (i) adaptation remains the central problem of economic organization; (ii) both spontaneous and designed adaptation of Hayekian and Barnardian types are relevant; (iii) specific attributes of transactions warrant varying levels of emphasis of market and organizational adjustment mechanisms for enhancing efficiency in a TC minimizing and welfare maximizing manner; and (iv) each form of governance (market, hierarchy or a mix) presumes varying levels of spontaneous or intentional adjustment factors for modulating adaptation to changes over time and influences at a given point of time.

With reference to the key role of adaptation, it is useful to recall that reasonably well developed formal models and methodology exist in the area of 'adaptive economics' (AE). Among the major contributions, Day and Groves (1975), and Day and Singh (1977) are noteworthy. AE begins with the assumption that changes evolve from current or contemporary conditions, and focuses on the economic problem of optimization for the admittedly imperfect co-ordination of partially informed economic agents. Adaptation has been defined broadly as the adjustment of economic agents or interaction of economic agents with the broader system of which a specific economic entity is a part. Behaviourally conditioned economic agents and their behaviour based on a feedback information system have been modelled formally in terms of what are known as 'recursive programming models'. These models are widely used in neoclassical economics and lead to computable results.

An important aspect of the theory of the firm is the managerial theory of the firm, explained below in relation to TC.

Managerial theory of the firm

The managerial or executive functions of a firm's management allow a substantial degree of managerial discretion and flexibility, given the informational asymmetry between these functionaries and the primary stakeholders (principals – shareholders and creditors). What optimization models do the managers adopt? They incorporate the interests of the principals, but also the private agendas of the key executive decision-makers of the firm. The firm profit or revenue maximization is subject to fulfilling these implicit objectives, and to this extent the efficiency may be compromised (although in some cases the built-in incentives also propel higher efficiency in some activities, but usually not widespread for the entire enterprise). Accordingly, the managerial view of the enterprise suggests that the objective of the firm (in a positive economic approach) is to maximize the managerial utility as a function of executive bonuses, severance pay, discretionary expenditure, managerial emoluments in the short run and in their different stages of continued (or potentially discontinued) employment relationship with the firm. When these features are recognized, it is not hard to find explanations for such contemporary events as senior executives often finding it easier to arrange themselves an attractive severance pay in a firm beset with losses, mergers and acquisitions of firms leading to windfall gains for the senior management, and wide disparities in lowest paid and highest paid employees of many of the corporate entities. Thus the role of the managerial theory of the firm here is to identify TC in the form of self-assignments of managers' benefits independent of specific productivity and profitability criteria, in the presence of informational asymmetries and agency costs (see section 2.3 below).

Let us note that the presumption of 1930s vintage in Coasean economics that the firm structure circumvents the price issue within the firm is longer valid in most of the big firms – because there is now the practice of cost accounting of units and divisions within a firm, as well as the process of transfer pricing within the firm relating to the market outside.

The firm, viewed as a nexus of contracts (Jensen and Meckling, 1976, p. 311), suggests 'the "behavior" of the firm is like the behavior of a market, i.e. the outcome of a complex equilibrium process'. This similarity suggests the increasing possibility of blunting the sharp divisions between firms and markets, and a major common element of assessment of the relative efficacies of these interdependent institutions brings us back to the role of TC.

The changing concept of the firm, with the emergence of giant corporations and their growing role over time suggests the traditional view of firm as a rather close knit organizational entity does not hold. Enterprises with diffused (sectorally and spatially) activities behave somewhat like decentralized markets, and face costs of asymmetric information that are no better than those of market exchanges. This is precisely the feature that is relevant in explaining principal–agent relationships.

2.3   Principal–agent theory

An agency relationship exists whenever a principal or the primary stakeholder delegates authority to an agent whose actions have a bearing on the primary goals of the principal. Most activities, in addition to those under the enterprise, obey differing forms of principal–agent relationships. The managerial discretionary powers in an enterprise and bureaucratic powers in a public system bring in TC as a result of asymmetric information and incomplete contracts regarding work standards.

Are firms merely collections of a series of principal–agent (PA) relationships? Agency theory or PA theory stresses that the firm comes into being as a mechanism of limiting the divergence of interests between the principals and agents. The PA theory also relates to the issues of internal organization of the firm and the role of TC.

According to the significant contribution of Jensen and Meckling (1976), agency relationship is a contract under which one or more persons or entities (the principals) engage another person or entity (the agent) to perform specified tasks or transactions on their behalf based on delegated authority and decision-making.

Agency costs include the expenditure incurred by the principal for monitoring, and 'residual loss', which includes the costs of divergence between the ideal welfare maximization and the sub-optimal maximization based on the agent's motives. Agency costs also arise in co-operative efforts, but their magnitudes vary in relation to specific attributes. In the general terminology of TCE, agency costs are just a component of TC. The residual losses depend on agents' risk preferences, time discounting, and the costs of effective monitoring by the principals, in addition to the costs of measurement of performance of agents and of devising effective operational policies for implementation.

The PA theory, by itself, cannot make predictions about the nature and operation of the firm, and it requires supplementation regarding the choice of incentives and organizational forms (Hart, 1989). Together with these ingredients, PA theory remains an illustration of the role of

TC in economic governance applicable in most situations, for both public and private enterprises.

In the financial management area, an analytical formulation in a multi-period setting that incorporates the insights of both the PA theory and the asset specificity aspect of TC has been stated by Vilasuso and Minkler (2001). The formulation seeks the objective of determining the optimal capital structure that minimizes the sum of agency costs and asset specificity costs. It was found that the conditions that support the reduction of TC arising from asset specificity features are also those that contribute towards the reduction of the agency costs of debt. The relative roles of debt and equity components of the firm capital structure are illustrated in relation to TC. For highly specific assets, equity reduces TC by limiting opportunistic behaviour, but over a longer time horizon, additional equity offers bondholders protection from excessive risk taking and thus reduces the agency costs of debt.

Audit methodology or technology, information structures and agents' preferences (with potential moral hazard issues) may be seen as some of the factors that contribute to endogenous TC. Faure-Grimaud *et al.* (1999) examined some of the analytical aspects of endogenous TC in the context of the role of external audit of business activity and performance, with costly state-verification features. Information structure is partly endogenous in a costly-state verification model, since the auditor receives an informative signal from the auditee as a strategic or other function of the audit mechanism itself. In this setting, two agents, the auditor and manager are protecting their interests rather than those of the firm and its shareholders or principals. Some of the recent corporate accounting scandals in the USA reflect these problems.

2.4 Technical innovation

Private firms became an important (and in some sectors, dominant) source of innovative activity. There exists considerable theoretical and empirical literature which seeks to explain industry research and development (R&D) and innovations with firm size, market structure, and technological opportunity aspects (see, for example, Cohen and Levin, 1989). Most of these studies are still inconclusive in their assessment of the role of firm size and market concentration on R&D. Corporate innovation is usually facilitated via the market processes that provide the channels for the products and processes. The premise that the size of the firm is a major determinant of R&D intensity is a misleading one, because in analysis at the firm level a number of other important influencing variables are side-tracked. Related determinants include access to capital risk pooling, a firms' scope economies, and its possession of complementary assets (Cohen and Klepper, 1996).

An analysis of innovations cannot be carried out fully in formulations of standard equilibrium models because of attributes such as uncertainty, irreversibility of investment or asset specificity, and other firm-level unique resources. Empirical literature remains largely inconclusive about the supremacy, if any, of large enterprises relative to small and medium ones when it comes to innovativeness. The role of relative inflexibility and bureaucratization of large entities compared to others was seen as an influencing impediment for more rapid innovations. Thus adaptive efficiency remains an important factor in this context.

Structural autonomy at the industry level implies two features (Raider, 1998): the extent to which producer firms are organized within an industrial market, and the extent to which these firms buy/sell to others outside the specific organized industrial market. The information benefits of industries in structurally autonomous settings facilitate innovation as the industries adapt technology and other resources used in one market to meeting profit needs in another. Based on an empirical study, Raider (1998) concluded (without referring to TC literature as such) that firms can reduce TC when in a network as this reduces costs of information and adaptation. The contributing factors for innovations involved the role of network forms of organizations, the inter-industry communications and networks of learning, as explained with empirical evidence for the biotechnology sector by Powell *et al.* (1996), and generally by Robertson and Langlois (1995).

The role of TC in the pace and extent of innovations is multidimensional; important features include organizational and dynamic capabilities, adaptive efficiency, asset specificity and uncertainty.

2.5 Conclusions

Coase's (1937) insight on the boundaries of the firm, especially those regarding firm-level decisions about whether to produce internally, or instead use other firms for that purpose, was summarized as the criterion based on cost minimization, including TC minimization. The field of study of the economics of the firm and of industrial organization has expanded ever since on lines that are directly or indirectly related to the role of TCE.

About six decades after the original Coasean contribution, one of the critical reviews of the role of TCE in the historical evolution of the capitalist firm was that of Pitelis (1998). Pitelis concluded (p. 1013), rather narrowly, that the main contributions of TCE are in the make or buy decisions of firms and in the analysis of economic development, and that its main limitations are that 'it lacks history, dynamics, and a historically informed evolutionary perspective'. Several analytical and empirical studies clarify that the contribution of TCE is not confined almost to the two ends of a wide spectrum, namely firm-level make or buy decisions and economic development processes. Admittedly, the role of power (financial or otherwise) and of the pre-existing alignment of rights (and control of resources) affects the evolution of firms and markets, and also affects almost every aspect of economic and non-economic life; this is not an area that can possibly be explained in terms of TCE.

There are areas where a balance in the use of TCE and public policy is rather delicate. Problems of quantification of relative efficiencies of alternative institutional arrangements abound. Joskow (1991, p. 81) stated: 'The hard problems in antitrust and regulatory economics often involve potential tradeoffs between apparent increases in market power and potential reductions in costs or between regulatory imperfections and organizational or contractual imperfections. To perform such trade-offs, we need more than an ordinal ranking of the efficiency of different organizational arrangements.' TCE is eminently suitable for such analyses.

The theories of the firm and of the market remain firmly grounded in TCE, in all their alternative interpretations and perspectives. The optimal firm or enterprise is defined not only in terms of its size but also in terms of its resource composition and sustainability or adaptability. Both productive efficiency as well as adaptive efficiency are critical for the efficient organization of the firm.

The view that non-market institutions and corresponding organizations arise primarily to alleviate problems of market failure is not entirely tenable. These entities exist for a variety of reasons, including the role of TC. Market institution is not always considered to be the first resort of social and economic policy in many countries that are deeply entrenched in bureaucratic administration. The main insight of Coasean economics and TCE is to be able to evaluate, qualitatively, the merits of alternative institutions and choose from them, without prejudging the role of market or other arrangements. This assessment is not necessarily dependent on the very complex task of quantifying all relevant cost elements in both the short run and the long run, including potential uncertainties of all kinds. Even when system information inevitably is incomplete, economic decisions still have to be made. The role of TCE in the area of industrial organization is to focus attention on to the critical issues of organization, and leaving specific applications of methods of PA analysis or other approaches to their context-specific relevance. If a firm and market nexus is founded on implicit and explicit contractual arrangements that explain the working of the total organization, the economics of contracts in conjunction with TCE perform better than an approach based on PA analysis or TCE alone. Thus a mix of context-specific analytical models and TCE approaches are relevant for explaining and suggesting relevant industrial organizational analysis.

3
Economic Externalities

3.1 Introduction

The issue of the uncompensated effects of one party's actions on another is generally the source of several legal and economic problems. Historically, Pigou (1932) was among the first to address the problem, and he suggested that the damage should be assessed and paid for by the party causing such effects. Pigouvian tax in the public policy context equates the levy of tax at that level for activities such as pollution. Coase (1960), on the other hand, seeks a bargaining solution and assignment of property rights in order to solve the problem of externalities in a decentralized and efficient manner. Since Coase's theorem has been a very important finding in the literature of economics, and since it rests on a number of explicit and implicit assumptions, it is proposed to examine almost all of the important facets of the results in this chapter.

In the Pigouvian approach, there exists an economic externality if there is divergence between the private and social costs of an economic activity conducted by a private party. As Dahlman (1979) pointed out, the relevance of externalities lies in the fact that they indicate the prevalence of transaction costs (TC) in the system. Because of the existence of TC, externalities may not always be internalized or compensated. The existence of TC may not always imply the existence of externalities, however.

The main difference between the Pigouvian and Coasean approaches to the issue arises in their respective methods of dealing with economic externalities. Demsetz (1996) argued that Pigou's readiness to depict the role of the state and Coase's refusal to adopt this line is the main difference between the two. However, this is an oversimplification of the distinctions and is not an entirely tenable position. Both Pigou and

41

Coase have also maintained different positions at different times regarding the relevance or irrelevance of the state intervention for the correction of economic externalities, seen later in this chapter. The role of the state in assigning property rights versus the levying of taxes and/ or subsidies has been the underlying difference between the two. It is thus not always possible to demonstrate the superiority of one solution over another in terms of its presumed efficiency properties without reference to a specific system under consideration.

This chapter explains the relationships between TC and externalities, the assumptions, role and limitations of the Coase theorem; the use of Coasean approaches, explanations and remedies for market and non-market inefficiencies (including 'failures'); the role of TC in network externalities phenomena; and the policy implications of some of these analyses for the design of institutions and mechanisms of economic governance.

3.2   Externalities and transaction costs

Externalities vary widely and arise from several factors. In the Pigouvian social welfare economic approach, externalities are stated to prevail whenever there is a divergence between the social and private costs of an activity.

Definitions

Externality.   The phenomenon of generating products/outputs that are not intended in an inter-relationship among specified entities (for example, ozone depletion as a result of the use of the chlorofluorocarbons):

Economic externality: characterizes the economic aspects of an externality;

Environmental externality: refers to the environmental features of an externality;

Positive externality: refers to the role of an externality in its positive contribution in relation to a specific context or objective – for example, regional (but not necessarily global) cooling effects caused by the use of aerosols;

Negative externality: the converse of the previous item – for example, the greenhouse effect resulting from the continued emissions of carbon dioxide;

Pecuniary externality: an external effect that makes an impact via the price system, in contrast to technological externalities that arise as a result of changes in physical processes – for example, when a firm lowers its product price and produces an additional unit of output, rival firms can be affected as a result of this decision;

Stock externality: the externality that arises from changes or accumulations of the inventory or stock of a specific commodity or other physical entity; a similar concept holds for a 'flow' externality. For example, atmospheric concentrations of greenhouse gases is a stock pollutant with negative externalities. Urban smog is a stock externality as well as a flow externality;

Strategic externality: the impact of strategic behaviour on other components of a system in relation to specific activities undertaken by direct participants; this occurs especially in resource-to-resource consumption with limited liability or cost-sharing;

Static externality: refers to an externality arising out of a single instance or single period process – for example, the effect of local high temperature on dry forest fires; and

Dynamic externality: refers to an externality that is carried out over time, as in the process of deforestation and its externality on the biodiversity of species.

Free-rider. The possibility of using goods/services without having to pay for the usage.

Incentive-compatible. The responsiveness of an entity to the provision of incentives, usually with reference to one or more of the stated objectives of the system or its functions.

Market failure. The inability of market institutions to attain socially/economically desirable efficiency objectives, such as social welfare maximization.

Market inefficiency. The sub-optimal role of market institutions in the realization of social efficiency or other aggregate objectives.

Public goods. Those goods which are not necessarily provided by the market in response to demand and supply factors, and possess the properties of non-excludability (the goods provided are accessible to all potential users), and non-rival usage (consumption does not always reduce the availability to other potential consumers).

Role of externalities

Externalities come into play because the TC of resolving them are very high. In a sense, every episode of externalities is one of TC. Zerbe and McCurdy (1999) proposed to relate externalities with TC: the net value of the externality constitutes the lower boundary for associated TC. Where TC remain irreducible it is possible that the corresponding externality is of a lower magnitude. There is another category of effects that belong in the TC arena; namely, internalities. Let us introduce the definition.

Internalities. The goals that apply within non-market organizations to guide, regulate and evaluate agency performance or its human capital.

Regarding the relative roles of externalities and internalities, Wolf (1979, p. 117) rightly argued: 'Whereas externalities are central to the theory of market failures... "the internalities"... are central to the theory of nonmarket failure.'

Dahlman (1979) suggested that the relevance of externalities lies in the fact that they indicate the presence of some TC, and that externalities are uninternalized because there exist the costs of doing so. Stated differently, in the presence of positive TC, externalities remain irreducible without any intervention. Dahlman also suggested that TC *per se* have nothing to do with externalities, and that if we could reduce TC to zero, externalities would be of no consequence. Dahlman's approach is to approximate TC with information costs, but this is far from comprehensive in the total set of costs for TC category.

The formal role of externalities

The role of externalities has been one of vitiating classical results and methods of analytical optimization. The technical role has been to violate 'regularity' conditions, such as convex production functions, which enable cost minimization under standard neoclassical economic formulations.

The Second Theorem of Welfare Economics might not hold without convexity assumptions about production and consumption systems of the economy. Since negative externalities induce non-convexities, competitive equilibrium may not exist in such systems, as Starrett (1972) and Otani and Sicilian (1977) proved. Also, an expansion of commodity space to include externalities in the form of traded commodities (as would be the case with the application of the Coase theorem) does not enable the achievement of competitive equilibrium efficiency. It has been suggested that Starrett's result amounted to an invalidation of Coase theorem.

Technically, one of the formal specifications that provide support for the problem of non-convexities induced by externalities and hence affect the existence of efficiency properties of equilibrium can be seen in terms of the applications of 'fixed-point' theorems (Brouwer's Fixed Point Theorem or Kakutani's Fixed Point Theorem). These theorems require the existence of convex mapping in order that a relation such as $f(x^*) = x^*$ exists, whereby x^* forms a fixed point.

These issues pose problems of the existence and optimality of competitive equilibrium in decentralized market economies in the presence of negative and uninternalized externalities.

Coase (1960) has been a major milestone for examining externalities and in the development of TCE. The following section explains the main issues.

3.3   Coasean proposition and neo-Coasean perspectives

Although Coase is best known for recognizing the role of property rights and bargaining without governmental intervention (for which he received the award of a Nobel Prize), it should also be well known that these prescriptions emerged based on the conscious assumption of zero transaction costs and admittedly in an ideal world.

The assumption that TC are negligible or equal to zero leads to a frictionless economic system. Economics based on a frictionless economy is similar to the study of friction-free physics of matter. Such studies tend to provide insights into the workings of an idealized system and offer some understanding of the non-ideal system that obtains in much of the real world. The assumption of zero TC made in the Coasean analysis (and hence referred to, rather unjustifiably, as a Coasean world) is advanced for a reason: to examine the implications of such a system on efficient functioning and to throw light on the sub-optimality of certain stipulations in a non-zero TC world. The Coasean contribution (mainly Coase, 1960) is to recognize the role of transaction costs, without which the predictions of the economic working of the institutions/ property rights could hold true. Let us recall some of the important conclusions of Coase (1960).

Coasean propositions

(i) 'if market transactions were costless, all that matters (questions of equity apart) is that the rights of the various parties should be well-defined and the results of legal actions easy to forecast' (Coase, 1960, p. 19); and

(ii)   'If factors of production are thought of as rights it becomes easier to understand that the right to do something which has a harmful effect... is also a factor of production' (ibid., p. 44).

In a zero TC world, well-defined property rights and their tradability are thus deemed to be important instruments in mitigating the effects of externalities without government intervention to correct externalities. Parties tend to enhance economic efficiency in the Pareto-welfare improving sense, based on 'efficient bargaining'. Later, Coase (1988, p. 178) argued that, with positive TC, the 'market transactions' by which private action would reallocate resources might become too costly to effect transactions.

Coase did not call his assertion a theorem, but most others did. In one of its variations, the theorem was stated by Posner (1993, p. 195) as: 'If transaction costs are zero, the initial assignment of a property right – for example, whether to the polluter or to the victim of pollution – will not affect the efficiency with which resources are allocated'. This assertion is proposed as an answer to the externality problem. A well-functioning legal system and a 'level playing field' for the bargaining parties are among the implicit prerequisites, lest the 'mighty' bargaining party (polluter or the victim, for example) extracts a socially sub-optimal price for the offence committed.

According to Stigler (1966, p. 113), the statement of the Coase theorem reads: 'Under conditions of zero transaction costs, private and social costs will be equal. Thus, in a real world of positive TC, the two cost assessments differ.'

The Coase (1960) results are founded on the assumption, among others, of common knowledge among participants regarding damage resolution or compensation negotiation. The application of these property right regimes does not automatically ensure efficient solutions. The existence of property rights is a necessary but not sufficient condition to resolve environmental or economic externalities (Rao, 2001). Well-defined PR and voluntary bargaining are the foundations for Coasean results.

In a later contribution, Coase (1988) provided further clarifications and some conditions which apply for the validity of earlier propositions or theorems (with a double negative qualification): 'It cannot be denied that it is conceivable that a change in the criteria for assigning ownership to previously unrecognized rights may lead to changes in demand which in turn lead to a difference in the allocation of resources' (ibid., p. 174). The demand influence and other factors with wealth effects (see below) also apply. Coase (1988) also noted that there are a number of limitations on the applicability of the original Coase theorem, especially the original suggestion that economic efficiency holds under varied legal rules as long as bargaining is undertaken between contending parties. It was still emphasized that there exists a role of bargaining between contending parties. This suggestion is founded on the assumption that there does not exist another externality in the form of strategic behaviour or other derived externalities associated with such actions. Less than well-defined and/or unclear PR contribute as a source of externalities; thus the process of mitigating externalities can itself be a source of derived externalities. TC remain a contributory factor in this process as well.

Calabresi (1968, p. 68) framed the Coase theorem as follows: 'If one assumes rationality, no transaction costs, and no legal impediments to bargaining, all misallocation of resources would be fully cured in the market by bargains.'

However, there is nothing automatic about reaching a settlement under bargaining mechanisms – even when TC are zero. On the contrary, the problem shifts to a new arena of behavioural dynamics compounded by the complexities of economics and the psychology of the parties involved. Among the relevant influences are (Rao, 2001): the costs of transmitting information among parties, issues of pay-offs (differentiated with respect to each participant in the bargaining process) for varying lengths of non-resolution of the dispute, differential time preferences and risk acceptance levels of parties, and behavioural traits that might include relative profitability or spitefulness.

There are a number of preconditions for the validity of the theorem, including (Hoffman and Spitzer, 1982): the existence of competitive markets; perfect common knowledge of contesting parties' production/profit/utility function; absence of wealth effects among parties; and the critical assumption that economic agents seek to strike mutually advantageous bargains in the absence of TC. Bernholz (1999) showed that, in order for the Coase theorem to hold, some of the necessary conditions include (in addition to the assumption of frictionless economy, or zero TC): all contracts/agreements are binding, and there exists a finitely divisible common numeraire that is valued by all parties.

In general, bargaining scenarios may not induce contending parties to declare their preferences and ranking of alternatives; this implies that bargains may not be optimal (Farber, 1997). Coase (1988, p.161) concedes the possibility of a breakdown in negotiations across hetero-geneous entities or strategic cases, but suggests that they are rare. The role of the Coase theorem remains extremely limited in the context of several problems of international and national economies. Yet the Coasean insight is far from insignificant. Even the critics agree that, despite there being some element of fiction in zero TC, Coase deserves full credit for elucidating the role of TC in economic life.

Limitations of the Coasean propositions

Some of the important limitations of the Coase theorem (or, equivalently, the Coasean propositions) arise from behavioural and structural problems of economic activities and the incidence of externalities. The following is a summary of various critical assessments of the Coasean propositions (including the so-called Coase theorem); these are given below not only to provide a broad list of objections to the validity of the propositions, but also to raise awareness in respect of multiple facets of economic analysis relevant in this and other contexts of TCE. But for the significance of the Coasean contributions, this wider debate (and in the process, enriching economic thought as a positive externality) could not possibly have surfaced.

In the behavioural dimension, people are more displeased with a loss than pleased with an equivalent gain, suggesting the feature of loss aversion in behavioural aspects (Thaler, 1992). An application of 'loss aversion criteria' suggests that the Coase theorem could not hold when the allocation of the legal entitlements influences the outcome, as those individuals who are 'initially allocated an entitlement are likely to value it more than those without the legal entitlement' (Sunstein, 1999, p. 132).

A legal entitlement creates an endowment effect (Thaler, 1991): a greater valuation of a right or resource stemming from the mere fact of endowment. As a consequence of the endowment effect, the initial allocation of rights has an effect on the final outcome of negotiations in any bargain.

The allocation of resources contemplated by the theorem is not neutral with respect to legal rights and their enforcement, as Samuels (1992, p. 79) stated: 'allocation is specific to the underlying rights structure which gives rise to it'. More importantly, the allocation 'cannot be independent of rights, when, *inter alia*, the cost functions (and demand functions...) which enter into the determination of allocation are themselves a partial function of rights' (ibid., p. 91).

Role of property rights

If the cost minimization or efficiency criterion is invoked based on the existing costs and prices scenario (in addition to prevailing inequities of resources and information), the latter is a function of existing property rights (PR) and liability regimes (LR), and the attainment of efficiency cannot be independent of PR and LR (Rao, 2001). Even in the absence of TC, institutions affecting PR and LR are likely to have a significant impact on the resource allocative process when income or endowment effects are prevalent (Hurwicz, 1995).

A primary function of PR is that of guiding incentives to achieve greater internalization of externalities (Demsetz, 1967). All interactions entail potential externalities. The costs of the exchange of rights between parties must exceed the gains from internalization in order for an uncompensated externality to exist. Although PR could include a bundle of instruments, LR is administered after the occurrence of an event and may not always lead to restoration of *ex ante* features or assets. The role of LR in this context, however, is to signal, *ex ante*, the consequences of negative effects on the damage-inflicting party; the latter may apply a probabilistic approach using an expected value of potential damage liability. The role of common risk-neutral attitudes among negotiating parties is assumed in the Coasean propositions. The propositions do not hold with differing risk-taking attitudes under uncertainty (Greenwood and Ingene, 1978).

Can TC tend to reach zero level with a complete market or assignment of PR for all activities and externalities? If TC are defined as the resources to effect transfer, and establish and maintain PR (Allen, 1991, p. 4), these approach zero as PR become more extensive and complete over the economic activity space (Zerbe and McCurdy, 1999). However, Inada and Kuga (1973) argued that the introduction of 'markets' for externalities may not lead to Pareto-optimal resource allocation. They also suggested that determining an appropriate level of externality compensation via bargaining is not much different from a redistribution of wealth. However, the role of TC in the alternative is likely to be more significant.

Coase's efficiency concept seeks to maximize the total wealth or 'total product rule' (TPR) (White, 1987), where the total is not necessarily that of the society but rather is that of the contesting parties. Let us quote a relevant extract from Coase (1960, p. 15) 'the economic problem in all cases of harmful effects is how to maximize the value of production'. However, Coase also recognized clearly its limitations (ibid., p. 43): 'it is desirable that the choice between different social arrangements for the solution of economic problems should be carried out in broader terms than this (the value of production) and that the total effect of these arrangements in all spheres of life should be taken into account'. Thus the 1960 Coasean contribution, in the most cited paper of economics literature, ends with a caution on the need for broader comprehensive approaches incorporating the role of TC, but the paper itself did not offer further directions on this.

The Coasean propositions are oblivious of the real-world features of differential transaction costs or asymmetric transaction costs, which invariably induce sub-optimalities. Besides, the contesting parties can contribute jointly towards externalities, extend these to another set of parties (who may or may not be identifiable). Even in its best feasible scenarios of applicability, Coase's theorem ignored general or economy-wide effects of 'efficient' solutions to the bargaining problems arising out of economic damages and property rights (or lack of the same). Thus the Coasean approach remains largely unsuitable for applications in global policies such as those in the global environmental arena. It may also be observed that TPR tends to favour the economically advantaged (for more details, see White, 1987). Besides, a well-functioning judicial system is often a prerequisite for Coasean bargaining solutions to emerge. The legal backdrop offers an infrastructural facility and this implies the working of the system, if at all, being conditional upon pre-existing set-up costs.

Behavioural features

The Coasean-style bargaining is inconsistent with rational individual behaviour, argued Olson (1996). The main obstacle to efficient bargaining among parties is the feature of strategic behaviour and not merely TC (Cooter *et al.*, 1982). In a rational bargaining model formulated by Cooter (1982) non-cooperative outcomes could still occur. This is because each player's strategy is best against opponents on average, but not best against every individual opponent. Reduction or elimination of TC in this model does not lead to the enhanced probability of co-operation. Dixit and Olson (2000) argued that, even with small TC, voluntary participation of bargaining parties for an efficient solution or agreement may not be forthcoming whenever strategic behaviour is involved.

Using game theory, it has been found that, if the core of the game is empty – as is often the case when more than two parties are involved – Coase's theorem cannot hold (Aivazian and Callen, 1981). It is also known (see Shapley and Shubik, 1969) that in an economy with external diseconomies, increasing returns to scale and non-convex preference functions may lead to an empty core. Some of these are rather common features and thus pose obstacles for the existence of Coasean solutions even when TC are negligible.

The role of probabilistic pay-offs and expectations among players is no less important in influencing their strategies and potential co-operation. As Cooter (1982) pointed out, the strategy selected by each player depends upon his/her assessment of subjective probabilities of various events and their corresponding pay-offs relative to his/her opponents' strategies. Thus some a priori specification of the mechanism for their expectations formation is a relevant part of the bargaining game in the Coasean negotiation process. In contrast to Coasean predictions, lowering TC could lead in this description to the reversal of incentives for an early resolution of the bargaining solution.

The Coase theorem assumes the validity of optimism that there exists co-operative behaviour between contending parties, when the TC of bargaining are negligible; this ignores, among other things, the commonly observed role of strategic behaviour (Cooter, 1989). The fact that bargaining is itself a transaction cost (Usher, 1998) suggests there are inherent fundamental flaws in the assertions with Coasean proposals. Some of the strongest logical objections to the validity of the Coase theorem have been enunciated by Usher (1998): the perceived role of TC conceals a fundamental assumption and corresponding cost about bargaining/negotiation; and the failure to agree is itself a TC. The cost of bargaining exists and is a function of surplus to be divided among parties.

It has been recognized, after the formulation of several interpretations of Coase propositions, that the Coase theorem requires, among other prerequisites, the absence of a 'wealth effect' in order to lead to the stated conclusions. The non-existence of a wealth effect is generally uncommon. The conditions explained by Milgrom and Roberts (1992) for the phenomenon of 'no wealth effect' are given below:

(i) given any two alternative decisions, there would exist a finite monetary sum that would suffice the economic agent or decision-maker to switch from one to the other choice of decision;

(ii) if the decision-maker were given an additional quantum of wealth, the switch would still occur at the same compensation level as above; and,

(iii) the decision-maker has sufficient monetary resources to absorb any loss of wealth necessary for a switch from the less preferred to the more preferred option.

Pigou and Coase

Nalebuff (1997) established the following:

(i) a market-based property rights approach is not a universal solution for all economic problems whenever TC are positive; and
(ii) at efficient levels of pollution, both Pigouvian taxes and Coasean property rights tend to coincide: the marginal damage equals the Pigouvian tax, and this equals the market price for pollution rights.

Is there a positive economics explanation for the limited difference between Pigouvian and Coasean prescriptions for externalities and related economic governance? Aidt (1998) posited that the public choice axiom of political self-interest narrows the gap between Coasean and Pigouvian approaches to the internalization of externalities. Competition between different interest groups, lobbyists and policy-makers/law-makers results in a temporal equilibrium as a compromise in the alternative objectives and their attainment in terms of varying levels of TC. The government usually has a tendency to levy Pigouvian tax, and Coasean bargaining applies after that. As a result of such processes, the divergence between an original Coasean solution and a new Coasean solution (related to the Pigouvian prescription) as well as that between Coasean solution and Pigouvian solution is reduced; the persistent gap is a function of political lobbying and public pressure as well as political and bureaucratic self-interest.

3.4 Market failures and institutional inefficiencies

Since ideal markets do not exist, it makes little sense to compare actual working markets with ideal formalized markets in terms of relative efficiencies. Thus such a comparison cannot form a basis for deducing conclusions about any observed market 'failures'. To qualify for the latter, we need additional operationally meaningful criteria. Similarly, an all-benevolent government that ensures the ideal efficiency features of functioning does not exist. The concept of market failure has often been misinterpreted in the literature to suggest that the role of government intervention is as an automatic standby (presumed cost-free) alternative, with little realization that the remedy can be worse than the ailment (perhaps as enunciated in the classical Shakespearian drama sense). Some policy analysts concluded in a few cases that market failure phenomena constitute necessary but not sufficient justification for governmental intervention. To describe government 'failures' we need additional criteria as well. The concept of market failure is both economic and political. It constituted (Dahlman, 1979, p. 143) 'a normative judgment about the role of government and the ability of markets to establish mutually beneficial exchanges'.

The debate of Coasean and Pigouvian contributions continues beyond externalities problems into the design of institutions with or without reference to the critical role of the government. In fact, the perceived and desirable role of the latter has been a major contentious issue. Coase (1960, p. 18), regarding the problem of choosing an appropriate social arrangement for dealing with harmful effects: 'All solutions have costs and there is no reason to suppose that government regulation is called for simply because the problem is not well handled by the market or the firm. Satisfactory views on policy can only come from a patient study of how, in practice, the market, firms and government handle the problem of harmful effects.'

Earlier, Pigou (1932, ch. 20 nt 36, quoted in Simpson, 1996) stated: 'The mere failure of private industry, when left free from public interference, to maximise the national dividend does not itself warrant intervention; for this might make things worse.' However, Pigou was a greater believer in the role of government intervention, and attracted the attention of Coase (1937, 1960).

One useful way of understanding the concept of market failure is to appreciate the notion of market success – the ability of a collection of idealized competitive markets to achieve an equilibrium allocation of resources which is Pareto-optimal. The First Fundamental Theorem of Welfare Economics links this concept with efficiency (see Arrow, 1951): if there are enough markets and if all producers as well as consumers behave rationally and competitively, and if an equilibrium of demand and supply exists, then the allocation of resources in that competitive equilibrium will be Pareto-optimal.

Government institutions may be able to deliver better results than private institutions and markets only when a scheme of incentives and corresponding contracts cannot be devised to augment markets and non-governmental institutions to equip themselves for appropriate corrections in the form of internalization of externalities and other relevant features. There is never an objective implication for the role of the government when market failure occurs, nor is there a doubt that the latter happens more frequently than most advocates of an all-pervasive market role proclaim.

Applied Aspects

As an illustration of the application of market failure concept in public policy, let us consider the US Government Executive Order 12866 of 1993. This requires US federal government officials to conduct economic analyses so as to provide justification, if any, for specific government regulations. The Order requires as a prerequisite for recommending government intervention that an assessment be made about whether the problem or issue on hand 'constitutes a significant market failure'.

In an applied and empirical study of policy/government failures in a set of sixteen case studies in the developing economies, Ascher's (1999) book analysed wasteful or inefficient resource allocation. Most arguments in this book refer to 'flawed institutions' and the inefficiency of public-sector administration. Proneness to managerial corruption in these government-controlled monopolies was rather widespread. Transparency or reduction of informational asymmetries and the provision of incentives for performance were suggested as important requirements for reform, if these entities still deserve to be located in the public sector. Clearly, both the requirements of reform refer to components of TC, and thus a general solution to be devised should follow the prescriptions of TCE.

Market as well as non-market institutions depict varying levels of performance and efficiency indicators. In severe cases of inefficiency these are also referred to as corresponding institutional failures, including market failures. A few qualifying factors exist for general scenarios, but a number of situation-specific or system-specific features contribute to the same end even when the general features (stated below) are not prevalent. The issue is not whether market or other institutional failure exits, but rather the underlying extent of inefficiency and provision of potential remedies that take into account attendant TC. TCE directs attention to the characteristics of government institutions that could possess advantageous features for the governed relative to other institutions in terms of lower TC (Zerbe and McCurdy, 1999).

If the Coase theorem suggests that complete markets produce efficient outcomes, are missing markets the root cause of all externalities? As Nalebuff (1997) pointed out, incompleteness of markets coincide with the existence of positive TC, since externality is the result of untraded goods and services. Even when PR are assigned and the externality dimension is brought into tradable category, the trading itself will be so thin as to negate the virtues of market institutions in many cases;

even after the assignment of PR there remains the problem of public policy and governance, including the role of LR (Rao, 2001).

Four types of factor are identified for their role in market inefficiencies and/or market failure (Wolf, 1979): externalities and public goods; increasing returns; market imperfections; and distributional inequality. The identified factors for non-market failure are: internalities and private goals; redundant and rising costs; derived externalities; and distributional inequality in relation to the exercise of power and influence.

Unlike much of neoclassical economics that entails adjustments at the margin (often referred to as second-order analysis) and claim normative efficiency fulfilment, TCE examines discrete structural alternatives (often referred to as first order analysis, by institutional economists) that provide the foundations for the existence and operation of some of the normative efficiency criteria emphasized in neoclassical economics. The provision of an appropriate mix of market, firm and bureaucratic organizations is an area of major concern for TCE. Relative strengths and weaknesses of these alternative forms, and different mixes of these, are generally sought to be examined via some of the criteria of TCE for their efficiency, sustainability and welfare enhancement for the society, or profit maximization for the enterprise, as the case may be. There have been criticisms in radical economic literature that TCE does not do enough to address the issues of fundamental institutional reforms, but that issue is one of pure political choice and social acceptance. It is difficult, though not impossible, to offer a TCE base for major reforms. Perhaps TCE need not be burdened with tasks that are not legitimately within its sphere of competence. None the less, the issue must be recognized that total indifference to initial conditions, or initial distribution of power and assets, is not always a meaningful scenario for the appreciation of desirable economic and institutional alternatives.

TCE and Coase propositions provide a significant insight into the fact that the mere existence of the phenomenon of market failure does not warrant government intervention in any automatic alternative sense, nor necessarily an optimizing TC sense. Instead, a parallel analysis of regulatory failure or government failure is necessary to enable the evaluation of a range of options in between as well. As Williamson (2000) suggested, the Coasean view expands the study of economic organization with more articulate alternatives and public policy in prospect. An analysis of imperfect alternatives is better facilitated in the Coasean approach than in an idealized neoclassical economic sense when we are short on several quantifiable parameters to apply standard methods of neoclassical economics. The imperative to examine the role of TC in each alternative alignment of resources and institutions is the message of TCE, and the concept of zero TC is helpful to initiate such analyses (Williamson, 2000). As in mathematics, the innovation of zero TC as a reference level has its fundamental advantages in the progress of learning.

If one needs a better integration of perspectives beyond the recognition of TC underlying both market and non-market institutions, let us note the narration of Bowles (1998). He concluded, based on a survey of cultural consequences of market and other economic institutions, that a broader concept of market failure is required, to include the effects of economic policies and institutions on preferences in society, and thus seek an appropriate mix of markets, communities, families and states in economic governance. In brief, there exists the need to incorporate the role and welfare effects of institutions and networks.

3.5   Network externalities

Networks are defined as a set membership of economic entities with an underlying physical or economic linkage. Network externality refers to the phenomenon of accrual to any member a bundle of positive or negative effects from within or outside the network.

Networks comprise physical or non-physical entities (including membership organizations) that are explicitly or implicitly co-ordinated by technology or human action. A participant (voluntary or implicitly associated) belongs to one or more networks in one or both of the possibilities: (i) may pay a fee to participate in a network; or (ii) may not even be aware, initially, of an association with a network and thus it is involuntary association by virtue of a transaction the 'participant' undertook and/or continues to undertake. Examples include: Apple computer users; the North American Automobile Club; and frequent flyers.

The terminology of 'network externalities' arose largely from the network industries of the computer age, and was originally limited to information technology and the personal computer industry. In that context, the benefit that a party's use of a product or service confers on the value of that product or service was called network externality (see, for example, Katz and Shapiro, 1985, 1986; Johnston, 1993; and Klausner, 1995).

An economic activity depicts network externalities when its value to the participant or transactor is a function of the number and type of use for other participants or transactors. The role of these externalities is akin to that of other externalities in that there exists a divergence between individual optimality and social optimality in the presence of such externalities. Much of the neoclassical economics literature tends to ignore the nature of externalities when it comes to corporate contracts (see Chapter 6 for details of the law and economics of contracts). This is a major omission, considering the role of externalities that exist in the form of network externalities in this arrangement.

The role of TC in corporate law, and the connections between TC and network externalities is beginning to be understood only in recent years (since about the early 1990s). In the corporate management context, Klausner (1995) detailed the role of these 'unrecognized' externalities and suggested the possibility that corporate contracts which maximize individual firm values do not necessarily lead to Pareto-efficiency or social optimality. This observation questions the contractarian perspective-based assertions of Easterbrook and Fischel (1991, p. 34): 'Corporate law is a set of terms available off-the-rack so that participants in corporate ventures can save the costs of contracting...Corporate codes and existing judicial decisions supply these terms "for free" to every corporation, enabling the ventures to concentrate on matters that are specific to their undertaking.'

Klausner (1995) identified a few significant types of network externalities and their sources in the context of corporate law. Typically, these are the sources that apply to variations in the incidence of TC. Network benefits constitute a positive externality, wherever these exist. In the corporate sector, such benefits include the benefit of judicial rulings from time to time – thus contributing to the reduction of some of the uncertainties of transactions and reduction of TC; the emergence of common practices among participants and the benefit of interpretation of the terms of the contracts that apply in the specific category (evolution of standards and norms, enabling expectations and predictability at different levels – an influencing factor for TC); and the effects on marketability of products and services. There may, however, exist some judicial decisions that do not contribute immediately to the reduction of some of the legal uncertainties, but these still lead to the evolution of stable legal norms later and thus reduce corresponding uncertainties. Where informational asymmetries exist and communications are costly, network marketing externalities operate to the advantage of the network participants.

Four distinct phenomena have been identified for the potential market failure or sub-optimality of contract terms in the presence of externalities (Klausner, 1995, p. 813):

(i)   Since the network benefits accrue at a future time, the time-discounting may lead some contract designers to prefer terms with immediate benefits;

(ii)   A similar effect may be possible when a firm considers the uncertainties associated with the number of adopters of similar terms of contract;

(iii) When firms differ in their valuations of alternative terms and their time-based discounting, the contract choices of early adopters may bias the contracting terms of later entrants, and thus lead potentially to sub-optimal uniformity in contracts; and

(iv)   With changes in the business environment and other innovations, accumulated network benefits can create either a socially sub-optimal 'lock-in' effect, or herd behaviour to abandon a socially desirable optimum contractual term.

Among other important findings of the role of networks in the resource allocation and economic governance processes are the following:

(i)   Network externalities can lead to a non-optimal choice of standards in a decentralized market economy (for details, see Blankart and Knieps, 1993); and

(ii)   Network externalities render institutional change less rapid and more incremental, thus imposing their own sets of TC on the system at the aggregate levels; this results partly from the role of the existence of 'interest groups' and lobbying activities that often follow the formation of a network.

It is of interest to note that sociologists use the framework of 'structural analysis', which maintains a focus on the patterns of relationships among social (and thus also economic) actors, and posits that the constraints associated with locations or positions in a network of relationships are usually more important in determining specific decision choices than the information or attitudes the decision-makers possess. Without stating the role of network externalities explicitly, this approach also suggests the role of such factors. Besides, it also seeks explanations regarding the role of a self-perpetuating system of structural constraints without claiming any 'efficiency' attributes (where positive economic approaches might seek explanations for the *ex post* efficiency features); see Leifer and White (1987) for a 'structural approach' to market functioning.

3.6 Conclusions

TC play an important role in affecting economic behaviour, and influence the specifications of different economic instruments for economic governance. The role of TC is distinct, though not always separable, from the role of externalities. TC exist even when the latter are absent, and the latter exist independently of TC. In many cases, both are correlated. The need to examine the role of TC in each alternative alignment of resources and institutions is the message of TCE.

Coase's contributions remain significant in directing attention to the evaluation of pragmatic alternatives, even though some of the pointed results (such as the so-called Coase theorem) fail to meet several requirements toward realistic applications. Also, it must be clarified, it is not fair to Coase to term a 'Coasean world' (as several writers seem to have done) as one of zero transaction costs, since the greatest contribution of Coase was to clarify the role of transaction costs.

The phenomenon of thin markets can often vitiate the role of Coasean analysis in general, and Coase's theorem in particular. The basis of Coasean analysis is that PR are well defined and enforced, and remain tradable.

Coase's theorem assumes that the bargaining process leads to optimality but the mechanism of attaining this is far from clear nor assured in many scenarios. Strategic and iniquitous behaviour of parties is a major obstacle for Coasean bargaining solutions even when TC are negligible. Coase's theorem is founded on a status quo structure of power and rights, and is largely fictional; however, the Coasean analysis of TC is fundamental. The following prescription (also referred to in the literature as the Total Product Rule) from Coase (1960, p. 15) may not hold except in a static and non-adaptive framework with valid market-based valuations of goods and services: 'The economic problem in all cases of harmful effects is to maximize the value of production.'

The notion that political internalization of environmental externalities exists is sufficient to enable a reproachment of the Coasean and Pigouvian solutions to policy. First the Pigouvian tax method and then the bargaining under the influence of various lobbying activities (environment and business interests, among others) are typical of the real working of public systems in many countries.

4
New Neoclassical Economics

4.1 Introduction

What is new neoclassical economics (NNE)? It is an integration of neoclassical economics (NE) and transaction cost economics (TCE), with a primary role for NE but without losing sight of TCE. Is this a compromise formula for something? Perhaps it is. The main purpose here (and in most chapters of this book) is to strengthen the current implementation of NE and its limitations whenever institutional alternatives are to be evaluated. NE cannot be an effective analytical tool of economic and social science if it remains largely oblivious to the distinctions of alternative forms of economic governance and implications on economic efficiency and economic justice. It is often fashionable to talk about 'getting prices right' even when there is little understanding as to whether or not the corresponding or underlying economic structures are amenable to pragmatic reform in the interests of economic efficiency and/or economic justice. 'Getting institutions right' is often a prerequisite for getting the prices right.

The premise of TCE is that transaction is the basic unit of analysis. Does it imply that NNE has to do the same in the integration of TCE and NE? Perhaps yes, with an enlarged definition of what constitutes a 'unit'. It should be feasible to define units at different levels of aggregation and apply relevant concepts for analysis.

This chapter addresses a few important areas of economic analyses with the objective of re-examining their current state of understanding, and the role as well as the potential policy implications of the recognition of significant TC that have been neglected thus far. Areas of investigation include, in addition to the application of classical optimality conditions and their modifications in formal analytical models, the issues of economic growth and development, trade liberalization and international credit lending, and the wisdom of conditionalities in lending. A few related aspects of analysis such as the relationships between modern information economics and TCE are also examined. Other applied areas of review in this chapter include: credit rationing, optimal public expenditure and subsidy mechanisms, sovereign debt contracts and economic reforms.

4.2 Marginality principles and economic optimality

The standard optimizing models and the optimality conditions (including marginality principles or first-order conditions of optimality) presume, among other features, the existence of a competitive equilibrium. If competitive behaviour of market systems is assumed, as in a traditional NE model, and at the same time the competition relies on the existence of positive TC, 'it follows that property rights cannot be completely defined and enforced, that neither consumers nor producers can be perfectly informed about the prices and properties of the things they buy, etc. Such deviations necessarily prevent the realization of idealized competitive equilibrium' (Furubotn, 1991, p. 681). Also, in a zero TC world, there are hardly any barriers to the collusive behaviour of producers, thus defeating the premise of the competitive process itself. A free market system, then, is incapable of producing a first-best Pareto-optimal equilibrium touted in much of NE. Does this imply automatically that non-free-market systems are better? Far from being plausible, such an alternative is not automatic either. All that is asserted here is that the traditional frictionless competitive economy models do not lead to the promised level of efficiency, and the shortfall in efficiency can have differential cost implications for the participating economic actors.

As Furubotn (1991, p. 684) observed: 'Institutional arrangements exert a direct effect on economic operations by influencing the level of transaction costs and the structure of incentives. Institutions, then, represent key "variables" that have to be included in the optimization problem.'

If the configurations of constraints in a rational optimizing model are inclusive of (i) the broader cost concepts that do not assume zero TC; (ii) the institutional features such as variational property rights; and (iii) the differential motives of economic actors, the traditional idealized NE models possess a closer resemblance to reality as well as tending to integrate institutional economics, including TCE. This is what is called New Neoclassical Economics (NNE). In a relevant approach, De Alessi

(1983) suggested the usefulness of generalizing the NE approach to include, as a first step, the utility maximization approaches to both consumer decision models as well as firm-level decision-making scenarios (which also recognize the principal–agent features); the prevalence of non-negligible TC induces new sets of efficiency solutions based on added sets of interactive constraints.

Whereas institutional economics and the governance of economic structures remains the primary focus of TCE, resource allocation under a given constellation of institutional arrangements remains the primary focus of NE. This lower level optimization problem is extremely important but not to the extent of ignoring the interactive nature of implications of alternative resource allocation mechanisms on the efficiency properties of institutions, and their bearing on resource allocative efficiency properties. TCE enables the getting right of the institutions, and NE derives getting the marginal optimality conditions right for a given institutional regime.

In terms of analytical formulations, standard optimization methods of variational calculus, including the Euler–Lagrange equation, should accommodate for the role of TC as (in the original terminology of physics and mechanics in which the variational methods originated) 'external forces', 'friction', or 'dissipative forces' P.

Let us use the notation:

L = profit or revenue function (or other relevant objective function);
X = state variable representing investment or production function (or other dependent variable, depicted as a time-dependent function) F;
Q = costate variable that represents the opportunity cost of changes in X; and
H = The Hamiltonian (see Chapter 1).

The standard Euler–Lagrange equation does not seek equalization of the variation to zero (as traditional neoclassical economic models suggest in their first-order optimality conditions) but to P. The corresponding Hamiltonian equations require the following to hold (see, for example, Santilli, 1983):

$$\dot{X} = \frac{\partial H}{\partial Q}$$
$$\dot{Q} = -\frac{\partial H}{\partial X} + P$$

with $H = L + QX$

Unlike the standard results of neoclassical economics, in revenue/ profit maximization the optimal level of production or investment does not equal the shadow price of capital or production, but the shadow price plus a quantity representing TC. When TC equals zero, the standard result obtains. It is thus seen that the marginal rate in this generalized case is greater than that in the simplified case of standard zero TC assumption.

The economics of information

The economics of information has been a great new contributor to standard NE since the late 1970s. In particular, the theory of incomplete information and incomplete contracting leads to the result that the market may not be in equilibrium in the sense of equalizing demand and supply at any price. The role of TC in all these case is the single most significant contributor to the emergence of features such as price stickiness, price dispersion, wage dispersion and excessive product differentiation.

Among the presentations that assume part of the role of TCE in the framework of NE is the information economics survey by Stiglitz (2000). He claimed (ibid., p. 1459): 'The new information economics not only showed that institutions mattered, and helped explain why the institutions arose and the forms they took, but showed why they mattered.' He went on to claim that it was Arnott and Stiglitz (1991) who showed that non-market institutions could even exacerbate the consequences of market failure (see also below for a contradiction by Stiglitz himself on this point). However, this result was articulated by Coase (1960, p. 27), thirty-one years before their contribution: 'What has to be decided is whether the gain from preventing the harm is greater than the loss which would be suffered elsewhere as a result of stopping the action which produces the harm.' Coase (ibid., p. 18) did argue that if the costs of handling through the market are high and if net costs are lower, only then may government regulations be relevant (see also Chapter 3). Similarly, about three decades before this assertion, Pigou (1932, ch. 20, nt 36) had observed: 'The mere failure of private industry, when left free from public interference, to maximise national dividend does not itself warrant intervention; for this might make things worse.' Ironically, Coase (1960) alleged it was Pigou who was unconditionally in favour of government intervention. It is apt to quote Coase (1964, p. 195) here: 'It is no accident that in the literature ... we find a category "market failure" but no category "government failure". Until we realize that we are choosing between social arrangements which are all more or less failures, we are not likely to make much headway.'

Also, Stiglitz (2000, p. 1459) claimed that the information economics 'dispelled a growing misconception (not unrelated to the Coase conjecture) that nonmarket institutions arose to address market failures, and that in doing so, they restored the efficiency of the economy'. This position regarding Coasean analysis is a misinterpretation. If anything, Coasean conjectures are accused in much of the literature of endorsing a whole spectrum of market-based interventions to address efficiency problems.

It is rather well known that whenever information is imperfect and/or markets are incomplete, competitive markets do not obey the Pareto-optimality efficiency criterion (see Hurwicz, 1973). Similarly, it is also known in NE literature (see, for example, Kogiku, 1971) that a competitive equilibrium ceases to produce Pareto-optimality when there are externalities that affect the system. In this scenario, Stiglitz (2000, p. 1458) jumps to the conclusion, without any concern for associated TC nor any proof of analysis: 'Government interventions – in the form, say, of taxes or subsidies on commodities that might lead to greater care (in risk taking situations) – will in general lead to Pareto improvements.'

It should be rather evident that the government monopolizes resources and power whenever its role does not include sufficient accountability, and this monopoly is often worse than that of the private sector for the simple reason that the former entails larger TC and hence much more social cost relative to the latter. As Zerbe and McCurdy (1999) rightly argued, TCE provides a core argument against the NE-based market failure analysis. They stated that when we recognize the existence of market failure phenomena as they potentially could occur, all forms of externalities of government interventions and non-market failures must be reckoned with (see Chapter 3 for more details). In the TCE perspective this prescription has been a basic premise for further analysis. Thus, Arnott and Stiglitz (1991) merely reconfirmed with their use of NE what was well established (but perhaps not always taken into account in practical policy). Suffice it to state that the role of non-market institutions can only be supplementary and not substitutory for market institutions, and that often the underlying causes of market failure include the failure of the government infrastructure in its complementary role as the provider of necessary legal and other institutional framework (including proper provision of property rights and liability rules, as well as their enforcement).

Some of these Stiglitzian claims of information economics are not totally ill-founded, but they do not convey the whole story. It is because TCE is not confined to information economics but rather it subsumes the latter. It is also clear that as further investigations continued in both of these areas, their original gap in the potential to offer economic insights is reduced significantly.

One point was emphasized in Stiglitz (2000): even with slight imperfections of information (which is rather common), most results of NE do not seem to hold. Relevant examples include the existence of price dispersion (or price distribution, as it is sometimes called) even in competitive markets in their equilibrium (because of the role of search costs of consumers and the recognition of this feature to the advantage of sellers in spatially or sectorally segmented markets), marginal cost does not equal price under profit maximizing optimality conditions whenever (not uncommon) issues of reputational and quality considerations arise. We explain the marginal cost issue further below.

The analysis of reputation, the economics of pricing and of private contractual enforcement are addressed together in the study by Klein and Leffler (1981). The study shows that when it is costly to observe quality (that is, in the presence of TC corresponding to information on quality), prices will diverge from marginal cost even in competitive market equilibrium. Their main result is that prices charged in excess of marginal cost provide an incentive for the firm to maintain its reputation for high-quality goods. Based on partial equilibrium analysis, the price rule states: the price of a high quality good equals the marginal cost plus a price premium; the latter equals the product of the interest rate and the difference between the good's marginal cost and the marginal cost of lowest tolerable quality good of the category.

Considering the role of quality and of related information at the consumer level, Wolinsky (1983) showed that the equilibrium price of a product is greater than the marginal cost of producing a good of given quality; in the absence of the role of fixed costs, as the product-specific quality information approaches perfect information level in the market, prices approach marginal costs. However, when fixed costs include TC, and if the marginal cost assessment itself adds to TC, this assertion also does not hold good.

If information economics has made us 'realize that much of standard economics is based on foundations resting on quicksand' (Stiglitz, 2000, p. 1461), it is even stronger reasoning to infer that TCE has rendered a better contribution by expanding the horizons encompassing the role of information economics and beyond.

Clearly, information is associated with non-convexities, just as externalities are (see Chapter 3). The role of information is akin to that of externalities, including information externalities. The existence of a fundamental non-convexity in the value of information was proved by Radner and Stiglitz (1984).

Credit rationing

Credit rationing is the phenomenon of the existence of excess demand at all levels of loan rates or cost of capital borrowings in a market, for a given supply of credit; or the feature that some of the potential borrowers are excluded from a loan market while some others with identical characteristics succeed in obtaining credit. Stiglitz and Weiss (1981) examined an effectively static model of equilibrium credit rationing and suggested that the problems of moral hazard and adverse selection in loan markets arise from the existence of 'residual imperfect information' after lenders' processing of potential credit borrowers. Adverse selection problems, handled in a multi-period model, lead to long-term contracts (see, for example, Webb, 1991).

It is also important to recognize the existence of dual credit markets, comprising the formal institution-based (banks or financial lending institutions) and credit transactions related to the informal lenders (pawnbrokers and other lenders). The interaction of the two markets for credit and the clear distinctions between the effective costs of obtaining loans in either of the two markets determine the type and extent of credit rationing. The role of TC surfaces predominantly at the borrower level and influence the demand pattern according to applicant types, an illustrative case of self-selection/self-sorting among loan borrowers based on their creditworthiness and risk attributes as well as their perceived TC in securing the desired loan. Locational proximity, simplicity or complexity of loan processing, and the use of bribery in formal financial institutions are among the factors that influence TC in this context.

On the credit rationing problem from the perspective of TCE, the following result, from Williamson (1987), is significant: positive TC in a situation of asymmetric information are sufficient to lead to the phenomenon of credit rationing in equilibrium, even when there are none of the problems of adverse selection or moral hazard that are often associated with imperfect information.

Many of the standard results of NE do not hold if we ignore the role of information economics. Also, even when the concepts and methods of information economics are utilized, many of these results do not hold good if we ignore the role of TCE. This is because TCE includes the role of institutions and contractual governance, in addition to features including TC (which include information costs).

4.3 Economic growth and development

The role of TC in macroeconomic growth and economic development deserves particular attention. TCE literature provides some powerful insights into the relationships between these economic processes and their transformation in relation to TC, including both direct and indirect routes of transmission of TC. The former include such factors as obvious deadweight loss factors and the latter include the role of regulation and government controls. One can extend the reasoning to include further loss factors in terms of their forward and backward linkages as well. Linkages for regulatory controls, for example, could include bureaucratic corruption and influence peddling in some systems. All these tend to act as additional multipliers whenever new frictions are added to an otherwise naturally governable (or low TC governance) system.

Economic growth

In his Nobel lecture of 1971, Kuznets stated the definition (Kuznets, 1973, p. 247): 'A country's economic growth may be defined as a long-term rise in capacity to supply increasingly diverse economic goods to its population, this growing capacity based on advancing technology and the institutional and ideological adjustments that it demands.' Kuznets added that institutional and ideological adjustments must be made for the efficient use of technical resources and improvements in human capital, and in his concluding remarks emphasized the need for economic studies that deal with 'quantitative bases and institutional conditions' of various national economies – in addition to 'seemingly optimal policy prescriptions'. Thus there has been a major concern for institutional factors and the need for an integration of quantitative information of economic factors with qualitative information regarding economic governance.

A few illustrative studies of more recent years also suggest a search for the key engines of growth: institutional infrastructure. In a study of comparative economic growth of different countries over about a century, Reynolds (1983, p. 978) concluded that the single most important influencing factor for economic growth is 'political organisation and the administrative competence of government'. In an empirical study encompassing around ninety countries over about three decades, Barro (1997) observed that the growth of real per capita gross domestic product (GDP) is enhanced by the maintenance of the rule of law, lower government consumption, and lower inflation. Thus the existence of rich governments and poor societies does not augur well for economic growth. Another empirical study, by Kormendi and Meguire (1986), found that the rate of growth of per capita GDP was correlated positively with a proxy for the degree of protection of property rights (PR). Political infrastructure is to be considered as economic infrastructure. Following an evolutionary perspective, Nelson and Sampath (2001) argued that economic growth results from the co-evolution of physical and social technologies, where the latter were interpreted as standardized institutions. It is also stated that these standardized or calibrated institutions provide for low TC-based mechanisms for interaction among economic entities.

Allocative efficiency and adaptive efficiency are two distinct and not necessarily congruent indicators of performance of an economic system. These aspects are better understood when we examine the process of economic development and economic stability. The role of adaptive efficiency remains very important for an economy to cope with emerging changes over time and across different variables at any given point of time. Let us recall an important observation of North (1990, p. 80):

> Adaptive efficiency is concerned with the kind of rules that shape the way an economy evolves through time. It is also concerned with the willingness of a society to acquire knowledge and learning, to induce innovation, to undertake risk and creative activity of all sorts, as well as to resolve problems and bottlenecks of the society through time.

Transitional dynamics

Endogenous growth models often incorporate the roles of externalities and imperfect competition. Both of these features affect the potential realization of economic efficiency in terms of optimal allocation of resources. Optimal policies obtained under the commonly used assumption of steady-state economy remain sub-optimal when economies are in transition, as they often are.

Contrary to the claims of some contributions in NE, transitional dynamics play a major role in conditioning economic growth and the development of economies. The following is an illustrative example of misinterpretations arising from NE based on steady-state economic analysis. Rebelo (1991, p. 502) claimed that the transitional effects of economic policies cannot have a large impact on the economic growth rate because 'the rough constancy of the real interest rate during the last century suggests that transitional dynamics play a modest role in the growth process'. There is no such constancy for several countries, such as those in Africa and parts of Asia, where the rates have been near zero or negative and fluctuating. Yet after the use of NE methods, it was concluded that the economic growth rate will be low in countries with high tax rates and/or a high proportion of government consumption in gross national product (GNP), and imperfect property rights regimes. The imperatives of both these features are simply those relating to TC, with the main issue being to optimize TC if an optimal economic growth rate is to follow.

In most NE models (such as those examined in Rebelo, 1991), economic policy has implications for economic growth only during the transition path toward the so-called steady state, and the costs of transition do not matter. This is typical of most of the studies undertaken by institutions such as the World Bank (WB) and the International Monetary Fund (IMF) in their prescriptions of policy for their capital-borrowing client countries of the set of developing nations.

Transactions occur within the framework of a social structure and its evolutionary dynamics. This structure provides the incentives (if any) for honest and co-operative behaviour and disincentives (if any) for deviant or undesirable activities of interacting individuals and economic entities. This process is sometimes referred to as 'embeddedness' of economic relations (Granovetter, 1985).

Role of trust

Since trust reduces TC, it is significant that economic growth and trust are correlated positively. How do we 'produce' trust? This is partly anthropological and cultural, and partly informal. However, there is a role for formal, credible (that is, trustworthy) institutions to enforce incentives and disincentives for trust depicting and cheating behaviour, respectively. If the enforcing organizations are themselves of dubious quality, no role can be contemplated for the 'production' of trust. In fact, the perverse incentives that some of the formal organizations provide in some countries are such that they contribute to the production of distrust. This could lead to another question: How do we obtain such credible institutions in a trust-scarce system? It has never been easy to break the cycle of trust-deficient society and the prevalence of similar governing organizations. It is no easy prescription to generate more trust, but one thing is clear: lack of trust can contribute towards low economic growth (see Chapter 5 for more analysis).

The bidirectional linkages between low trust and poverty have been postulated and partly verified empirically by Zak and Knack (2001). Let us recall an earlier observation from Mill (1848, p. 131): 'The advantage to mankind of being able to trust one another, penetrates into every crevice and cranny of human life: The economical is perhaps the smallest part of it, yet even this is incalculable.'

Economic development

The developing countries that did not succeed in maintaining economic stability and sustaining economic growth were found in the 1980s and 1990s (Rodrik, 1999, p. 17) to be those where their 'social and political institutions were inadequate to bring about the bargains required for macroeconomic adjustment – they were societies with weak *institutions of conflict management* . . . adjusting to changing circumstances, and to external shocks in particular, requires the presence of institutions that can mediate distributional conflicts in society.' Rodrik's economic growth formulation (in the context of negative externalities for developing countries arising from global economic shocks) depicted direct proportionality of growth with latent social conflict, and inverse proportionality with institutions of conflict management. Although Rodrik did not relate the analysis to the role of TCE explicitly, his work is an illustrative empirical exercise in the role of institutions and institutional economics, with special reference to the adaptive efficiency requirements of economic governance. Much of NE modelling ignores these fundamental requirements for policy prescriptions, especially in less developed economies.

The *modus operandi* of transactions in a society in general, and managing the incidence of TC in particular, play a major role in determining the economic progress of any society. It is useful to note here that even those societies where the economy is only partially monetized (as in several developing countries), the TC play an important role in the efficiency of economic governance. As North (1990, p. 54) rightly observed: 'The inability of societies to develop effective, low-cost enforcement of contracts is the most important source of both historical stagnation and contemporary underdevelopment in the Third World.' Stern (1991) did not recognize the role of TC explicitly in his synthesis of the economics and policy of development, but observed that a close study of the institutional and other impediments to the intersectoral movement of resources could have a substantial pay-off, benefiting the management and organization in each sector.

Hierarchical and decentralized economic management

If the TC of operating organizations were zero, resource allocation and income distribution would be the same in a free enterprise economy as in a communist command economy; individual preferences are revealed without cost or do not matter. Poor economic performance of a command economy is attributable mainly to excessive TC. The bureaucratic nature of the erstwhile centrally-planned economies of East Europe were vulnerable to TC associated with economic development relative to market economies, and these factors hampered the potential for economic growth (Pryor, 1994).

Technically, in linear programming methodology, the equivalence of optimal values in linear models under primal optimization and its dual optimization suggests a similar interpretation. The above description does not always extend to general non-linear models, however. In certain cases of non-linearities involving assumptions of convex structures, the equivalence of the primal and dual optimal values holds; see 'duality theorem' 30.5 in Rockefeller (1970, p. 318).

In the context of political economy, Colombatto and Macey (1999) examined information and TC for citizenry participation in influencing economic policies and hence economic growth in democratic countries, and contrasted these aspects with the fact that information costs as well as TC are very high in non-democratic systems for effecting any desirable economic change. In this interpretation, the economic change agents from the society are facing a high TC scenario in their efforts to attain economic growth anywhere near its potential (see also Olson, 1963). It is also perceived in Colombatto and Macey's (1999) paper that incumbent rulers in these countries have an incentive to keep such costs high and thus continue to stay in power; any enhancement of economic growth potential is carried out in terms of rent-seeking activity. 'The typical totalitarian country differs from the democratic world in that there is no clear contract between populace and ruling elite' (ibid., p. 639). The contractual context of public policies remains an important aspect for further study in relation to the role of TC; see Chapter 6 for more details.

One of the applications of the role of TC as a limiting factor in economic development is seen from the observation of Ehrlich and Lui (1999): 'The relationship between corruption and the economy is ... explained as an endogenous outcome of competition between growth-enhancing and socially unproductive investments and its reaction to exogenous factors, especially government intervention in private economic activity.'

The failures of government tend to be more acute in countries where social and administrative institutions are developed inadequately, and it is also the case that these are the countries that are not usually well-equipped with functioning markets either. The severity of non-market institutional failures only exacerbates the phenomenon of market failure in a vicious cyclical fashion in some of the developing countries. In all such situations, it would be simplistic to claim that TC alone are the main factors for retarded economic development; rather, it is several institutional features that contribute to the underdevelopment phenomenon. However, the feature that stood out most prominently over the years in respect of countries that moved out from 'command economy' or hierarchical systems is that market institutions tend to play a positive role in the medium run in enhancing economic efficiency. The problems of transition and costs of transition from command economy to market economy are significant, but often remain ignored in public policy, however.

4.4   The economics of free trade

There are at least two features of the economics of free trade that require considerable attention, especially because these have major policy implications and because the existing NE models fail to provide reasonable bases for policy. The first is the role of TC relative to prescriptions of free trade that allow for free factor mobility (usually excluding a significant part of labour, however). The second arises in the context of trade liberalization reforms that are usually prescribed for developing countries as packages for international credit lending from multilateral financial institutions such as the WB and the IMF.

Positive economic analysis of the patterns of international trade suggests that the classical economic predictions based on free trade theories do not fully explain the emerging trade flows (see, for example, Trefler, 1995). Ironically, it was found that international trade theories seem to work better within rather than across countries, and that the role of TC explains much of the trade patterns between countries (Helliwell, 1998). It was suggested that there exists the need to reduce uncertainties of economic exchange, and the reason for greater trade among neighbouring regions (geographic nexus) is not only proximity contributing to reduced transportation and operational costs but also the structure of relations such as trust and cultural understanding. In other words, the costs of information and (generally) TC play important roles here. Social and commercial networks provide low-TC-based exchanges via enhanced trust among interacting economic entities. The implication is for the design of institutions that reduce uncertainties and TC, thus contributing to efficiency improvements and sustenance of trade relations.

Let us provide a definition here.

Free Trade.   The trade policy of a country or a group of countries which impose no tariff or non-tariff restrictions on the trade of legitimate goods and services; the trade transactions occur purely as a result of demand and supply forces; the government's role is such that its contribution to TC remains at zero level.

The classical Heckscher–Ohlin factor price equalization theorem (FPET) states the following: suppose that each of two countries produces something of the same two products with the same two factors, that returns to scale are constant and returns to proportions diminishing, that trade between the two countries is allowed with no impediments. Then the same real and relative factor prices prevail in each country. It is also important to recognize that this theorem was concerned with factor rentals and not prices of durable capital assets.

Specific assumptions for the validity of the theorem include the following:

(i)   Transaction costs are zero or negligible;
(ii)   Factor markets are free from distortions; and
(iii)   Factor mobility across sectors does not entail transaction costs.

A number of elements of transaction costs are noteworthy. Some of these include the following (Rao, 2000b): the trading entities' perception of counterparts' trade terms and their legal enforceability, and the national governments' explicit and implicit policies towards trade with specific countries and governing specific products for export or import; the role of effective taxation on each of the trading activities and their aggregative contribution to the enterpreneur's profitability; and the existence of transparent trade laws and enforcement methods – especially the customs procedures and the role of corruption in enforcement levels. These elements affect potential trade transactions, and these are not usually independent of the national differentiation or geographic reference.

The national borders and institutional differences affect trade significantly, even under the regimes of 'free trade'. Helliwell (1998) rightly argued that geography and national borders have separate but analogous effects in setting patterns of economic activity, and the determinants of the realized trade include transaction costs and the role of history. An earlier study by Amelung (1991) examined the role of TC using the empirical evidence of trade flows in the Asia Pacific region.

Institutional differences (including cultural factors, the familiarity with which plays the economic role of information and trust), the role of uncertainty and TC have been the most robust determinants of trading patterns within and across countries over the past few centuries (see also Greif, 1992).

The increased role of regional trade and trade agreements (such as in the European Community (EU), and in North America) is noteworthy. About half of global trade is channelled through these regional trading arrangements, explaining the major contributory role of TC. These costs include the combination of perceived costs of doing business, familiarity, cultural and political integration, geographical proximity and other factors.

Trade liberalization and TC

Adjustment costs are often an important aspect of trade liberalization. Advocates of unfettered free trade ignore these. Such an approach is tenable if the costs of adjustment are such as to reinvigorate innovation and/or adopt efficient adaptation mechanisms that contribute to long-run efficiency improvements and/or productivity improvements. However, in reality, sections of society and some of the vulnerable sectors of the economy lose out in their potential for survival. If factors of production do not reflect the costs of adjustment, externalities propagate to various other sectors. The case for gradual trade liberalization rather than sudden quantum changes is justifiable largely on the grounds of adaptation and minimization of TC in transition as well as in the long run. In some of the studies this has been suggested even without reference to TC, based only on social considerations. For example, Mussa (1986) found that gradual liberalization is relevant in order to limit income and wealth losses to erstwhile owners of assets and productively employed labour in covered or 'protected' sectors.

The speed of adjustment of economic policies (often in response to external pressures and conditionalities for access to international credit markets) in several of the developing countries has been an issue that met with very limited reflections in both economic theory and practice. Major and sudden reforms entail significant economic and social costs. In fact, such proposals have met with significant resistance from organized labour and other sections of society, who perceive them as damaging to their well-being. They have also led to social upheaval in some countries. Examples abound in most regions of the world whenever such major changes have been proposed – for example, by the IMF in Turkey, Poland, Zimbabwe, Sudan and a few other countries. This preimplementation disruption constitutes just one element of the total set of elements of TC associated with improperly devised and implemented reform packages. Trade liberalization has been the major focus of most of these reforms, which seek to remove artificial constraints on the functioning of the market and provide more openness to the economic system.

Technically, externalities, uncertainties and co-ordination failures induce multiple economic equilibria and there is nothing unique about any particular prescription of economic policy in the way this was undertaken during the last few decades of the twentieth century under the direction of the IMF and/or the WB. Among the few analytical studies on related issues in the NE tradition are those of Frooth (1988) and Mehlum (2001). There are no robust results in literature and the area is wide open for further studies, especially with the integration of TC.

Using a two-period model, Frooth (1988) examined the possibility of self-fulfilling failure when a credit market is constrained in its access to international borrowings, and found that the failure is most likely to occur in the face of drastic rather than gradual reform. Mehlum (2001), in another formulation, suggested the role of risk-averse investors and international aid as elements to soften the negative effects of major reforms. However, this imposition is far from satisfactory as an analytical tool, or for practical policy. The required elements of any proposals for trade liberalization and economic reform should include the following, to begin effecting desirable change: institutional reform; reduction of bureaucratic and archaic procedures; enhancement of adaptive and allocative efficiencies; straightening of information systems and flow of information for decision-making; provision of incentives for efficient performance; sound legal institutions; and the rule of law.

The role and limitations of export-trade-led growth deserve attention in this context. It may be useful only in the short run to emphasize features of export-trade-led growth, to tide over budgetary or other resource requirements. The prerequisites for economic relevance of such measures are: (i) the economic system is not locked into inflexible capital investments – that is, it does not contribute to asset specificity beyond reasonable and optimal limits; and (ii) the substitution effects of such a focus on the macroeconomic linkages of development are minimal or do not entail additional TC and/or derived externalities. These specifications closely resemble those of the adaptive efficiency requirements in the economics of organizations (see Chapter 8 for more details). The critical issue is to relate the speed of reform, speed of adjustment and costs of adjustment in relation to benefits of reform for different sections of society and sectors of the economy.

4.5   The economics of structural adjustment lending

One of the important areas of application of TCE is in credit lending under multi-lateral financial institutions such as the IMF and the WB. The role of TCE pertains in the interface between creditors and borrowers, and in the assessment of costs, benefits and policy desirability under various lending programmes directed by these organizations.

When reversibility costs of capital investments are very high, as is often the case with the asset specificity feature of TCE, uncertainties of future policies contribute to sub-optimal investments from the private sector, and public sector resources will usually continue to lack direction. Rodrik (1990) argued in favour of the need for a 'sustainable policy environment' with the components:

(i)   Stable macro policies, including realistic exchange rate policies and small fiscal deficits;
(ii)   A credible and predictable set of microeconomic incentives, with the expectation of their sustenance over a long time horizon; and
(iii) The absence of forces that would create social and political pressures to reverse courses in the process of changes.

The economics of policy sustainability in this context translates into the economics of TCE, especially in terms of the role of uncertainty, duration of transactions, credibility and provision of incentives for avoidance of *ex post* opportunism of different active and passive (stakeholder) parties to policy reforms.

Rodrik (1990) examined a sample of fifteen countries and their performance during 1982–7 and noted that, among these, the countries that resorted to substantial trade liberalization (as sought under IMF prescribed reforms) did not perform better in terms of investment improvements relative to others. To the extent that reforms generate uncertainty, this source itself entails costs if no attempt is made to offset these by appropriate complementary policies, in both the short run and the long run. The issues of gradualism in reforms versus shock therapy are also amenable to the analysis of TCE more than any other approach. As Rodrik (1996) noted, we need a better understanding of the potential institutional arrangements that compensate undeserved losers of reforms.

In the stabilization programmes, short-term restoration of financial balances has been the main objective (at all costs, for each participating country). The argument that allocative efficiency can be improved by the removal of artificial controls in the efficient functioning of the market for various goods and services is the main argument in favour of regulatory reforms toward economic liberalization or 'market-oriented reforms'. Among the stated objectives of policy reform and structural adjustment is the restoration of conditions for renewed growth. Rodrik (1990) argued that: (i) the source of efficiency improvement benefits is not necessarily the economic liberalization reforms themselves, but from credible and sustained liberalization; and (ii) the efficiency argument provides no strong reason to undertake trade liberalization in an 'unsettled economy' in its early stages of transition towards equilibrium. These arguments simply focus attention to the role of TC in all transitory stages of reform, and the need for credible and uncertainty-reducing provisions in the policies.

Technical claims of integration aside, there is no comprehensive approach to economic and social problems of borrower countries in the IMF and WB approaches. As Tarp (1993, p. 5) pointed out, the analytical models used by these organizations continue largely unaltered, and an integrated framework for analysing stabilization and structural adjustment measures is still lacking. Lack of sustainable development perspectives and the role of transaction costs in affecting economic efficiency are the two most important omissions of the IMF and WB approaches to credit lending to developing countries. Just as product marketeers claim 'new' for most products aimed at consumer marketing, these institutions claim changes and 'new' and/or 'comprehensive' approaches from time to time, with few substantive changes. The main motivation for change would arise when the institutions recognize the role of TCE, especially in the sense of risk sharing with the borrower countries.

The main elements of structural adjustment programmes related to structural adjustment lending (SAL) have been:

- the reduction in domestic financial imbalances, including in the extent of deficit financing;
- increased trade liberalization;
- the reduction in price distortions; and
- the mobilization of domestic and external resources for funding various restructured programme.

The specific instruments of policy generally included:

• domestic bank interest rate and lending policies;
• exchange rate adjustments, usually in the form of devaluation of local currency;
• the reduction of public expenditure;
• the privatization of financially non-performing public-sector enterprises; and
• debt rescheduling.

Each of these elements requires due recognition of the role of TC. It is futile to attempt to 'get prices right' without first putting the corresponding institutional alignment into practice. The transition costs of adjustment are usually ignored, even with the provision of 'social safety net' programmes with some of the reforms.

The analytical models used in this context are based on so-called 'general equilibrium models' (GEM) where the 'friction' costs within an economy are ignored. The efficiency claims of such models have serious shortcomings, and the extent of the gap between the promise of optimal resource allocation and the realized performance varies directly with the prevalence of frictional costs in an economy and its various sectors. Accordingly, intersectoral and inter-country differences are not taken into account when using GEM, despite using country-specific and more disaggregative data that are oblivious to the differential TC underlying their operation. Constrained TC minimization should be regarded as one of the primary requirements of economic reform, and the elements of TC reduction would invariably involve risk-sharing between IMF/WB and the adjustment country. In the absence of such an integration and stakeholder responsibility, these organizations have been playing the role of lender without liability, and offering advice that entails short-term costs and certainty of costs with uncertainty about promised benefits.

Adjustment costs

Is there an awareness of the economic and social costs of adjustment? Social and political upheavals in several countries, leading to social destabilization and economic costs, are very significant in many of the countries that were administered the 'shock therapy' treatments in the name of adjustments.

In a case study relating to the African and Latin-American regions, Stewart (1995) found that per capita expenditure on the social sectors fell significantly among the 'adjusting countries' by about 30 per cent, and by about 17 per cent in Latin America. It was also observed that cuts in food subsidies were part of the programmes of adjustment; any replacements with target subsidies were inadequate as they rarely maintained their purchasing power, and a larger proportion of people were left out. The growth and performance of non-adjusting countries was superior to that of the countries which received adjustment loans from the IMF and WB within the low income and Sub-Saharan groups of countries (see also Mosley, 1994; Stewart, 1995). Several studies documented a significant drop in education and public health services for the poor in most of the countries in Africa. Regarding the effects of structural adjustment programmes in Africa, a World Bank (1994) study stated that there had been cuts in social services, and that poverty reduction was not an explicit central objective of early adjustment programmes. In summary, these programmes inflict both short-term and long-term costs in a differential manner on various sections of the society, but are oblivious of these costs in their cost assessment. Recognition of TC (including transition costs) should direct the institutions towards a new set of policies incorporating the costs of adjustment as well.

Severe limitations of some of the adjustment programmes were noted for several years. The Food and Agriculture Organization of the United Nations (FAO, 1989) argued that the adjustment process 'often results in a sharp fall in real purchasing power of some of the poor and limits their ability to purchase food and other essential items ... Negative effects on the poor are often certain and immediate, whereas positive effects are uncertain and have long gestation periods.' A comprehensive cost–benefit assessment that incorporates TC in economic adjustment and reform processes would eliminate such lopsided policies.

In a later study, Stewart (1995) argued that among the strongest verifiable criticisms against the IMF and the WB is the claim that adverse effects on poverty and environment occurred when the borrower countries undertook adjustment policies at the insistence of these global institutions, and that many of the problems were foreseeable and avoidable; yet these institutions did not share any responsibility for these adverse consequences. The prevalence of TC is thus widespread and no serious attempt was made to reduce these costs.

A recent study by Easterly (2001) questions the wisdom of the policies under Structural Adjustment Lending (SAL) and suggested that these policies have been ineffective, and that the organizations have not changed much over the years – that is, there has been very little 'learning by doing'. Capital transfer mechanisms seem to be influenced most by the common interests of the lender and recipient, and much less by the genuine needs of the populations whose welfare these institutions purportedly enhance. Such processes, by their nature, ignore contemporary TC for the society; instead, a high-cost capital transfer is attempted imposing future liabilities on the recipient society.

Balance of payments (BOP)

Balance of payments (BOP) was one of the main Articles of Agreement of 1945 at the formation of the IMF. One of these objectives was to 'give confidence to members by making the general resources of the fund temporarily available to them under adequate safeguards, thus providing them with opportunities to correct maladjustments in their balance of payments without resorting to measures destructive of national or international prosperity'. However, in practice, the maladjustment is often either misdiagnosed or a strict short-term view of BOP is taken into account, ignoring several aspects of TC in the cost assessment of alternative intervention strategies. The computation of the BOP has been a financial accounting rather than economic assessment. As a result, medium-term and long-term costs, as well as unquantified non-financial costs incurred by some major segments of the society have been systematically ignored. In the context of social capital and human capital, when disturbances occur, as in the case of the imposition of terms of 'structural adjustment', the arguments of Putnam (1993) remain relevant here: lack of measurement or recognition of collective costs in current account schemes does not mean that they do not matter: 'shred enough of the social fabric and we all pay'. Aren't there TC in operation here? Hence the need for a more realistic approach in the design and implementation of economic reform policies.

The structural adjustment measures deal with very short time horizons – one to three years, with assessments every six months. These force the borrower country's policy-makers to seek quick and politically expeditious decisions rather than to consider policies that yield results on a sustainable basis. The UN Report (1997) pointed to the problem of inadequate financing in the face of external shocks forcing countries to make a swift adjustment in their BOP, leading to accelerated export earnings (usually priced by an exchange-rate deflation, implying a greater volume of exports being required to earn the same fixed level of foreign exchange):

Such distress exports were particularly notable among the middle income debtors in the 1980s, when most of them were forced to accommodate not only sharp declines in commodity prices but also cutbacks in lending and mounting debt-service obligations. In some cases, efforts to obtain a swift payments adjustment were an important reason for further downward pressure on commodity prices through the fallacy of composition effect. Similar conditions still prevail today among the HIPCs [heavily indebted poor countries]. (UN Report, 1997)

The TC of a unit of net benefit delivery is extremely high in current institutional alignments. International institutions confronting new economic, social and environmental problems proceed with agency inertia; their unwillingness or inability to dovetail policy interventions to suit new and potential problems is indicative of lack of adaptive efficiency and thus contributes to high TC in their credit lending transactions. Also, as long as the international institutions fail to become trend-setters in their accountability and in the transparency of their operations, it is futile to issue sermons to their clientele on these aspects (see also Shultz and Dam, 1997).

Public expenditure

The role of the international financial institutions is rather ambivalent in their net contribution towards mitigating poverty. The structural adjustment programmes (SAPs) devised in the credit lending processes by the IMF and WB impose a special burden on the poor and vulnerable: 'It is children who have paid the heaviest price for the developing world's debts. Fragmentary evidence... has shown a picture of rising malnutrition, and in some cases rising child deaths, in some of the most heavily indebted countries of Africa and Latin America.' (UNICEF, 1992). By lifting price controls while freezing wages, and by devaluing the local currency, SAPs diminish the purchasing power of poor families attempting to buy food, health services and other basic minimum necessities. The social programmes designed to protect the most vulnerable groups (such as feeding programmes for underweight babies) are usually scaled back sharply precisely at the time juncture when the gap between affordability and demand is the greatest. These are important elements of transitional or switching costs that should be accounted for in the framework of TC and thus in the total cost assessment of alternative programmes envisaged for the host countries by the multi-lateral credit institutions.

Discussing lessons for adjustment in the 1980s, the *World Development Report* (World Bank, 1990, p. 120) stated: 'In the short run, however, some of the poor may lose out'. This is one of the clearest assertions of the problem of negligence of some of the critical costs that involve irreversibility (as in the case of infant mortality or severe under-nourishment). The issue is short-run for whom? It is a subjective and biased perception. The transition cost for the individuals who are adversely affected is infinite, and for society it exceeds the monetary valuation of human life. When these adjustment costs are not reflected in any adjustment programme, the projected benefits are over-estimates and costs are gross under-estimates. The short run for the poor in some of these cases equals some days when it is an issue of coping with severe deprivation and mere survival. A TCE perspective would take into account all the costs of transition however these may accrue, and advance economic policy as if people and costs of all kinds matter.

Subsidies

Public expenditure policies in developing countries are, to a substantial degree, affected or even governed by the IMF and the WB. Their influence means that the borrower countries are at the mercy of the lending institutions for their external borrowings. Although the motives and genuine needs of the borrowing governments and their rulers could be many and varied, the end product in all cases seems to be the same: in their perceived need to control deficit financing, overdrafts and inflation, the lenders seek creditworthiness and minimization of the risk of defaulting on loan repayment. These considerations are usually oblivious to their implications for poverty and environmental damage.

In their dominant concern about debt management and loan repayment, the international lending institutions have been stipulating requirements where the negative externalities are ignored. It was observed that in Ghana, kerosene subsidy withdrawl accelerated deforestation. Whenever certain subsidies are removed, the substitutory and compensatory mechanisms must be addressed if specified targets of public expenditure are to be achieved without surprises on the social and environmental fronts.

Various policies for reducing public expenditure and subsidies must address the issues of substitution effects and complementary activity requirements within the broader perspective of TCE. Only systems such as these can minimize TC and attain the broader objectives of economic reform.

The characteristics of some games that creditors and borrowers play (with or without full knowledge or information) are at a disjunction with the imperatives of social welfare maximization, mainly because of the following ingredients:

- agency maximands;
- organizational internalities;
- social and economic externalities;
- the role of uncertainty;
- incomplete information;
- perverse incentives for inefficiency;
- *ex post* opportunism at the creditor as well as borrower levels; and
- differential discounting of time among creditors, borrowers and general citizenry.

Some the TCE-related impediments to the efficient design and implementation of required reforms include: information basis for policy prescriptions in SAL; the role of bounded rationality and of malalignment of incentives at most levels; asymmetric information and opportunistic behaviour; monitoring and enforcement problems, discontinuities of economic agents and principals at the participating country levels.

Sovereign debt reduction

Debt relief with provision for debt repayment incentives in sovereign debt of developing countries is a matter of importance in contemporary international economics. As Franke (1991) pointed out, minimization of TC is a relevant criterion when choosing between different avenues of debt relief. These costs include bargaining between creditors, and between debtor and creditors, the collection and sharing of information (which is necessarily asymmetric, with implied private information), the costs of trading debt claims, the costs of monitoring the debtor's compliance with various provisions of debt contracts, and the verification of the relevant parameters for debt relief and rescheduling. The TC issue is very prominent in sovereign debt management cases, in contrast to corporate debt cases.

Based on a detailed analysis of plausible alternatives, Franke (1991) suggested a 'menu approach' to the design of debt-relief instruments, with features including: (i) burden-sharing by the beneficiaries of debt relief; and (ii) debt relief contingent on exogenous and easily observable variables (such as foreign exchange earnings). Again, the role of TC remains significant in this context, and hence the need for the greater use of TCE.

4.6   Benefit–cost analysis (BCA)

Benefit–cost analysis (BCA) remains a widely used, and even more widely misused, concept and approach of economic analysis. Even the so-called 'social benefit-cost analysis' (SBCA) is hardly social in much of its applications. This is because most methods and applications in this direction fail to take into account the role of differential TC in the assessment of a common scale of costs and benefits. This assertion holds even after recognizing the roles of multiple incommensurate objectives of ranking alternatives in terms of their relative ratios of benefits and costs, and/or of their net values. The latter refer to benefits adjusted with costs, both evaluated at a time point and lumped in with the choice of a 'proper' discount factor for discounting future values to their current value.

Hicks–Kaldor criterion and its fallacies

The standard financial methods of benefit–cost calculations draw upon the calculation of the discounted stream of cash flows, both the sequences of costs C_t and of benefits B_t, for the period of concern T for a project or component of economic activity. The discounted lump sum is called the net present value (NPV) and depends on the choice of the discount rate r. This is given by the expression:

$$\mathrm{NPV} = \int_0^T e^{-rt}[B_t - C_t]dt$$

If inflation needs to be taken into account, r is replaced by $r - i$, where i is the rate of annual inflation. The new measure $r - i$ corresponds to the real rate of interest wherever the formulation is carried out only in financial terms.

The Hicks–Kaldor (HK) criterion seeks to justify activities when benefits, however these may accrue, exceed the costs, and assumes, unrealistically, that the marginal utility of income is constant and that it remains the same among all persons.

This description holds for cash-flow-based BCA. In general, the true worth of resources is not reflected in the above estimates of benefits and costs. At the minimum, one needs to assess the shadow prices for each of the inputs and outputs involved in the flows of benefits and costs. The shadow prices corresponding to such an objective function are reflected in the costate variables. It is not always possible to construct and solve complex optimizing models to generate these shadow prices. Instead, approximations are often made to assess these 'true values' of resources with an intuitive approach.

In the context of environmental issues, especially the management of global commons and related policies which arise largely in the public arena, the methods require considerable further strengthening because of the following factors (Rao, 2001): (i) the timescale involved is usually hundreds of years or longer; (ii) there is no unitary decision-making mechanism; (iii) most factors to be considered are largely outside market parameters – as they may not influence the market characteristics at the present time; (iv) there are unusually predominant unknowns and uncertainties in the cost and benefit configurations; and (v) assigning numerical values to bring the multiple factors to a common numeraire and scale is extremely complex and founded on many assumptions.

Commensurability

Much of the application of BCA presumes some type of 'commensurability'. 'Strong commensurability' assumes the existence of a common numeraire which enables the assignment of numerical values to each factor and function involved in the decision-making context, in models and policies. A 'weak commensurability' approach relies only on the ordinal ranking of preferences among alternatives, does not require numerical values to be assigned to all the parameters involved, but this may not be enough to suggest relevant policies and the scale of operations or interventions in economic governance. All the approaches are sensitive to the specifications of institutional constraints. The market and state institutions form the relevant background.

Any assessment of costs and benefits is based on a pattern of economic equilibrium that enables such assessment. However, over a relatively medium/long-term (ten or more years) framework, it is important to recognize that the equilibrium is not expected to remain unaffected by the continued disturbances to the systems involved and the significant possibilities of the mechanisms of adaptation. With reference to the general usefulness of BCA or SBCA, some of the arguments of Arrow *et al.* (1996) are relevant: (i) SBCA can play an important role in legislative and regulatory policy debates about protecting and improving health, safety and the natural environment; (ii) although it is neither necessary nor sufficient for designing sensible policy, it can provide an 'exceptionally useful framework' for consistently organizing information; and (iii) in this way it can improve the process and outcome of policy analysis. It was also suggested that, if 'properly done', SBCA can be of great help to agencies participating in the development of environmental, health and safety regulations, and can be useful in evaluating agency decision-making and rule-making.

Intergenerational efficiency and SBCA

Missing markets phenomena exist whenever there is no willing inter-action and exchange for mutual gain taking place between present and future generations; it thus impossible to realize intergenerational effi-ciency except possibly as a mere coincidence. This is in addition to the well-known problems of 'market failures' in terms of their inability to correct for 'externalities', such as pollution during industrial processes. The possibility that the current generation could use conventional or relatively narrow interpretations of SBCA methods to reallocate part of the endowment to itself is not too remote if the methods do not prop-erly incorporate valuation issues (Rao, 2001).

Standard conversion factor (SCF) and its fallacies

SCF is used to derive shadow prices or 'true worth of resources' by converting market prices (whenever these exist) through this product or resource-specific conversion factor. This is done by comparing do-mestic market prices with international prices for traded goods, and with other comparable estimates of shadow prices (for a coverage of writings on methods and applications of BCA see, for example, the edited collection of Layard and Glaister, 1994).

International financial institutions such as the IMF, the WB and the regional Development Banks can do more to tie-in financial lending mechanisms with the attainment of some of the interrelated aspects of the alleviation of poverty and sustainable patterns of development. The benefit–cost calculations and project appraisal methods applied by these institutions need to take into account various TC. These need to reflect the long-term future, and the discounting of the future must be handled judiciously and ethically in these calculations, taking into consideration the rights of future generations as well.

4.7   Conclusions

The critical limitation of the much vaunted efficiency of competitive processes is its insensitivity to the role of TC. The closest practical illustration of the attendant problems of such approaches is the demon-strably ineffective role of the policies devised by the IMF and the WB using GEMs. Transactions do not get carried out without the use of real resources, and these entail costs, some which are significantly different from one setting to another and are highly sensitive to institutional and organizational specifications as well as their dynamic evolution.

The 'standard' world of much of neoclassical economics is one of zero TC, an unreal world of frictionless economies. Generalized models that incorporate positive TC and their all-pervasive roles are the ones that are needed to address real-world economic systems. Absence of readily usable data for assessing various elements of TC does not provide an excuse for oversimplified analyses leading to misguided policy prescriptions. The fact that NE emerges as a special case of TCE under simplifying assumptions is enough of a reason for the traditional economics profession to move in the direction of embracing TCE. The combined approaches of NIE and NE can lead to a desired NNE that approximates TCE. Substantial further progress must be made in this effort, however.

Areas of application of these approaches, as illustrated in different sections of this chapter, include the design and implementation of multi-lateral credit lending and economic reforms; trade liberalization; institutional development for economic growth; and economic development. The role and usefulness of the standard NE models are enhanced with their integration of NIE, as will be explained in the next chapter.

5
New Institutional Economics

5.1 Introduction

An economic analysis of real-world situations often warrants an analysis of the governance of institutions (or lack of the same) and their interactions which may lead to 'rational' decision-making models and applications of neoclassical economics (NE).

Among well-known contributions to traditional institutional economics are those of Thorstein Veblen, John Commons and, in a different class, Karl Marx. It is not proposed to review these contributions, but suffice it to state that most modern economists found in these contributions shortcomings arising from a lack of analytical framework and operational economic models that ensure the welfare of all sections of society. Most traditional studies of institutional economics were considered to be historically specific descriptions lacking in predictive power for modern and evolving economic systems.

New institutional economics (NIE) deals with the origins, incidence and ramifications of transaction costs (TC), even though the definition of TC is still rather elusive. NIE seeks to integrate the economics of institutions with neoclassical economics; it incorporates transaction cost economics (TCE), political economy and behavioural economics (in addition to a few other approaches).

NIE has been developed since the 1960s, mainly through significant contributions by Ronald Coase, Douglass North and Oliver Williamson. It differs from the old institutional economics that was developed mainly by John Commons and Thorstein Veblen during the early twentieth century. For an interface between the 'old' institutional economics and NIE, see Hodgson (1998). The extensive use of theory and applications of TCE makes NIE richer in terms of its explanatory power and predictive interpretations. However, the fundamental unit of analysis in either of the two approaches remains the same: transaction. The definition of a transaction can vary, however, to reflect different types and degrees of aggregation.

Is the approach of NIE opposed to formal economic models and analytical methods? The answer is no. Posner (1993, p. 75) stated: 'Rejection of economic formalism, or a certain version of that formalism, is the negative side of the new institutional economics.' Any two sub-disciplines of economic thought, by definition, tend to reject some versions of each other's initial formulations – but that need not imply a feature amounting to a 'negative side' of an approach. What is still lacking is a greater focus on analytical methods and formal structures beyond generalities about a few cases.

This chapter provides a brief narration of the concepts and approaches of NIE, and extends the background to explain the roles of several economic and social features in their effects on TC. These include trust, reputation, credibility, co-operation and cultural factors. The relevance of NIE in the study of markets and institutional efficiencies, and in the governance of economic institutions, is explained. The roles of contestable markets or potential competition in promoting efficiency, of X-efficiency and related features affecting efficiency are also examined.

5.2 Concepts and approaches

NIE is an approach to generalize the neoclassical economic methodology to include mainly the role of property rights and transaction costs (Eggertsson, 1989, 1990; Williamson, 1996). In some cases, this inclusion could be at the expense of some of the long-held views and assumptions of neoclassical economics, however. This issue is perhaps best illustrated by the applications in the economics of contract (see Chapter 6 for details).

Let us introduce the definitions (Davis and North, 1971, pp. 5–6):

Institutional environment. The set of fundamental political, social and legal ground rules that establishes the basis of production, exchange and distribution.

Institutional arrangement. An arrangement between economic units that governs the ways in which these units can co-operate and/or compete ... provide a structure within which its members can cooperate ... or a mechanism that can effect a change in laws or property rights.

The analysis of institutions leads to three aspects of study (North,1999): (i) the formal rules of the game defined in legal terms; (ii) the informal norms of behaviour that supplement, complement and modify institutions; and (iii) the effectiveness of enforcement mechanisms. It has been clarified that the combination of these three elements determines the effectiveness of institutions in influencing TC.

Institutions are the rules of conduct of a society and include humanly devised structural constraints; these comprise both formal stipulations, as in statutes of law and regulations, and informal constraints such as social conventions and norms of expected behaviour. Organizations are the actors in the societal network, and these include parliamentary or other political arrangement, corporations, judiciary and so on. Many of the formulations and the results of NE form a sub-set of the general economics of institutions, where TC are assumed to be negligible and/or institutional differences have not been accounted for explicitly.

NIE comprises primarily an institutional environment and its governance via institutional arrangements. The means of achieving this is the application of TCE. It is a combination of first-order economizing to get the institutional environment right, and of second-order economizing to get the governance structures right (Williamson, 1998, 2000). In contrast, the standard NE problem of resource allocation would focus on the third-order economization problem, that of getting the marginal conditions right, based on the specified institutional environment and governance structures. The complementarity of NIE and NE is thus an obvious prescription for solving real-world economic issues from micro as well as macro perspectives. NIE supports economic formalism and lends support to NE models when the latter incorporate more of the real-world features.

Among the tasks of NIE is to offer explanations for institutional inefficiencies and failures (including bureaucratic failure, non-market failure or market failure) and offer remedial alternatives based on the comparative analysis of institutions. This task is by no means simple, nor based on unidisciplinary considerations. The role of anthropological and cultural factors, for example, cannot be ignored completely. It is not to claim that these factors are amenable to change in the short run, but the role of institutional analysis using such ingredients is useful for the comparative study of institutions. This is especially relevant when one tries to replicate models of institutions or transplant structures from one setting to another – in effect comparing 'apples to oranges' without realizing the difference!

Endogenous institutional response (EIR)

In one of the alternative definitions, institutions are defined as: 'persistent and connected sets of (formal and informal) rules that prescribe behavioural roles, constrain activity, and shape expectations'. (Keohane, 1988). However, expectations about institutions also matter. It was argued that (Snidal, 1996): 'institutions matter because they provide a stable environment for mutually beneficial decision-making as they guide and constrain behaviour'.

Broadly, two forms of institutional governance structures are relevant: exogenous and endogenous. These are not mutually exclusive, given the interactions between them. Both tend to be influenced rather significantly by the role of transaction costs. Exogenous structures allow a greater role for third parties or international collective bodies to address issues arising out of agreements or their absence. Endogenous structures are active internal mechanisms of state practice which form policies and respond to emerging issues of multi-lateral co-operation, co-ordination and other forms of interrelationships. The concept of state practice facilitates the development of endogenous governance structures.

Exogenous and endogenous governance structures and the role of transaction costs in state practice are some of the issues examined by Aceves (1996). Hurwicz (1972) proved that there do not exist informationally decentralized mechanisms to realize Pareto-optimal performance in economic systems involving externalities.

Endogenous institutional response (EIR) refers to the phenomenon of institutional responsiveness to changing information and circumstances in sustained pursuit of the stated or normal mission of any institution (Rao, 2001). The responsiveness need not arise only out of external influences; informational inputs from exogenous sources could constitute a source of change, however. If the EIR is positive, it implies that institutions can adapt rationally to change and thus minimize disruption costs and various types of TC. EIR is the institutional equivalent of the 'resilience' phenomenon in ecological and environmental systems. Adaptive efficiency (AE) features emphasized in TCE require the existence of EIR for AE to remain operative. This should form an essential short-term and long-term objective for policies and activities of organizations and institutions.

Based on a survey of the economics of the firm and contracts, Wiggins (1991, p. 657) concluded: 'institutions are devices designed to lower contracting costs, primarily by lowering enforcement costs. More specifically, private institutions often emerge as cost minimizing responses to particular problems of incomplete contracting and enforcement.' We do not prejudge merits in the classification of private and public institutions without reference to the TC implications and complementarities of both at the operational level. Private institutions may not automatically be TC minimizing for society as whole if there does not exist a sufficient enabling public infrastructure in the form of legal provisions and other law enforcement mechanisms. In the latter case, the efficiency of private institutions draws upon that of the public institutions as well. The interdependencies as well as TC in both systems are reduced when there is a social infrastructure comprising trust, co-operation and other forms of social capital. These are the focus of the next section.

5.3   Trust, co-operation and social capital

Shared social values and norms of conduct such as the role of mutual trust in interactions among individuals and economic entities reduce some of the structural uncertainties and contribute to reduction of TC. Mutually beneficial exchanges can be undertaken at significantly lower TC and in larger numbers in a social structure of mutual trust relative to situations with least trust or shared values of conduct (see also Knack and Keefer, 1997).

Lack of trust can induce some costs. Arrow (1971, p. 22) observed: 'In the absence of trust... opportunities for mutually beneficial cooperation would have to be foregone... normal social behavior, including ethical and moral codes (may be)... reactions of society to compensate for market failures.' This assertion is equally valid in the context of non-market failure as well.

Trust is a commodity in one of the perspectives. However, it does not possess the typical characteristics of a marketed product; it only enters a formal production function and governs economic and social functioning. In another version, perhaps more meaningfully, trust is a component of social capital, and contributes to economic progress and sustainability. Since there do not exist complete or completable contracts, from an incomplete contracts perspective, the role of trust is critical for the viability of most transactions and for the efficiency of conducting transactions.

The role of trust as a facilitator and TC-reducing factor is elucidated by several authors, not all from the economics tradition. Fukuyama (1995) argued that trust arises when a community possesses a common set of moral values in such way as to create expectations of regular and honest behaviour. Seligman (1997, p. 13) begins his book about trust with this opening statement: 'The existence of trust is an essential component of all enduring social relationships.' The role of trust in building reputation and durability of transactions or relations has also been examined by Lahno (1995) and several others. The pivotal role of trust in governance by state polity and the role of trust in civic life has been examined in Braithwaite and Levi (1998).

Cultural factors

The role of cultural endowments (mainly the inherited features of culture, rather than new cultural developments) in the economics of development was addressed by Ruttan (1988). He suggested: (i) 'Cultural endowments make some forms of institutional change less costly to establish and impose severe costs on others' (ibid., p.S250); and (ii) 'The value of social science knowledge is that it offers the possibility of lowering the cost of institutional change, including the cost of conflict resolution' (ibid., pp. 263–4).

Cultural traits and/or endowments can be treated as a common resource for the functioning of economic institutions. These features influence the paths of change or evolution in institutions and organizations. The role of inertia and general resistance (not necessarily interest-group type or lobbying type resistance to change) can also be seen in this light. These factors also show varying levels of effectiveness of incentives and disincentives aimed at steering an economic system in desirable directions. Accordingly, the usual 'one size fits all' approach of much of NE may not be up to the task if the approaches do not take into account cultural variations. When the relative efficacy of chosen policy instruments tends to be blunted or blurred because of these factors, the accompanying TC also remain high and represent a drag on the economic system. Kinship, for example, plays a role in the operational decisions of organizations and affect economic decisions leading to inefficiency. This feature is more common in some of the Asian societies in contrast to Western societies. It was not until the sudden economic crises during the 1990s in East Asian countries that the role of cronyism, in addition to other inefficiency features, was discovered by the wider global public.

Thus the role of cultural and social factors affect economic performance via various levels of application of TC, and these costs are differential in their incidence across societies. Some of the features reduce TC, whereas others enhance it. The formation of formal and informal contracts, their enforceability and corresponding features affecting TC are critically determined by cultural factors; see Witt (1986) for detailed analyses.

A considerable time period is required for the evolution (and stability) of norms of behaviour, and for any change in this regard. Provision for changes in formal rules is relatively easier, but informal constraints and norms of conduct remain operative from the inheritance of properties of the system before any changes in the formal rules. Because of this feature, for systems with a long history of established behavioural traits, reform and restructuring processes take a long time and the outcome remains very uncertain (North, 1993, p. 21): 'It is one thing to get the "prices right" at a moment of time; it is something else to create an institutional framework that will get them over time.'

Among the behavioural traits and perceptional factors that affect TC and performance efficiency of economic systems are reputation, credibility and expectation formation. These are explained in the next section.

5.4   Expectations, reputation, credibility and commitments

The role of reputation, credibility and commitment is to enable expectation formation, and the role of this is to reduce the costs of uncertainty and of incomplete information. None of these factors by themselves could lead to competitive market equilibrium or cost efficiency of standard NE. Yet these factors contribute to the reduction of TC. The applications of these important factors, similar to the role of trust elucidated in the previous section, are many and significant.

In the context of economic reforms, Rodrik (1990) argued that: (i) the source of efficiency improvement benefits do not necessarily arise from economic liberalization reforms themselves, but rather from credible and sustained liberalization; and (ii) the efficiency argument provides no strong reason to undertake trade liberalization in an 'unsettled economy' in its early stages of transition towards equilibrium. These arguments simply focus attention on the role of TC in all transitory stages of reform, and the need for credible and uncertainty-reducing provisions in the policies.

Product or service standardization is one of the examples of a reduction of uncertainties in the quality features. Interactions and transactions are better facilitated when these are standardized to some reasonable extent. Marginal additions to standardization usually lead to decreasing utilities or returns, suggesting the existence of an optimal level of standardization, conducive enough to lead to the formation of expectations. The role of the state in standard setting is often unavoidable and remains a complex task in itself. Blankart and Knieps (1993) suggested that standardization can come closer to the competitive market case where strategic behaviour is least significant. However, this assertion neglects the role of TC. The role of state and regulatory agencies in standard-setting, monitoring and enforcement entails significant TC. It is doubtful if this form of governance is cost-effective, especially if such standardization leads to reduced incentives for the entrepreneurship in favour of quality enhancement (see also Chapter 7). Differential applications of rules and norms leads to the phenomenon of multiple equilibria, some stable and some unstable, some known and some unknown, and thus reduce economic efficiency.

A balance between different objectives here is to stipulate a minimum acceptable standard in each case and leave it to the market to exceed those standards. The expectation formation process then relies on an acceptable minimum and takes note of other factors (including credibility, price and quality). The transparency of the rules of conduct provides greater potential for fairness and economic efficiency via a reduction in TC.

Reputation

The role of reputational considerations in pricing and related aspects of NE was discussed in Chapter 4, in explaining deviations of price from marginal cost.

Milgrom and Roberts (1988) suggested that a society of long-lived, formal organizations may be effective in using reputational mechanisms, and thus possess the corresponding incentives for reputation. It was also suggested that (ibid., p. 449) 'the reputational mechanism cannot operate effectively in fluid, impersonal, anonymous market settings ... Only in more developed markets, with the extensive communications among traders and repeated dealings, do market reputations matter.' If this holds, Milgrom and Roberts suggest that the market need not be viewed as a single form of organization but rather as a whole category, and the distinction between markets and other organizations blurs. Yet, the role of relative reputations of different organizations affect economic decisions.

The phenomenon of rent seeking in the state sector and the state–private sector interface is generally governed by a series of multiple equilibria derived by the interplay of interest groups and others. Any disturbance to the equilibrium could be met with endogenous opposing forces and a new set of resultant equilibria emerge.

In the foundations of law, law rests on a special and complex convention, where a convention is interpreted as both a social fact and a framework of reasons for specific action (Postema, 1982). Against a background of common knowledge of mutual expectations, actions of economic agents can be interpreted as being intended to induce reliance, and generate obligations on the part of those agents to honour the expectations thereby created (Hart, 1961).

State practice and international law

Explicit international treaties and contracts are widespread but never adequate to govern all international relations. Continuous and long-standing state practices emerge into customary international law (CIL) and promote *de facto* legal behaviour among states in the absence of explicit treaty provisions, or requisite protracted negotiations towards such an understanding. As Aceves (1996) discussed, these state practices facilitate the development of governance structures that address the problems of TC and related operational impediments. An automatic endorsement of specific state practice traditions obviates the need for explicit agreement formation, enforcement and monitoring. However, this emergence of state practice, and hence of CIL, is a time-dependent feature; it cannot be formed whenever some specific international issues have to be addressed. This situation calls for the role of treaty law. TC have a major role in this aspect as well. There is a need to recognize the *ex ante* costs of forming an agreement and the *ex post* costs of monitoring and enforcing the agreement. The latter problems are acute in international situations where state sovereignty restricts access to certain aspects of information and enforcement. The behavioural feature of post-contractual opportunism by states is not uncommon.

State practice reduces TC associated with the formation and implementation of treaties in three ways (Aceves, 1996): (i) state practice does reduce the costs of contingency-based full contractual specification by adapting to relevant circumstances in a given state; (ii) it fills in the contractual gaps to some extent and adopts practical interpretation of the treaty; and (iii) original agreements may partly be modified while staying within the stated objectives, and allow parties to address new circumstances without seeking formal cumbersome co-ordination mechanisms.

The role of NIE in international public law has been reviewed by Dunoff and Trachtman (1999). They suggested that NIE, with its emphasis on comparative institutional analysis, is a source of methodology for comparative law, and that TCE plays an important role in the formation and implementation of international agreements.

5.5 Political economy and institutional efficiency

NIE has a number of ingredients to contribute to the development and reform of institutions, not necessarily related to ideology but related to relative pragmatism. The latter requires the meticulous application of principles and approaches of TCE to the design of institutions. This is not to suggest that drastic reforms of institutions are feasible merely by the appeal of the economics of alternative governance mechanisms. Any changes arise from the polity and social philosophy of the governed and governing entities. However, within a broader existing framework, some reforms, such as selective privatization, the simplification of bureaucratic procedures, recognition of specific efficiencies and devising policies for the reduction of TC as well as enhancing the desired performance indicators of the economic systems can be accomplished meaningfully with the application of TCE.

In order to find more insights into the arguments that supported alternative institutional forms we provide a brief review of some of the major economic arguments that emerged historically.

Socialism in retrospect

Among the early contributors to the logic of merits of socialism (state control of resources and their governance) were Oscar Lange (1938) and Abba Lerner (1934). Soon after, the writings of Abram Bergson (1948, p. 447: 'socialism can work') and Joseph Schumpeter (1942, p. 172: 'There is nothing wrong with the pure theory of socialism') also went along in a similar vein. However, Lange (1938, p. 109) had observed that 'the real danger of socialism is that of a bureaucratization of economic life'. Over subsequent years, this potential danger surfaced and combined with the perverse role of incentives for performance, and the systems largely failed to enhance the social and economic welfare of the systems and people they were designed to govern.

An interesting and rather basic economic principle of NE was also posited in the context of socialist economies. Bergson (1948, p. 424) also stated the optimum conditions for socialist systems to realize efficiency: 'The total cost incurred in the production of the optimum output would be at a minimum and, in the optimum, price must equal marginal cost.' The critical issue is what constitutes the total cost and how to account for inefficiencies accompanying 'bureaucratese' and other forms of inefficiency.

Several problems of inefficient implementation of seemingly sound economic policies originate in the phenomenon of lack of transparency of systems, or asymmetric information between the administration and the public in a centrally planned economic model. This problem can be viewed in terms of incomplete contractual provisions as well. In democratic countries constitutions do exist; in others, a different set of rules operate and change arbitrarily. Even where constitutions govern the conduct of economic and other activities, the problems of incomplete contracting and enforcement abound.

Constitutions are essentially incomplete contracts, and so are government institutions in relation to the members of the society. The contractual incompleteness or the corresponding gaps in interpretations are usually filled in (efficiently or otherwise) by judicial institutions, bureaucracy and other institutions (including those aimed at lobbying and other interest-group activities). Substantial variations in interpretations are very much the norm rather than the exception in this scenario. However, whether these interpretations are subject to influences (including bribes) or sufficiently objective is to be examined only in relation to specific systems that one is examining.

One of the issues for decisions that are based on non-benevolent attitudes of government functionaries relates to their relative or effective time horizons as well as discounting of time. As Wolf (1979, p. 115) observed: 'an appreciable disjuncture between the time horizons of political actors and the time required to analyze, experiment, and understand a particular problem'. The rate of time discount tends to be higher than that of 'society' as a consequence of the incentive structure in the political or administrative set-up.

Emphasizing the nature of limitations regarding adaptation under socialist economic institutions, Williamson (1996, p. 148) stated: 'Mechanistic arguments about the efficacy of socialism failed because they neither recognized the real needs of economic organization (for rapid adaptation) nor appreciated that the marvel of the market serviced these needs in subtle, spontaneous ways.'

North (1990) examined 'transaction-cost politics' and noted the lack of 'instrumental rationality' of participants in the economic and political systems; the participants use imperfect and/or incorrect models of the real system to guide their decisions, and the feedback information they receive is insufficient to revise the models. Dixit (1998) extended this reasoning to economic policy-making context with illustrations, and the deviations from ideal concepts of efficiency are explained in terms of the role of TC. Dixit emphasized an aspect of TC that constrains political commitment as an imperative of the political process itself. Time-inconsistent policies entail costs of their own, and the roles of expectations and credibility are some of the contributing factors. One of the suggested rules of operation of a political commitment problem (see Majone, 2001) is to operate via independent public trust entities. It is not clear how 'independent' institutions arise out of political entities, however.

In the theory of state governance the NIE recognizes the relative roles of commitment and flexibility in various policy formulations (for related explanations under the conceptual approach of the New Economics of Organization, see Yarbrough and Yarbrough, 1990). The capacity to commit credibly, maintain flexibility in relation to relevant new information and change of qualifying circumstances, and the ability to recognize the difference between the imperatives of flexibility and commitments are important elements of state capacity with implications for economic efficiency.

Economic and other organizations differ in the developed countries from those of the developing countries mainly in terms of the credible and/or transparent functioning of the institutional arrangements, and thus in terms of the role of TC. Buchanan (1987) suggested that economic efficiency must be judged by the processes through which transactions are carried out, and the role of institutional development remains important in several systems, especially in the developing regions and sectors.

X-efficiency and transaction costs (TC)

The concept of X-efficiency was proposed by Leibenstein (1966), and subsequently revised by him several times. This was proposed as an alternative standard neoclassical economic approach, treating individual rather than household (or firm or other entities) as decision-making units. Leibenstein initiated the formulation by noting that the relatively small welfare/efficiency losses associated with monopoly (as documented in the literature of the 1950s and 1960s) were based on the assumption that the firms were minimizing costs for a given level of output. A number of cases supported the view that this was not the factual scenario, and the failure to minimize costs, called X-efficiency, was rather common and was the significant factor in welfare losses. Leibenstein (1966, p. 412) offered the following three reasons for the existence of X-efficiency: (i) contracts for labour are incomplete;

(ii) the production function is not completely known; and (iii) not all inputs are available on equal terms. However, these explanations are straightforward implications of positive TC, as pointed out in De Alessi (1983).

Selective rationality (a special case of bounded rationality where deliberately limited alternatives are evaluated) rather than the utility maximizing behaviour of an individual was postulated in the X-efficiency approach. It was also suggested (Leibenstein, 1978, p. 329) that an individual 'will not necessarily move to a superior position in the standard utility sense because of the inertial costs of moving'. The existence of positive TC can lead to this situation. A similar explanation holds for farmers, who do not make full use of information they have when making farm crop decisions, as reported in Shapiro and Muller (1977). Among other studies, Stigler (1976) observed that the reasons ascribed by Leibenstein (1966) to X-efficiency are primarily caused by incomplete contract formulation and enforcement, and the effects of inefficient markets for knowledge on production functions. De Alessi (1983) noted that the X-efficiency feature is observed *ex post* and is attributable to the structure of property rights and positive TC. Let us recognize that, nomenclature apart, the role of inertia contributed by sub-optimal incentives and asymmetric information, and hence that of TC, remain critical in all these respects.

5.6   Contestable markets and governance

The greater the competition among organizations and economic entities, the greater the incentive to institutionalize efficiency improvements and undertake relevant innovations for both the short run and the long run. The provision of optimal incentives for economic efficiency requires an appropriate provision of potential competition via contestable markets.

In the presence of entry and exit costs, which typically qualify under TC with or without invoking the categorization 'fixed costs', economic entities have to enhance efficiency if there exists potential competition; this would apply even when there is already a competitive mechanism in existence.

In one significant contribution, Demsetz (1968) argued that potential rather than actual competition would be sufficient to promote efficiency and solve some of the monopolistic enterprise problems. This insight was later formalized further by Baumol *et al.* (1982) in their treatment of contestable markets.

Among the potential applications of the role of improvising contestable markets, Wolf (1988) argued that the influence of the contestability of the market by potential entrants may lead to greater incentives for incumbent firms to innovate and thus retain their market shares, and that potential competition may have an effect similar to that of actual competition.

Institutional analysis deals with features regarding various contractual provisions and their credible enforcement with the least TC. A full understanding of institutions must rest on a more complete understanding of enforcement (Wiggins, 1991). In this context, the ease of enforcement of some of the market-related features is usually better done with lower TC wherever competitive market forces exist, and in their absence the next best approximation in the form of contestable markets exist.

5.7 Regulations and rent seeking

Let us refer to the conventional market institutions as the primary markets, to distinguish these from secondary markets. The latter operate whenever the former are less than competitive and/or costs of functioning through such market systems are so high that the existence of the standby alternative facilitates lower TC-based operations. Thus we are in a dual market system, each with its own legal (or not necessarily legal) foundations for its existence and operation. Dual systems exist in almost every economy, but they are significant in regulated rather than free market economies. Rural credit lending, pawn shop trade, foreign exchange currency trading and other examples can be found in most systems.

The exercise of non-benevolent authority generates its own secondary market and this provides services to circumvent the enforcement of some of the enforcement measures controlled by the regulating authority. Inappropriate regulatory provisions or ill-designed rules lead to high TC, both in their legitimate implementation and in their softened enforcement with private rewards for the enforcers.

Regulatory costs should be assessed, which is not the case in many studies, in terms of both the direct costs of regulation as well as in terms of rent dissipation and economic efficiency loss. The 'market for corruption' (political, bureaucratic and other) is yet another form of institution characterized by demand and supply factors, but less competitive than regular markets.

Rent seeking refers, in general, to the phenomenon of private entities seeking to capture rents created by government interventions in the economic system. Unless otherwise stated, rent setting is carried out by the instruments of the government; the dynamics of rent seeking and rent setting suggest the active role of their interactions for the private gains of different sections of individuals holding regulatory powers, and thus the economic efficiency of the system may be compromised in such cases. The original work on rent seeking was contributed by Tullock (1967), and extended by several others.

Much of the literature on rent seeking deals with a static and certainty framework, and this generally leads to the over-estimation of corresponding social costs. This is because, in a dynamic setting, the phenomenon of potential opposition or multiple partially counter-balancing forces to rent seeking and the resulting equilibrium phenomena on the type and scale of operations convey features closer to reality in many political and economic systems (for a simplified analytical model formulation, see Cairns and Long, 1991).

In the context of quotas and tariffs regulations in the trade sector, Krueger (1974, p. 302) observed that all market economies have some rent-generating restrictions. One can conceive of a continuum between a system of no restrictions and an extremely restricted system. In the former, entrepreneurs would 'seek to achieve windfall gains by adopting new technology, anticipating market shifts correctly, and so on'; and in the latter case, 'regulations would be all-pervasive and rent seeking would be the only route to gain. In such a system, entrepreneurs would devote all their time and resources to capturing windfall rents.'

Informal economy

Rules and organizations define what constitutes a formal economy and lead to an informal economy as well. The informal sector comprises (Feige, 1990, p. 990): 'economic activities that circumvent the costs and are excluded from the benefits and rights incorporated in the laws and administrative rules' covering property relations and other economic activities. The shadow economy and the underground economy are special components of the informal economy, usually the illicit aspects. Legal rules alone do not lead to an informal economy, but other institutions and corresponding rules do. The existence of informal activities is a by-product of the role of the state and the institutional arrangements governing the formulation and implementation of rules affecting some or all of its activities. Corruption itself is an informal economy. In degenerate systems, corruption and bribery are 'necessary' for mere survival (let alone meeting the greed objectives of individuals and economic entities). This phenomenon occurs not because of a lack of rules but rather *despite* the existence of rules, as implementation is completely lacking or is enforced selectively either to meet desired statistical indicators of 'performance' of the units, or to raise private incomes for the benefit of the implementing functionaries. There has been a classic assertion: public penalties give rise to private rewards. In some of these systems, the provision of penalties is merely to reap private benefits.

The growth of non-compliance in one sector or area of economic activity tends to contribute to spillover externalities in other areas: 'The characteristics of each distinct informal economy are determined by the particular set of institutional rules that its members circumvent' (Feige, 1990, p. 990). A significant and expanding shadow economy is a reflection on the inappropriateness and inefficiency of existing economic and other policies in an economic system. Oppressive tax and regulatory regimes, including the complexity of regulation, appear to drive economic agents from the official sector to the shadow economy; one of the roles of the state is to provide improved institutional infrastructure such as the rule of law and enforceability of contracts (Fleming *et al.*, 2000). For a detailed survey of the shadow economy and its estimates, see Schneider and Enste (2000).

Demand for, and supply of, informal economy/shadow economy/illicit economy, the role of TC in an informal economy, and of TC in relation to a shadow economy deserve further study. Clearly, the difficulties in obtaining relevant data are formidable.

5.8 Conclusions

Economic formalism continues to remain a useful requirement in NIE. Several studies contributed to this process and will continue to do so. The coexistence of formal and informal institutions is a normal feature of an economic system, but the relative roles of these groups of institutions in economic governance, the role of TC in each system and its components, and the role of the state in directing the institutional constellation in socially and economically desirable directions are some of the issues that deserve the serious attention of new institutional economics. Clearly, generalities and analytics of these interrelationships can only provide a limited insight, and much greater focus should be directed towards various types of economies and the polity that administers these economies. The role of economic reform should always be examined in terms not only of potential benefits of reform before and after some desired changes, but also in terms of applicable TC in the transformation from one set of alignment of economic activities to another. It may also be the case that, in some scenarios, the transition costs outweigh the potential benefits, and that these costs to be incurred are certain, whereas the benefits remain uncertain. Formal analysis of these potential alternatives requires further attention.

Reduction of TC and/or the achievement of greater economic results for a given level of TC remain the major areas of attention in any economic system, and this suggests the need for greater attention in formal economic analysis (whether based on neoclassical approaches or not) to incorporate the TC elements in the analysis (Coase, 1988, p. 30).

Part II
Applications

Applications: Introduction

Part II provides some of the important applications of transaction cost economics; several additional areas of application exist and can be extended too. Almost every transaction entails costs and benefits to the transacting party (parties) as well as to others who may not be involved directly in the transaction. The issue of transaction cost (TC) minimization is not always the central one, but that of the role of different types and magnitudes of TC in resource allocation efficiency and production efficiency is of paramount importance. This is not only because of the existence of some additional elements of cost that are often ignored in much of orthodox economics, but also because of the influence of such costs on the rest of the system. Accordingly, TC affect economic systems through their influence on the behavioural features of the governance of the system as well as of the economic actors at different levels.

Part II includes several applications of transaction cost economics (TCE), including the law and economics (with particular reference to contracts and property rights), behavioural economics (with a special focus on the issues of relative profit maximization and compliance with regulations), organizations theory (with special emphasis on the issues of centralization and decentralization in organizational functions), and environmental economics (emphasizing the role of market and non-market policies for environmental governance). The final chapter suggests a few directions for further research (these are in addition to some suggested in different sections of Part I).

6
Law and Economics

6.1 Introduction

When it is costly to transact, the role of institutions surfaces very prominently. Institutions are composed of legal regimes, rules and standards, conventions and informal traditions, and enforcement features (North, 1992). This generalized view of enforcement allows a combination of legal and informal enforcement mechanisms to establish and sustain different sets of property rights. Institutional features and property rights affect the efficiency of markets and overall economic performance. The role of law and the need for an 'efficient' legal system as a prerequisite for the minimization of transaction costs (TC) in modern societies deserves particular emphasis, however.

The new field of 'law and economics' emerged primarily out of the seminal contribution of Coase (1960) and draws heavily on the role of transaction cost economics (TCE). There have been several significant developments in this field in recent years. Often, the approach of law and economics has been interpreted as one that promotes market-based approaches to economic governance. This impression is only partially valid, however. It is not in the spirit of TCE to pre-commit to one or the other direction of governance without the due consideration of a comparative analysis of alternative forms of institutions and governance. In one of the recent applications of the theme, Rao (2001) provides detailed coverage of the approach to the international (rather, global) environmental governance arena.

This chapter deals with a few important aspects of the field of law and economics. These include the law and economics of contracts, litigation and of the role of property rights, among others. The economics of contracts remains an important focus of neoclassical economics (NE).

The role of TCE is largely to complement and enrich the relevant analyses. Much of the existing literature on the economics of litigation seems to be focused rather narrowly on analysing the 'rational behaviour' of the plaintiffs' decision-making process with the built-in calculus of costs and benefits, and ignores the role of TC. This chapter seeks to provide some remedies. The design and implementation of property rights (PR) and liability rules (LR) depends critically on the role of TC in effecting this. Some of the main elements of these features and interlinks are discussed in this chapter.

6.2   Economics of litigation

The major segment of the current literature on the economics of litigation is centred on the varying implication of two major alternatives in judicial litigation cost-sharing: American and English legal systems. Among other features, the distinguishing feature is that, in the latter, the loser (in many but not all cases) may have to pay the costs. These costs are the direct incremental costs: on many occasions, these are either nominal or court-determined costs, rather than actual or lawyers' market-based costs. These costs are underestimates of the real direct costs, and of the TC involving several additional major costs, including opportunity costs of time and other resources. Thus the conventional analyses tend to analyse the effects of a small segment of TC and seek to examine the implications of alternate legal systems. When TC are taken into account (including the costs of delays or waiting time in the judicial litigation process) it seems that the above analyses possess the feature of overplaying the implications of the two legal systems.

Market for litigation

It is important to identify the sources of demand for judicial litigation. This enables a better assessment of the demand for, and supply of, judicial solutions, and the TC faced by the litigants. The phenomenon of the prevalence of litigious plaintiff and systematic offender tend to be explained in terms of the roles of economies of scale, ratio of variable or incremental costs to fixed costs, ratio of total direct (financial costs) to total transaction costs, and expectations about the judicial outcome. At the same time, these factors are among the most important considerations for a litigant, whether a typical plaintiff or a typical defendant, to 'stay' in the 'litigation market'.

It is important to recognize the role of quasi-judicial or other institutions which have the capacity to screen, process and offer remedial measures in dispute resolution. These include court-ordered or other arbitration methods (binding or non-binding categories), and the role of arbitration by some of the non-partisan, non-governmental organizations such as the Better Business Bureau in the USA. One of the prerequisites for the efficacy of the results of these mechanisms is ensuring the quality of their output and their credibility. These tend to offer cost-effective screening mechanisms for judicial litigation, as well as cost-effective prejudicial providers of justice. The demand for judicial litigation is then a derive demand: when all other avenues of remedy or relief do not satisfy the litigants, the judicial solution is needed (with or without the participation of the jury, depending on the category of the legal case and the legal system). It is also important to examine the role of TC and of revelation of information in these processes of litigation. Asymmetric information remains great in the absence of expensive investigations and/or the provision of incentives for the litigants to reveal the full truth. Thus the effective working of prejudicial litigation is determined by a conglomerate of factors.

The role of non-economic factors (such as vindication of credibility) and motivational factors such as public interest litigation makes it imperative that the litigation market be analysed not only based on the calculus of the litigant's costs and benefits, but generally centred on a utility or social welfare function. The latter can be deployed in an optimizing framework with due recognition of the dynamics of demand and supply functions. Such a normative analysis tends to offer a prescriptive framework, or at least, the key parameters for devising appropriate cost-sharing in prejudicial and judicial litigation. Here, the methods of cost sharing include provisions for total cost sharing (including TC), *ex ante* fees and *ex post* fees to the prevailing litigants, and alternative bases for cost-shifting.

The existence of 'excess demand' for judicial litigation is an indicator of several factors: budgetary and administrative measures which lag behind in the strengthening of the personnel to administer justice, the role of vague and incomplete legislative enactments requiring legal interpretations, the lack of disincentives and screening mechanisms for frivolous lawsuits, incentives for nuisance litigation, non-compliance with legal requirements by offenders and their calculus of costs and benefits of such conduct, the provision of sufficient disincentives for improved compliance, and effective provision for out-of-court settlements.

These ingredients and the role of TC play a critical part in most of the judicial litigation processes, and the demand for and supply of litigation. The 'market' for litigation is thus largely determined by behavioural as well as normative economic considerations. These admit a formal representation and analysis of the issues and the dynamics of litigant behaviour. The role of fee-shifting or cost-shifting becomes only one of several important issues of the economics of litigation.

The current systems tend to ration judicial solutions by significant waiting for trial. Only a few of the cases waiting are need-based: the time to furnish full discovery and investigations. Most others affect the decision-making processes of the litigants in unintended ways. Those who have to undergo 'delays' (beyond the required investigative time) to obtain legal relief are assumed to maintain the low rate of time-discounting, thus imposing a compromised solution. If the role of delays in the provision of justice in this context is ignored, it is reasonable to visualize the equivalence of reduced relief to the victims and enhanced incentives for the offenders. It also relevant to note such implications as the calculus (and hence motivations) of the offenders who count on the victims' costs in their attempts to obtain justice. Such elements tend to provide a perverse incentive for the wilful violation of the law.

Disputes for resolution arising in such areas as in contracts and torts typically are resolved by 'private law', where the state provides only the court system, but investigative and other litigation costs are incurred by the parties themselves.

The economics of litigation needs to be viewed in terms of micro- as well as macroeconomic aspects at the level of the litigants and at the aggregate level of society. A just society would seek to minimize the costs to the innocent (plaintiff or defendant), and to the social cost of delivery of justice as a whole. These broad assertions tend to have varying implications in different court systems. The usual debate about English or American (or other) systems of awarding costs to the winners in judicial decisions are only a segment of the total problem. The social cost of ensuring a just (and, one hopes, an equitable) society is an area of paramount concern, and by no means should this imply any enhancement of TC for the innocent.

Loser pays costs?

Several courts at both federal and state level in the US justice system sought, albeit only occasionally, to invoke the possibility that the losers pay the direct costs of the plaintiffs (see, for example, *Fischer* v. *Johns-Manville Corp.*, 512 A.2d 466, 482 , NJ 1986: 'the plaintiff's litigation expenses' as a factor for assessing the magnitude of punitive damages). It is also sometimes suggested (see, for example, Green Oil, 539 So.2d at 223, and related references in Polinsky and Shavell,1998) this may be necessary to 'encourage plaintiffs to bring wrongdoers to trial'. The references here so far are in the context of rather significant judicial decisions which involved misconduct of the defendants to invoke tort law and punitive damage awards. However, the costs of the plaintiffs continue to affect their decisions to bring in a lawsuit or not; it would not be a socially desirable activity to expect most members of society to remain the silent sufferers of the consequences of wrongdoers. Similarly, it is also a counter-productive activity to invoke existing or interpretational provisions of the law to seek redress where there could be cost-effective methods of resolving disputes.

In general, it is useful to note that each legal transaction for the litigant, whether plaintiff or defendant, comprises a fixed cost and a variable cost. There are economies of scale too, for some of the corporate (and the 'nothing to lose' type of economic agent), either because of their set-up costs (sometimes called sunk costs) and the existence of relevant capacities (which may or may not be the same as legal capabilities, but are more likely to correlate well with these), or because the litigants cannot risk much when they had nothing to begin with. The first category typically is large enterprises, and the latter could be some of the crooks in deceptive activities, as in a few cases of telemarketing.

Polinsky and Shavell (1998) suggested: (i) the full social cost caused by an accident is the sum of the direct costs to the injured and of the costs associated with the use of the legal system (p. 922, fn. 168); and (ii) 'the main justification for considering litigation costs is in connection with estimating the chance that defendant might have escaped liability because he would not be sued. Punitive damages should be awarded to make up for the chance of escaping liability for this reason, but not as a general matter to encourage the bringing of lawsuits' (ibid., p. 923).

Some of the relevant issues include: What are the direct and indirect cost elements of litigation systems? Are there cost minimizing and efficiency enhancing alternatives to current practices? Are there potential instruments that can enhance the effectiveness of the existing systems – without seeking very drastic reforms? What is the magnitude of the problem of judicial processing and its changes over time over recent years in the state level and other levels of the courts? Are there any incentives and disincentives that can play effective roles in screening the excessive loading of cases to the court system? Can some of the existing provisions, such as Rule 11 of the US Federal Code be utilized more effectively to reduce the number and type of frivolous lawsuits? What could be the role of Rule 68 of the Federal Code in curtailing caseloads and providing disincentives for seeking judicial intervention when the cases could possibly be solved by other methods, such as negotiation and arbitration? How can the arbitration system be made more useful in this process? These issues require further study.

Are all potential litigations worth litigating? Under a 'live and let live' doctrine, Hylton (1996, p. 1006) stated:

> In a situation where symmetric low-level damages are experienced frequently, part of the benefit received in exchange for absorbing these losses is the ability to externalize similar costs to others without having to compensate them, and to incur transaction costs that would necessarily accompany such efforts ... the loss is one the law requires the plaintiff to absorb because small losses are offset over the long run by small benefits.

The critical assumption in this doctrine is a symmetry that is not always of a reciprocal nature, and some entities indulge in systematic practices over time and across their interactions with other entities. This type of 'habitual' or chronic nature of illegal conduct warrants a proper remedy. This attracts the role of tort law and other provisions, including punitive damages.

Bargaining and out-of-court settlements

A normative theory of settlement of legal cases tends to view the decision problem of the litigants in terms of selection of their choices, subject to applicable judicial rules, of maximizing their respective expected utility under discrete alternative scenarios – with trial by jury or other, and without a court trial. The rules governing the bearing of court costs and legal fees tend to influence the relative comparative assessments of these costs and of an uncertain outcome in the future. These evaluations depend crucially on their risk-preference attitudes. Typical risk-neutral behaviour, commonly enunciated in the economics literature, allows a simple expected value ranking of alternatives. In several realistic settings this may not easily be computed, however.

In terms of a positive theory of settlements of litigations outside the court, the factors affecting relevant choices and decisions may include the following elements: court-specific characteristics such as a recent history of type and magnitude of awards; legal rules governing the assignment of direct court and attorney fees; and situation-specific information or precedents. Fournier and Zuehlke (1989) pursued this approach using a sample of cases for empirical analysis, and suggested that both higher mean trial awards and higher alleged damages have a significant positive effect on the likelihood of settlement. This implies that as the stakes in a trial are increased, litigants tend to enhance their efforts to reach a settlement and this increases the possibility of a settlement. The English rule reduces the probability of a settlement by increasing the stakes of a trial: because the loser is to pay the court costs of both the litigants, the return to winning a trial as well as the cost of losing a trial are increased (Shavell, 1982). The study by Fournier and Zuehlke (1989) lends more empirical support to this proposition. It was also estimated from the sample study that a mean increase in the awards history by 100 per cent can lead to an increase of 93 per cent in the settlement.

Finally, there is need for further development of legal economics. This area, as currently known, is simply the financial damage assessment aspect of costing for damage or cost recovery under the current legal systems. Current legal practice does not often permit inclusion of TC as a component of the total costs. Yet, these are real costs incurred by parties to a litigation and the issue needs further attention in law-making and legal institutions.

Among the most important institutions and provisions for orderly conduct and promotion of economic efficiency through *de facto* and *de jure* specifications are property rights (PR) and liability rules (LR), the focus of the following section.

6.3   Property rights and liability rules

The main characteristics of PR are: exclusivity, transferability, divisibility, duration and well-defined boundaries of rights, and enforceability. One of the definitions of PR is (Landes and Posner, 1987, p. 29): an 'exclusive right to the use, control, and enjoyment of a resource', and this does not entail any further calculation of the potential benefits of the transfer of PR to others. In contrast, the LR allow a claim for damages caused to the resource. A primary function of PR is that of 'guiding incentives to achieve a greater internalization of externalities' (Demsetz, 1967), where internalizing refers to a process (usually a change in the specifications of PR). It was also noted that the costs of internalizing externalities is smaller with a small set of decision entities. Based on an empirical study covering several countries over a long period of time, Mahoney (2001) observed that the 'common law' produces faster growth through greater security of property and contract rights.

PR refer to (Furubotn and Pejovich, 1972, p. 1139) the 'sanctioned behavioral relations among men that arise from the existence of things and pertain to their use... defining the position of each individual with respect to the utilization of scarce resources'. The specifications of PR are influenced by technology resources (Stubblebine, 1975) and offer an expanding set of choices of instruments with technological or development progress. It is important to recognize the role of institutional governance, especially that of the state, in any analysis of PR regimes. A regime, in general, consists of 'norms, rules and procedures agreed in order to regulate an issue area' (Haas, 1980, p. 357). Thus a PR regime presumes the existence of an appropriate regulatory/enforcement mechanism, and this entails TC.

In an early study, Demsetz (1966) identified three implications (similar to the implications of the Coase theorem) of a PR regime when the costs of exchanging and enforcement are zero (which is unlikely in any realistic setting): (i) the value of all 'harmful and beneficial effects' of alternative specifications of PR will be brought to bear on the asset holders; (ii) PR will be used efficiently if the asset-holding decision-makers are rational utility maximizers; and (iii) the mix of output that is produced will be independent of the distribution of PR among asset holders apart from the effects of changes in wealth holdings of these on relevant demand schedules (Rao, 2001). Some of these idealized insights are useful as a starting point to examine the role and implications of PR. In a real-world setting, the complexity of issues warrants a greater comprehension of the role of TC and the behavioural characteristics of the economic decision-making entities.

A theory of PR is incomplete without an accompanying theory of the state and the role of LR. LR seek to offer protection to an interest (if it is well-defined), and do not directly support the protection of the exercise of rights or duties in any PR regime. In its operative form, an LR that specifies a penalty clause in an agreement or other legal stipulation is an *ex ante* formulation that signals the costs of violating a legal imperative and thus tends to contribute to self-enforcement of the required obligations, provided the penalty clause remains enforceable (at reasonably low TC). A theory of PR that gives the proper role to LR is a crucial requirement to enable the efficient functioning of entities or activities under any meaningful decentralization of resource management (see also Mattei, 1997).

TC based on LR govern the distribution of the terms of negotiation. It is relevant to quote Samuels (1992, p. 92): 'In a world of asymmetrically distributed transaction costs, the locus of liability is important with respect to distributional consequences.' The assertion that TC are a function of LR is significant, and calls for further analysis.

An integrated view of PR and LR suggests the use of the concept 'entitlements' (Calabresi and Melamed, 1972). While this integration serves the purpose of examining the distributive aspects of resources, the operational aspects involving TC for devising relevant regimes, institutions and organizations – including the role of different elements of TC – remains a major factor in selecting one component over the other in the PR versus liability approaches. These aspects can be examined better in relation to specific contexts and issues, in addition to the objectives of these regimes. The reasons for the greater use of the PR approach in the international legal systems include (Dunoff and Tracht-man, 1999): (i) the costs of creating PR versus dispute resolution systems; (ii) the costs of determining and levying damages from offend-ers; (iii) operative features of 'excessive costs', and net benefits of liabil-ity regimes; and (iv) the collective public goods nature of the provision of liability systems, with the potential free-riding behaviour of some countries.

The existence of significant magnitudes of TC implies that the role of LR will be rather limited; the practicality of rules of liability should act as guiding principle for the substitution rules in relation to negotiated solutions (Demsetz, 1972). PR need not be unconditional or renogotia-tion-proof.

The role of the passage of time is usually neglected in the literature under the Coasean framework. As Cordato (1998) argued, the normative standard regarding the sequence of events leading to an 'arrangement of rights that may bring about a greater value of production than any other' (Coase, 1960, p. 16) is largely unknown. The efficiency properties of 'coming to the nuisance' (or 'first come, first served' in rights) are linked to the economic analysis of dynamic disequilibrium markets. These issues require further attention.

Much of TCE can be treated as the economics of contracts regarding alternative forms of governance. The law and economics of contracts thus merits careful attention. Section 6.4 examines relevant aspects, including the theory and applications.

6.4 Economics of contracts

A firm, a market, a constitution and governance relations – all these are examples of the institution of contract. There do not, in general, exist complete contracts – not even the completable ones (see also Chapters

1 to 3). The role of TC in contract formulation and implementation has been one of the most discussed aspects of TCE. Masten and Saussier (2000) provide a brief, useful summary of comparative assumptions and of relative stands of the agency theory of NE and of TCE regarding contract economics. There have also been several studies that investigated the interdependencies empirically, lending greater support to TCE formulations.

The theory of contracts abounds with the potential for incomplete contracts, and this feature poses several limitations on both the formal and informal models of economics of contracting. Analytical formal models of incomplete contracting are of relatively recent origin in economics, and it is necessary to examine why parties sign such contracts – be it a result of bounded rationality or TC, or a combination of these and other factors.

When we view the firm as an entity of incomplete contract setting, following Coase (1937) and Williamson (1975), four types of TC can be seen to play major roles here (Rao, 2001): (i) at the contract formation stage some of the future contingencies are simply unforeseeable; (ii) if some or most of these contingencies are visualized, the costs of writing the detailed formulations for each of these becomes prohibitive; (iii) monitoring the implementation of contract terms is costly; and (iv) verification and enforcement of the terms of the contract and/or revision of the contract at a later date is costly, and might warrant litigation or other third party enforcement (with an unreliable quality of the outcome in some cases).

Let us state a few definitions:

Complete contract.   A contract that has the relevant decisions (specific transactions, resource flows and so on) depend on all verifiable factors, including information revelation by the parties involved; an a priori incomplete contract also qualifies as a complete contract if it yields the parties the same pay-offs as the optimal complete contract (Tirole, 1988, p. 29).

Incomplete contract.   A contract in which: (i) there exist contractual gaps, *ab initio*, or in its interpretation *ex post*; and/or (ii) it does not exhaust the contracting possibilities that could ideally be envisioned in the complete contracting case.

Inevitably incomplete contract.   'the optimal solution to a contracting problem would require the parties to condition on information that is unobservable to one or both of them *ex post* or that decision maker could not verify' (Schwartz, 1992, p. 79); a contract is legally incomplete to the extent that (ibid., p. 81) 'its terms require the parties to condition on unverifiable information'.

A key aspect for the formation of 'complete contracts' is the feature relating to 'perfectly contingent contracting'. This feature is itself conditioned by (Tirole, 1999): (i) adverse selection, when some of the decision-makers possess (at the initial stage of contract formation) private information not shared in the contract setting; (ii) informational asymmetry, when some parties accumulate additional information (after contract formation) contributing to informational asymmetry among contracting parties; and (iii) moral hazard, when contracting parties take action inconsistent with the specifications of contract but the action may not be verifiable.

The existence of TC, in addition to incomplete information, hinders the possibility of forming 'complete' contracts. The factors contributing to (relative or absolute) incompleteness of contracts include: the costs of formulating comprehensive, and hence complex, contracts; unforeseen contingencies; undescribable events and other uncertainties having an impact on the system affecting or affected by the contract specifications (see also Anderlini and Felli, 1994); the increasingly high cost of enumerating what are considered *ex ante* costs as rather remote or 'less important'; and potential or *ex post* costs of contract enforcement.

An important theme of the incomplete contract theory is that the assignment of PR determines the bargaining positions of the parties in the *ex post* contract formation scenario. Socially optimal contract provisions often require the provision of default rules, either within each specific contract and/or background legal provisions under common law. It is often sought to fill contract gaps with 'default rules', and the normative economic view suggests that these be based on the criterion of minimization of the aggregate costs of contracting.

In general, courts (or other third-party institutions) are required to fill in the contractual gaps, both *de jure* and *de facto*, to bring some operational meaning to the incomplete contracts. These interpretative gap-filling methods elude any sense of uniformity across locations, sectors and time. This is because of substantial imprecision in the use of criteria to resolve such situations.

TCE stresses the role of opportunistic behaviour of parties and related behavioural features. One of these features is the hold-up problem and relates to *ex post* opportunistic behaviour (see Williamson, 1985): in the context of incomplete contracts one of the parties may renegotiate terms after entering into an agreement – a stage where it is not necessarily in the interests of the other party to decline renegotiation. Inevitably, incompleteness of contracts sometimes leads to the need for governance of business transactions via the organizational form (that is, the firm). When parties cannot use the contract system they use governance structures (Wiggins, 1990).

Various long-term contracts are often interpreted as substitutes for 'missing markets', because the price system does not carry enough information for a long time horizon and the corresponding characteristics of the markets. Eggertsson (1989) suggests the role of different components of the missing markets with an illustration of European agriculture for a long time during earlier centuries: the prevalence of the open-field system was because of one or more of the missing markets for insurance, for grazing rights, and for labour services in agriculture.

The complexity or simplicity of a contract is dependent on several factors, but in almost all cases the formal economic analysis and legal requirements suggest a very complex specification of terms and conditions to be fulfilled by the contracting parties. However, the efficiency of a contract is not determined entirely by its complexity, but rather by its 'optimal' incompleteness. The role of incomplete information and bounded rationality affect the completion. Reliance on reputation, trust and mutual co-operation tend to simplify the requirements of contractual specifications to a large extent. Besides, the existence of a uniform commercial code under the prevailing legal system in some countries enables simplicity by linking up to a blanket set of provisions as a package – mandatory or voluntary, depending on the legal provisions.

Complete contracts, if these exist, can only be accomplished at a high cost. Among other extremes of the alternatives is informal (unwritten) agreement with contract costs at the lowest level. The economic efficiency question that remains in an incomplete contract implementation is that of the role of residual rights; that is, the liability of the party that fails to fulfil the promise. In US commercial law, Article 2-508 of the Uniform Commercial Code (UCC) allows a seller to correct a defective or non-conforming delivery of a product or service by reducing the price 'appropriately'. The default option thus allows a two-part pricing in practice in law. Chen (2000), in a simplified formal model, examined the welfare maximizing implications of residual rights in incomplete contracts, but did not employ Coasean bargaining options. The provision of PR for residual rights can generate secondary markets and potentially reduce TC.

Empirical studies

There have been a number of empirical studies on contract economics and these support TCE perspectives and provide evidence contrasting with the basic assumptions of the agency theory of neoclassical economics. Based on a survey, Lyons (1996) concluded that the risk-sharing motive of contracts seems to have only a very indirect effect on modern contracts between production firms; but TCE (including the role of reputation) seems to play a major role. Saussier (1998, 1999) found that the duration of contracts was related positively to the value of investments in asset-specific or relationship-specific cases. Bercovitz (1999) found that the duration of franchise agreements is longer in relation to the size of initial investment by the franchisee, correlating with asset-specific investments and TC. Crocker and Masten (1988) and Saussier (1998, 1999) found that contract periods tend to be of shorter duration in the presence of greater uncertainty, a finding that does not lend support to the NE approach to contracts advocating a risk-sharing mechanism.

Measuring asset specificity has been an empirical problem for testing the TCE theory of firms. Monteverde and Teece (1982), Masten (1984) and Joskow (1985) contributed to specific case studies in the application of this aspect. Substantial complexity in products and services leads to the potential for overstating quality (and price) by providers of such items, and this situation often warrants vertical integration, or at the minimum provides an incentive to seek integration in some enterprises. The complexity issue differs from the asset-specificity issue, but they are often correlated. Complexity itself undermines contracting because of problems of bounded rationality.

On the issue of vertical integration of business activities in relation to contracting, Masten and Saussier (2000), in their review of empirical studies and comparison of validity of assumptions of the two alternative schools of thought (NE and TCE), concluded that: (i) the empirical literature suggests a preference for integration over contracting as the asset-specific investments increase as a proportion of the total investment; and (ii) uncertainty and complexity of the contracting environment reduce the attractiveness of contracting relative to integration.

Saussier (2000a) observed that asset-specificity plays an important role in the determination of contract form. It was concluded (ibid., p. 394): 'In the case we studied, it seems that the contract form is chosen not to induce efficient asset-specificity investments but rather to ensure sufficient adaptation to *ex post* unanticipated changes... Contracts in our study appear to be a simple non-exhaustive governance, created to facilitate the *ex post* realization of the transaction.'

Firms and corporate contracts

The firm is often viewed as a contractual entity, described as a 'nexus of contracts' (see, for example, Jensen and Meckling, 1976). These contracts are viewed as (Klausner, 1995, p. 759) 'the product of a market-mediated process that tends to lead the constituents of the firm to adopt contract terms that maximize the firm's value'.

The term 'corporate contract' is used in corporate law literature to include the specifications of the relationships among investors (share-holders and creditors), workers and the management of the firm. A state's corporate charter is an important aspect of contract design, and that charter invariably possesses features affecting the incidence of network externalities.

The standard and crucial assumption in contract economics is that the value of a firm's contract term is independent of the number of other firms that adopt similar or the same terms.

The role of co-ordination assumes significance in the presence of network externalities. This does not imply automatically, however, that such a co-ordination is feasible, nor that the TC of co-ordination are less than the benefits of co-ordination; nor is state intervention imperative here (Klausner, 1995).

Contract enforcement

While it is a known element of TC, the cost of enforcement is not often integrated with the contract formation and/or its costs. In reality, private individuals and entities, and not the state, bear most of the costs of enforcement. To this extent, any estimate costs have to reflect the cost of private ordering and its effect on the cost of enforcement. This is not to state, however, that there is no private ordering implication when the state is the enforcer, but in the state case, it is a *de facto* rather than *de jure* cost of enforcement that applies in addition to the official costs of administration and enforcement.

Incomplete contracts

A series of short-term 'complete' contracts, renegotiated frequently, may approximate the role of long-term contracts, subject to the conditions: the existence of a common knowledge of preferences and gainful op-portunities at renegotiation dates (Milgrom and Roberts, 1988). It is likely that the costs of negotiating a series of short-term contracts constitute major segment of the costs of market transactions.

Even when the costs of contractual complexity are not predominant, short-term contracts may not approximate well as equivalents for the long-term contracts when either of the following two conditions hold (Milgrom and Roberts, 1988): (i) the existence of private information or asymmetric information between parties at recontracting stages prevents the parties from forming efficient agreements; and (ii) monetary incentives are of limited effectiveness or delivery of exchange involves payments in kind that can be made only in a long-term relationship.

Can a series of short-term contracts lead to efficiency over a period of time? The role of opportunistic behaviour, specialized assets and uncertainty about the future are among the factors that hinder a market arrangement based on a series of short-term contracts from yielding an efficient outcome (Milgrom and Roberts, 1990, p. 66). It is important to incorporate incomplete contracting models with models and provisions for enforcement. Even a so-called complete contract is to be deemed essentially incomplete if it only addresses specifications of performance under all contingencies but provides no credible enforcement mechanisms.

Ranking of incomplete contracts using a common norm or numeraire is an area of interest for further investigation. Using an approach of ranking different contracts with reference to their potential economic efficiency implications (in relation to the objectives of the contracts) is perhaps a straightforward method, but the assessment of the efficiency implications cannot be conditioned by the unknown type and degree of incompleteness of the contract. Thus a set of assumptions regarding the latter are to be formulated before attempting any ranking. Again, problems of bounded rationality and adaptive behaviour surface in this exercise. Contractual incompleteness and the role of bounded rationality are hard to formalize, including the complexity of the contract. However, a few analytical approaches can be made to address the situation.

When contracts are inevitably incomplete or unenforceable, trust and the co-operative behaviour of economic agents play a major role in determining the quality and efficiency of transactions, and thus affect the efficient functioning of the economy.

Legal contract theory versus economic contract theory

Legal contract theory advises (Schwartz, 1992, p. 76) 'authoritative decision-makers how to regulate contracting behavior', procedurally and substantively, whereas economic contract theory focuses on the design of optimal contracts, assuming 'rational parties' as the contracting parties) to be devised by various institutions. Despite widespread usage of different types of contracts, contracts literature in legal and economic arenas remains incomplete, and this explains the substantial utilization of the judicial institutions. A wide variety of categorizations of contracts is relevant for gaining greater insights.

It is not as important to figure out the completeness or lack of it in contracts, because it is almost impossible to form a complete contract. The relevant issue is how incomplete contracts are, and to examine why some contracts are more complete than others. One contract is more complete than another if it gives a more precise characterization of the transaction and of the means of implementing it (Saussier, 2000b). A useful finding may be stated here:

> *Proposition*: The marginal cost of a contract that aims for completeness increases with the transaction-uncertainty level and the contract-completeness level (Saussier, 2000b, p. 193).

It is useful to note that, in the complete contracts framework, optimal contracts can be specified contingent on all observable information, even after the original starting date of the contract. In contrast incomplete contracts are founded largely on the existence of unobservable and/or asymmetric information among contracting parties on the one hand, and third parties (for the purposes of verifiability or co-ordination) on the other. As pointed out by Saussier (2000a), non-verifiability feature remains an important provider of incompleteness in contracts. Strategic uncertainty remains an important contributor of the phenomenon of incomplete contracts. This feature remains largely unexplored in the literature on the theory of incomplete contracts, and on the role of TC.

TC play a role in mitigating the effects of incomplete information by suggesting relevant guidelines for the design of 'optimally incomplete contracts'. This is largely because of the explicit recognition of the role of bounded rationality in decision-making, and the existence of it also in complex scenarios. The role of contract renegotiation and its costs, in addition to the costs of contract design and enforcement, remain pertinent issues in the application of TC analysis. Contract adaptation and *ex post* flexibility issues are also required for consideration in the TC approach. Thus the complementary roles of contract theories and TC approaches remain essential for the design of optimal contracts, and these require further attention.

Other categories of contracts

Several additional categories of contracts are also useful in terms of their classifications and the role of TC in their conceptualization and operational implementation. These are summarized below.

Explicit and implicit contracts

These are distinguished by the features of the stated explicit contract, and by the underlying (usually unwritten) linkages with other activities (outside the contractual provisions) of the contracting parties that affect one or more of the parties. It may be noted here that there exists a distinction between implicit contracts and implied contracts. The latter is often interpreted in courts and other institutions in relation to the objectives of the contract or other relevant provisions (even if the interpretation may not admit its unique or only particularity), but implicit contracts are usually non-verifiable or enforceable by third parties. The interaction between implicit and explicit contracts requires considerable further study.

An apparent sub-optimal choice is made consciously by some parties, since it becomes optimal when viewed in the broader context that includes other interrelationships between parties. This is not necessarily a 'give-and-take' summing situation, but could be a systematic submission of some parties to the implicit coercive measures of more dominant parties in the contract scenario (assuming such a contract was deemed necessary by the relatively weaker parties in the first place).

Short-term versus long-term contracts

These relate to the nature of specifications of the time horizon over which the contract is sought to be implemented, including any clarity about the terminal period specifications, such as target fulfilment.

Static versus dynamic contracts

These differ in the nature of the specifications of contractual duties/rights that are functions of time, changing over time in accordance with a specified schedule (usually time-based, but it could also be in relation to the magnitudes of various parameters involved in any given time interval).

Renegotiable versus negotiation-proof contracts

These characterize any contract provisions, allowing renegotiation in relation to various contingencies and/or specified time periods, in contrast to fixed, non-renegotiable (closed) contracts. Contract modifications based on renegotiations apply differently to the major categories (Schwartz, 1992): (i) the renegotiation of complete contracts; (ii) the modification of 'completable' contracts (based on *ex post* states of the situations); and (iii) modifications of inevitably incomplete contracts using renegotiations.

Optimal contracts

These are defined in terms of normative features that enable the attainment of the maximization of stated objectives subject to relevant constraints, and provide enforceable specifications of actions for implementation by parties to the contracts, clarified in terms of time horizons, verifiable information features, contingencies for alternative scenarios, and provision of non-fulfilment of clauses. Obviously, these are transaction-specific, although methodologically common formulations can be advanced.

Relational contracts

In complex and repetitive interactions, parties form relational contracts in order to minimize the TC of contracting; they agree to general procedures of relationships and dispute resolution mechanisms without specifying all, or even a substantial number of, relevant parameters for a formal contract.

Frequent and ongoing interactions can obviate the need for complex contracts and state-imposed structures. In complex, long-term relationships, the details to be spelt out for a near-complete contract would be excessive and costly; parties in such situations try to economize on such TC by resorting to relational contracting, in which parties agree to procedures for any future changes that might be warranted because of a change in applicable factors, including procedures for dispute resolution and enforcement. Some of the details of the law and economics of relational contracting are given in Schwartz (1992), Goetz and Scott (1981) and Macneil (1981).

Can Coasean negotiation lead to optimal contracts, with or without the backdrop of pre-existing contract laws? The answer depends on the nature of incompleteness of existing laws to form a basis for contract formation between parties, and on the role of TC in the process. Among the behavioural prerequisites for the existence of optimal contracts as a result of negotiations among contesting parties are the parties' risk-neutrality (see Maskin and Tirole, 1999).

6.5   Conclusions

Several important observations emerge from the major aspects of the emerging field of law and economics. The integral role of TCE in this dynamic area is one of its main strengths. Wide applications in economic and legal sectors is indicative of its broad and specific usefulness. The economics of litigation studied thus far has not addressed the key role of TC and its implications for legal remedies, as in the case of assessment of compensatory damages in the court system. Contract laws inevitably remain incomplete, as are the contracts themselves. Hence there exists much greater scope to strengthen the role of informed and efficient negotiations for the resolution of disputes, and for the design of arbitration processes that fill in the contractual gaps in an efficient manner.

The emphasis of part of TCE literature on the role of PR needs to be integrated with the integrated roles of PR and LR, and the influence of TC in this system of formulations. The role of the state in the efficacy of the functioning of PR is often a less recognized feature in the relevant literature. A prerequisite for the enhanced role of PR and Coasean negotiation is the existence of legal infrastructure, including well-defined laws and their enforcement with low TC.

The role of TC in the law and economics of contracts remains a very important feature that affects the design and implementation of contracts, elucidated in this chapter.

7
Behavioural Economics

7.1 Introduction

Behavioural economics constitutes the foundation of transaction cost economics (TCE). One of the main elements of this approach has been to recognize the role of bounded rationality, as well as opportunistic behaviour (discussed in Chapter 1). Much attention was focused on the behavioural theory of the firm in literature, but the emphasis was largely on managerial behaviour and relatively less on the role of bounded rationality or other behavioural traits of firms (see Chapter 2). The totality of TC was not usually reflected; for a classic treatment, see Cyert and March (1963). Despite these developments, there are a few aspects of economic behaviour that have not been fully integrated with TCE. In order to explain and predict economic behaviour, TCE must recognize other relevant features of decision-making as well.

It is important to recognize that TC act as behavioural constraints, not only as added costs (except if we imagine the 'addition' of costs in terms of some non-linear scale of additional elements of TC beyond an unknown 'reasonable threshold'). Some of the practical cases summarized in Chapter 1 illustrate this point. Does co-operation among parties (as opposed to opportunism) guarantee that TC is minimized? Not always, as a counter-example in Warneryd (1994) showed. This is because every economic problem does not involve the critical feature of cooperation but does involve TC.

The role of behavioural traits is to exploit these features for TC minimization and performance maximization of the system. Of particular interest are the issues of financial markets and trading. This chapter addresses a few important issues: the role of relativity in performance as an indicator affecting TC; motivational impacts of standardization of the characteristics of goods and services; and the role and implications of time-consistent policies and of habit formation, customs and norms. Clearly, these aspects raise several unexamined questions and further study is needed to throw more light on these issues.

7.2 Relative profit maximization

When firms have market power, profit maximizers are not necessarily the best survivors because of the spiteful behaviour of powerful firms (Schaeffer, 1989): a firm that does not maximize its profits may still be better off than its profit-maximizing competitors if the costs to itself of the deviations from the maximal profit scenario are less than the costs it imposes on the 'rational' profit maximizers.

This is just one example of some of the corporate practices akin to the problem of survival of the fittest, as in the games played by corporate entities. These do not occur often in the market place, but there is no denying that some of the enterprises formulate their business activities in terms of predatory policies for the annihilation of their rivals and the capture of a comfortable level of market share. Where is the role of TC in all this, though? The issue is one of the articulation of TC before and after the capture of market power for the predatory firm and for the affected firms or other economic entities. These actions, subject to their conformity with the law, impose various economic externalities on the market, especially in the closer interactions of the sector where the effects are material. These activities entail short-run adjustment costs for rivals and include the possibility of knocking out some of these entities from the business altogether. We do not propose to examine the issue of anti-trust laws and those of mergers and acquisitions or hostile take-overs here. Suffice it to say that TCE needs to recognize the behavioural features beyond those of a 'rational' approach or of profit maximization. The role of evolutionary strategies advocated under the TC approach by Warneryd (1994) deserve further development in order to explain these dynamics. Accordingly, the role of 'evolutionary stability' and other forms of survival strategies also need to be examined for an explanation of the existence of these phenomena.

If we extend the scope to sociological features of populations where relativities matter (rather than absolute utility or income maximization), the possibility of denial of mutually gainful opportunities cannot be ruled out as a result of perceived 'relative gains' by one or more parties. In fact, this behavioural trait seems to act as a serious limiting factor against economic growth and development in some of the underdeveloped economies. Hence there is a need for a greater focus on this aspect of behavioural economics and its implications for TC, as measured from a positive economics as well as normative economics definition of TC (see Chapter 1). It may be hypothesized that relative utility or performance maximization is not usually competition-enhancing in its effects; besides, such behaviour enhances TC as well as reduces the total welfare of a society and its corresponding economic systems.

7.3   Habit formation and irrationality

The role of habit, or that of the influence of past and/or current activities on the future conduct of similar activities, is not often recognized in the economic literature when seeking neoclassical economic explanations for rationality or irrationality. The latter is a complement of the behavioural features that characterize rationality in the sense of utility maximization subject to appropriate constraints.

What constitutes irrationality relative to a narrow definition of rationality is unlikely to be a useful concept since we miss out a wide variety of plausible and pragmatic scenarios of economic behaviour and their 'rationale' by dubbing them an 'irrational' category. The role of behavioural economics and finance is important in explaining a number of important observed phenomena. Where does TCE come into play here? The ingredients of TCE that play a significant role in this context include: adaptation and inertia costs; bounded rationality; and asset specificity.

In formalized models, habits are viewed broadly in two approaches: (i) habits react only gradually to changes in economic conduct; and (ii) habit formation is a lagged adjustment process, where the specific time-lags vary with socioeconomic and other characteristics of decision-makers.

Irrational behaviour

A realistic description of 'irrational' behaviour may possibly be called 'non-standard' behaviour. The main approaches for formalism of non-standard behaviour include applications of prospect theory (or the prominent role of loss aversion), and the role of irrational expectations. Kahneman and Tversky (1979) advanced prospect theory. According to this, individuals do not judge outcomes only on the absolute values of outcomes, but compare outcomes with an initial reference scenario. The objective function in this case is concave for gains above the reference point and convex for losses corresponding to outcomes below the reference point. There exists a kink at the reference point and this is relevant in explaining some of the observed phenomena (as in the 'equity premium puzzle').

The existence of the kink in the objective function makes it optimal for some investors to hold zero stocks when the equity premium is small. This observation contrasts with the standard result that a risk-averse investor should always possess a favourable stock, and this might explain the non-participation of some investors in the stock market (Campbell, 2000). Amihud and Mendelson (1986) argued that TC reduce the prices of small stocks significantly. Campbell (2000) concluded, in a survey on asset pricing literature of the financial economics area, that we have only a poor understanding of how TC can affect asset prices.

The role of TC in relation to the decision-making structure of various categories of investors is still an unexplored area. Non-standard behaviour among investors includes: irrational expectations based on knowingly limited information; the latter comprises, typically, either an impulse-based and incomplete study of the history of the stock, or a gradual diffusion of rumours and signals leading to herd behaviour. The roles of a very low rate of time preference or a very high rate of time preference, and of a very high coefficient of risk aversion or of a very low coefficient of risk aversion are also similar to those of non-standard behaviour. If the perception of TC is rather arbitrary (which is likely when much of the relevant information is substantially unknown), the differential impact of such perceptions leads to widely varying decisions when decision-makers are non-standard in their behaviour.

Friction and financial markets

Friction measures the 'difficulty' or its cost with which an asset is traded. It can be measured by the price concession needed to implement a transaction without delay (Demsetz, 1968), or other extraneous risks of delay. Two types of friction may be distinguished (Stoll, 2000): real friction and informational friction. It was suggested that the former uses up real resources and that the latter redistributes wealth (no implication regarding desired welfare maximizing redistribution, however). Real frictions must, in theory, be reflected in lower prices of assets such that the return on an asset is sufficient to offset the real cost of trading the asset (including the cost of holding the asset for the applicable period). If interpreted as the price of immediacy, friction costs depict the role of incomplete markets, and when interpreted in terms of costs of informational asymmetries, the friction costs constitute an illustration of the standard elements under TCE.

Facilitators of immediacy in financial transactions, such as market makers, are passive traders who stand ready to trade at prices they quote. The demanders of immediacy are active traders who place market orders to trade immediately. Immediate sales are usually made at the bid price and immediate purchases are usually made at the ask price. The spread, or the difference between the bid price and the ask price, is one measure of friction (Stoll, 2000). Market power has a clear role to play in the extent of this friction, since the spread can be made sensitive to the relative costs of the players.

A new measure of trading friction called the traded spread was introduced by Stoll (2000). This measure is applicable when institutional investors calculate their trading costs. It is the difference between the average price of trades on the ask side and the average price of trades on the bid side. In the empirical study, it was found that market structure has an effect on the friction measures. It was also found that real friction, arising from order-processing costs and inventory holding costs, is significant in the US stock market.

Under the informational approach to friction (see, for example, Glosten and Milgrom, 1985), the spread is the value of information lost to better informed or more timely traders. The facilitator of immediacy of transactions confronts the risk that the ask or bid activity at a price will be accepted by some other traders with different information in their possession. If suppliers of immediacy are to avoid losses, imperfectly informed traders must pay a margin sum or premium sufficient to compensate facilitators of immediacy for losses to informed investors (Bagehot, 1971).

Time inconsistency and economic policies

What constitutes an optimal solution for an economic problem seen *ex ante* at a specific time T may not remain an optimal solution at time time $T + 1$ after new information is revealed. In the absence of rigid commitments, it is possible to revise optimal strategies or solutions *ex post*, if there are no significant legal or other constraints – or, equivalently, if the corresponding TC are not prohibitive. The problem of dynamic inconsistency was first examined by Strotz (1956), and the source of the inconsistency was viewed in terms of change in preferences of economic decision-makers from one time period to another (see also Pollak, 1968, for a critique of some of the results; these do not change our further interpretations here, however). If the discount rate is the same in each time period in the decision-maker's valuation of future parameters (cost, benefits, utility), the problem of inconsistency is resolved, only in so far as the inconsistency is not a strategic behavioural feature. Pre-commitment (contractual or other self-restrained behaviour) is a general solution to the dynamic inconsistency problem, but this may not always be a welfare maximizing optimal solution. If TC are not prohibitive, but not necessarily negligible, it might be pragmatic to devise a rolling plan approach whereby decisions are revised at the end of each time period (on a relevant practical time horizon). A sequential or rolling plan allows for the incorporation of new information and reduces the costs of bounded rationality arising in a complex one-stage formulation. The costs of implementing such an optimal strategy is a significant aspect of TC, and we are thus confronting choices between two streams of TC: one set when a complex decision with less information is to be made, and the other with a sequential flow of information but with added costs of strategy revision, and perhaps adding to the strategic uncertainties of players or parties at each stage because of the non-binding commitments beyond one time period.

In formal optimal models, Kydland and Prescott (1977) first drew the attention of economists to the potential problems of time inconsistency (under rational expectations formation assumption) and implications for formal optimization methods of economic analysis. Holly and Hallett (1989, ch. 8) observed that if the policy adjustment costs are zero (the zero TC case), the multi-period optimization separates into a series of equivalent one-period static optimization problems (subject to a further requirement that the number of policy instruments is not less than the number of response variables in the model).

In practical applications of the problem of inconsistency, it was also suggested that the use of monetary and other negotiable instruments in lieu of the barter of goods and services could have been a partial explanation in resolving the problems of dynamic inconsistency entailed in the barter system. Lack of consistency over multiple time periods leads to loss of reputation, and governments which seek to change policies in light of new information will suffer the consequences of loss of credibility and reputation.

In a formal model, Roberds (1987) formulated a simplified version of what was called stochastic replanning based on the assumptions of rational expectations of economic entities and random changes in policy-makers and the need to re-examine the policy at each random time interval of change. It was suggested that the potential gains to pre-commitment should be evaluated, not by contrasting outcomes under consistent and pre-commitment cases, but by contrasting the prevalent replanning and pre-commitment outcomes.

In the context of seeking renegotiation-proof multi-period agreements, Rubinstein and Wolinsky (1982) showed that the addition of a time horizon for agreement or its revision as a negotiated policy parameter enables parties to enlarge the set of policy choices and potential efficiency of the agreement or contract. This assertion does not take into account the corresponding change in TC, however.

One of the major impediments to some of the formal models for economic decision-making involving future generations is to ensure time-consistency: in an intergenerational setting, how to ensure that future decision-making systems will, in fact, respect the continuity and ensure the furtherance of future interests at every point in time or the start of new decision horizons? Some elements of TC have not been accounted for in formal models addressing some of these issues, and further developments are called for.

7.4   Norms, customs and traditions

The role of norms and customs as well as traditions has been to impose, naturally, some behavioural regularities on a society or organization. These factors, in a formal representation, are typically those of an endogenous preference function affecting decision-making via the objectives and constraints of relevance (including initial conditions or reference points).

Endogenous preferences

The role of endogenous preference is particularly important in analyses involving long horizons and/or the role of past information, as in habits. Changes in economic actors' responses are affected by changes in information, institutions, and other factors. In much of the economic literature the preferences are largely sought to be reflected in the time-discounting parameter that typically values future parameters. This is hardly a satisfactory accounting for changes that occur in the preference structures over a period of time. The assumption of a constant, exogenously prescribed rate of social time preference or stationarity of preferences over the entire horizon of relevance has been a feature of technical convenience rather than of realism in many economic studies (Rao, 2000). Also, this feature is inconsistent with the basic premise of TCE. With bounded rationality and adaptation mechanisms, there is little scope for such characterization of economic behaviour.

The typical endogenous discount function at time t for a traditional problem of optimal consumption assumes the form, with v (c) as the time-dependent consumption:

$$D(t) = \exp\{ - \int_0^t v(c_s)ds\}$$

where $[0 , t]$ is a sub-interval of the relevant horizon, and the integrand is the corresponding discount factor affected by the consumption level at each time instant.

More general forms of endogenous discount functions can be formulated to allow the integrand above (the discount factor) to depend on the state variables, the control variables and time; these recognize the role of changes in consumption 'tastes' and 'habits'.

Various general forms of discount factors, and hence discount functions, can be accommodated in the present approach; these functions are endogenous with respect to control variables, state variables and time (explicitly). The method that allows the amenability of these features within the framework of standard optimal control models augments the structure of the model with an additional state variable.

If the discount function is of the form:

$$\exp\{ - \int_0^t g(x, u, \tau)d\tau\}$$

A new state variable z is introduced and given by:

$$\dot{z} = -g(x, u, \tau)$$

The formal model allows the application of one of the dynamic optimization methods, as suggested briefly in Chapter 1. Further investigations along these lines are expected to throw light on the issues of relevance.

Market influences

The effectiveness of policies and their viability (political and/or economic) depend on the preferences they induce or evoke. In the environmental field, for example, see Sunstein (1993) for a description of the role of endogenous preferences in response to public environmental policy formation. Bowles (1998, p. 105) argued that, if preferences are shaped by markets and other economic institutions, these induce 'actions imposing non-contractible costs and benefits on others.'

Let us bring in a definition:

Nice traits. These are behavioral characteristics that confer benefits on others in social and economic interactions (Bowles, 1998).

Bowles (1998) argued that repeated interactions and a smaller number of personalized interactions tend to promote nice traits; these features are necessary but not sufficient to ensure nice traits, however.

Is it useful to design laws that might have deterrent or behavioural influences merely because these exist on the law books? According to one of the perspectives offered by Hirschman (1985, p. 10), 'a principal purpose of publicly proclaimed laws and regulations is to stigmatize antisocial behavior and thereby to influence citizens' values and behavioral codes'.

This prescription may not be entirely tenable, however. This is because such stigmatization may induce a differential or disparate application of the laws on a selective and discriminatory basis, and generate private rents from bribes for the enforcement entities. If the costs of designing these laws are considered as a component of TC, these costs, along with other potential misuse features, might outweigh the benefits of possible stigmatization in some societies. In fact, it is the lack of respect for the law or ineffective enforcement of legal provisions that brings down the credibility of the governing institutions, and that entails significant TC in the long run. Accordingly, there is a greater need to examine the role of more than necessary provisions of the law if these provisions are not aimed at being implemented in any case.

Reciprocity and social norms

Most contracts, both formal and informal, tend to remain incomplete, for reasons discussed in Chapter 6. Reciprocity is often an inducer of co-operation between parties to an interaction and more generally when they continue to remain parties for further transactions (as in international relations or employer–employee relations). Consummate co-operation, contrasted with 'perfunctory co-operation' (where a semblance of obligations under an agreement may seemingly be realized), and is defined by Williamson (1985). It refers to that type of co-operation where an affirmative attitude of parties that enables the filling in of contractual gaps with initiatives and the exercise of judgement with the objective of meeting the performance requirements of explicit as well as implicit agreements or contracts.

Let us introduce a definition:

> *Social norm*: a behavioural regularity that is based on a 'socially shared belief how one ought to behave' which triggers the enforcement of the 'prescribed behavior by informal social sanctions' (Fehr and Gachter, 1998, p. 854; see also Fehr *et al.*, 1997).

Social norms are effective constraints on individual behaviour beyond legal or other constraints. Many economic formulations do not take into account these constraints and thus obtain results that are usually deviant from real-world solutions (even in a normative framework). The role of reciprocity as a social norm and its effectiveness in the enforcement aspect of contracts and other transactions (and hence affecting TC) is an important feature that deserves better understanding.

Economics of standards and norms

Established or well-defined standards (whether established under a legal regime or by commonly accepted norms of conduct) that are shared by different economic entities and states tend to reduce transaction costs and uncertainties of transactions (Platteau, 1994). The role of trust and tested/repeat co-operation also remains similar. Buchanan (1987) suggested that economic efficiency must be judged by evaluating the processes through which transactions are carried out, and thus requires a greater focus on the issue of standardization and institutional development.

Let us state a formal definition here:

Standardization: this refers to a well-defined characterization or specification of features verifiable with reference to an entity – physical, economic, environmental, institutional, organizational, or other.

One of the key ingredients of standardization is transparency, which reduces informational asymmetry between participant decision-makers and facilitates the minimization of transaction costs involved in the conduct of interactive activities, direct or indirect, planned or unplanned. Such a background facilitates behavioural prescriptions, compliance and enforcement.

Interaction, if not entirely strategic interaction, among decision-making entities is facilitated when it is standardized. The broadly defined utility of increasing marginal standardization yields decreasing marginal utilities, with the implication that there exists an optimal degree of standardization in any given institutional and physical configuration. The role of the state is to exploit the economies of standardization, with a dynamic framework, in both internal and external activities (see also Blankart and Knieps, 1993). Harmonization does not imply identical standards, as these may not fit all societies or activities alike. There exists an optimal degree of harmonization of standards, economic, environmental or other. The critical determinant of these standards should include the need to optimize resources with few externalities (Rao, 2001).

The relative roles of rules versus standards depends to some extent on the role of legal mechanisms and whether the law is given its content relating to *ex ante* or *ex post* behaviour. Standards are usually given a well-defined content when they are applied to a specific type of conduct or activity. The main distinction between rules and standards is (Kaplow, 1992, p. 560) 'the extent to which efforts to give content to the law are undertaken before or after individuals act'. It was also suggested (ibid., p. 588): 'Whether a complex standard is preferable to a simple rule depends on the combined effects of complexity and promulgation of the law as a rule versus a standard (*ex ante* versus *ex post* creation).' A simple rule, often based on the presumption of a 'one size fits all' norm, could over-deter, whereas a simple standard may be under-inclusive relative to the features to be managed or regulated. The main factor determining the relative desirability of rules versus standards is the frequency with which a given law is expected to govern the conduct of the actors or participants, as pointed out by Kaplow (1992). The economies of rule making and of the specification of standards are also influenced by the TC involved in either specification, as well as the available information base. The static versus dynamic aspects of these features are also important. In general, the specification of rules affords economy in the processing of information, but could compromise the efficiency-enhancing role of provision of incentives for eligible participants for innovation or cost-effective compliance (Rao, 2001). Standards also tend to be transformed into rules in the legal system whenever it relies on precedents for legal decisions. The role of optimal design of rules and standards is largely to devise methods of implementation that minimize TC.

We summarize briefly below some of the findings or observations regarding the role of expectations, conventions and self-fulfilling prophecies.

Behavioural beliefs (Greif, 1997) are the expectations that members of a society have with respect to actions that will be taken (in addition to specified rules), and these expectations, as a cultural element, are common knowledge. In game theoretic formulations, for games with multiple equilibria, any equilibrium could become a self-fulfilling prophecy by co-ordinating the actions taken by the players leading to the selection of that equilibrium if it were expected by all players (Greif, 1997, p. 255). To avoid this trap, players have to pre-select relevant equilibria, preferably in a TC minimizing sense. Behavioural beliefs thus play a major role in the attainment or otherwise of collective goods. Is there a role for conventions in the economic efficiency phenomenon? The stability of a convention depends on its welfare consequences for individuals (Young, 1998). The underlying issue is to relate the ingredients of a convention to the corresponding social and economic efficiency implications, thus linking them to the welfare of the society. In the process, the route does pass through the TC implications of these ingredients.

Institutions and organizations tend to form their own endogenous inertia after their formation to such an extent that it is hard to undo some of these because of frictional opposition to desired normative changes in favour of *ex post* efficiency. Although changes do occur, and this is a form of evolutionary process (Young, 1998), this may not always be efficiency enhancing or TC minimizing. The role of the inertia is to enhance TC involved in a conscious change or reform for enhancing efficiency.

7.5 Economics of regulatory compliance

In a comprehensive normative approach, the economic analysis of regulation should seek to minimize a combination of deadweight losses caused by the failure of markets (or firms or other economic entities) in maximizing social welfare, and the incremental TC associated with regulation. In the NE tradition, a few studies attempted to use the so-called general equilibrium models (GEM) to assess the impact of regulations across different sets of interdependent economic activities. These formulations are founded on the assumption of perfectly competitive markets with zero TC. Thus these do not present a realistic assessment. For example, Jorgenson and Wilcoxen (1990) estimated that environmental regulation in the USA reduces the level of gross national product (GNP) by 2.59 per cent; this estimate did not, however, consider the potential benefits of environmental improvement investments in augmenting long-run economic output. Hahn and Hird (1991) noted in their survey that several previous studies on the estimates of the costs of regulation probably overstated the true costs by ignoring the net changes in economic efficiency implications.

The methodology for assessing the costs of regulation needs to include the entire TC of a regulation. This requires the assessment of direct costs as well as net costs of adjustment, including TC.

7.6   Conclusions

Contrary to some parts of TCE literature, it is useful to recognize that TC act as behavioural constraints, not merely as added costs.

When firms have market power, profit maximizers are not necessarily the best survivors because of the spiteful behaviour of powerful firms; a firm which does not maximize its profits may still be better off than its profit-maximizing competitors if the costs to itself of the deviations from maximal profit scenario are less than the costs it imposes on the 'rational' profit maximizers.

The relative utility or performance maximization may not be competition enhancing in its effects; besides, such behaviour enhances TC as well as reduces total welfare of a society and of the corresponding economic systems.

The problem of time-consistency examined in the NE tradition is akin to that of opportunism. One of the major impediments to some of the formal models for economic decision-making involving future generations is to ensure time-consistency in an intergenerational setting, how to ensure that future decision-making systems will, in fact, respect the continuity and ensure the furtherance of future interests at every point in time or at the start point of new decision horizons? Further investigations are required to answer these issues. The role of endogenous preference is particularly important in analyses involving long horizons and/or the role of past information, as in habits.

8
Organizations Theory

8.1 Introduction

The transaction costs (TC) paradigm offers a general framework for examining the choice of policy instruments and/or regimes for the management of resources and economic entities. The most fundamental unit of analysis in the economics of organization theory is the transaction. The TC paradigm enables articulation and choice of organizations geared to meet stated objectives.

Economic organization includes the roles of markets and organizations created to fulfil certain tasks of a specific nature. As Hayek (1945) argued, the central problem of economic organization is that of efficient adaptation to changes in particular circumstances. Hayekian adaptation is an autonomous market-style behaviour. In contrast, Barnard (1938) argued that the role of formal organizations was central to social and economic life. In the Bernardian approach, adaptation refers to that kind of co-operation that is conscious, deliberate and purposeful. A proper mix of both of these positions is relevant in a modern organizational setting. Market-like features apply in any organization, especially when it comes to the demand for and supply of services rendered by an organization.

This chapter deals with issues of the relative merits and demerits of hierarchies and decentralization, the significance of incentives relative to disincentives for performance, the design of economic institutions, and the relationship of analysis to neoclassical economic (NE) approaches. The role of transaction cost economics (TCE) remains very significant when we recognize the role of information, bounded rationality and opportunistic behaviour as well as the need for adaptive mechanisms. Complementarity in the approaches of NE and TCE is also evident at various stages in the following sections. To be of greater use in practice, several additional investigations are required.

8.2 Hierarchies and decentralization

We deal first with centralized versus decentralized economic systems and their role in economic development planning. Some important contributions in the economic development planning literature suggest that plan preparation draws upon resources of an innovative and imaginative nature, while plan implementation is a 'struggle with reality'. The missing link in this proposition is that the plan formulation itself is required to cope with the problems of realistic implementation and thus needs to take note of *ex ante* as well *ex post* TC, seeking to minimize TC while maximizing social welfare. Much of the failure of planned economic development originates in the admitted dichotomy and divergence between theory and practice. This is not to over-simplify the problem and to prescribe the role of TC as panacea for all problems, but it is much more useful to formulate plans that recognize the role of TC at every stage of planning and implementation.

Formal organizational structures for optimal decentralization of authority and information processing is very much conditioned by the role of TC in alternative designs of organizational structure. The bureaucratic nature of the erstwhile planned economies of Eastern Europe were vulnerable to high magnitudes of TC associated with economic development relative to market economies, and these factors hampered the potential for economic growth (Pryor, 1994). The fundamental, but largely invalid, assumption of the role of government control and regulation is that of state benevolence (rather the benevolence of state actors). The non-benevolence of political and bureaucratic functionaries who pursue their own private agendas contributes to the deviation of attained economic equilibria from feasible social-welfare-maximizing equilibria. As Laffont and Martimort (1998) pointed out, the optimal internal organization of the government can be assessed only after examining and providing for incentive/disincentive constraints that modulate the state actors' behaviour, in addition to the role of incomplete and asymmetric information. Salient features of government systems, such as the employment contracts of public employees (job security of bureaucrats, and related labour laws), and its disjunction with job performance (including measurement problems or related TC) remain contributory factors in the realization of potential social welfare maxima.

If the TC of operating organizations were zero, resource allocation and income distribution would be the same in a free enterprise economy as in a communist command economy; individual preferences are revealed without cost or do not matter. The poor economic performance of a command economy is attributable mainly to excessive TC.

In a simple optimizing framework using linear programming methodology, the equivalence of optimal values in linear models under primal optimization and its dual optimization suggests a similar interpretation. Does this imply that organizational forms do not matter, at least in simplistic cases? Not usually. This is because of the role of TC and the difficulty in meeting the conditions of the above simplified systems. One of the elements of TC is the bargaining cost between different economic actors or entities. Following Milgrom and Roberts (1990, p. 72), these may be defined as to 'include the opportunity costs of bargainer's time, the costs of monitoring, and enforcing the agreement, and any costly delays and failures to reach agreement when efficiency requires that parties cooperate'. Bargaining costs, an ingredient of TC, remain a critical aspect of the economics of organizations.

One of the practical questions in attempts to decentralize planning and implementation of economic activities is based on the assumption of the simplicity of the task. However, the formulation of a consistent (in terms of forward and backward linkages) and efficient plan (corporate unit or other) at lower levels is unlikely to be easier relative to the information requirements of information and other signals at the apex, unless there exists genuine decentralization across different sections and levels. Logically, the lowest level exposes itself to greater uncontrollability and openness. This suggests the need for an optimal degree of decentralization, whereby the information economy and TC are minimized at that level.

There at least two important considerations which deserve to be examined in conjunction with the attitudes and behavioural characteristics of the decision-making entities at different levels: the externalities of specific actions and policy selections at each level on the rest of the system; and the cost as well as the ability of the decision-making entity to collate and process relevant information. Thus there exists some prerequisites in order for decentralization to remain efficient, and these are in the form of infrastructural and institutional/organizational provisions to facilitate the TC minimizing implementation of policies and programmes for the maximization of the legitimate objectives of the entire system. Decentralization for its own sake tends to serve a social or political goal, but an optimal decentralization, or decentralization with co-ordination, may be a useful arrangement for enhancing economic efficiency, if we take TC into account. Given the apparent lowering of information requirements in relation to decentralization, its is somewhat ironic that TCE suggests not full decentralization but rather an optimal decentralization. The missing link in this approach is the cost of interlinkages and their omission or proper reflection in the decentralized units.

8.3 The design of incentives

The fundamental factor that distinguishes the performance of different institutions is the role of the incentives of decision- makers and other economic agents. Devoid of 'optimal' incentives, any description of an institution and its classification as a market/non-market or other category can be just as good or as bad as any other. As long as the role of incentives for efficient performance is not recognized and allowed for, most institutions perform at sub-optimal levels. In terms of the role of TCE, an efficient provision of incentives is more desirable than focusing on penalties and disincentives, because of the higher costs of monitoring and enforcement of penalties. For an analytical formulation of this assertion, see Varian (1990).

The information revelation role of optimal incentive design is more significant than moral hazard or adverse selection problems for the provision and enforcement of disincentives. Incentives are the underlying determinants of economic performance, in terms of the behavioural description of cause and effect relationships.

As North (1990) pointed out, efficient institutions are created by a polity that has built-in incentives to create and enforce efficient property rights. It is also important to recognize the role of contractual forms and specifications that underlie the provision of incentives. Although the specific features of the elements are usually conditioned by the totality of wage reward–income distribution features of a society, the nature of incentives and performance expectations are conditioned by appropriate contracts.

The design and enforcement of optimal incentives for compliance and efficient performance is often less complex than that of the provision of disincentives for corresponding tasks. This asymmetry has different TC implications as well. It is often easier and less expensive to effect incentives than to enforce disincentives. The former (which entails costs in terms of compensation promised as an incentive) has some features of self- enforcement, but there is no such possibility with the latter (which requires costs of enforcement). Usually, a mix of both is considered to be both cost effective and performance effective in most systems.

Let us introduce a definition:

Private ordering: this refers to contractual parties' efforts involving the self-enforcement of agreements by incorporating activities of self-evaluation, incentives for compliance, and disincentives for non-compliance; in the absence of an explicit contract reference, this refers to the non-judicial mechanism of arrangements of interactions among parties based on a variety of economic and social factors specific to a setting, and involve perceptions of relative TC factors influencing specific actions and inactions.

The role of private ordering is relevant in all cases of contractual incompleteness as well as high costs of enforcement of explicit contracts. The 'quality' of private ordering may be defined in terms of the resulting contribution to the system's objective and efficiency. It may be posited that the role of this process is inversely proportional to contractual completeness as well as the quality and effectiveness of judicial institutions. Constitutional and statutory completeness of laws combined with cost-effective methods of rendering justice through formal institutions will reduce the need for private orderings.

The incentive design problem is significantly more relevant in sovereign international relations. Corresponding organizations need to address international issues of governance where disincentives may have less of a role to play, considering the TC involved in their implementation. Yarbrough and Yarbrough (1994) suggested that the strategic organizational approach should focus on two aspects of transactions that affect contractibility in the international setting: the parties' alternative choices, along with their perceived merits; and the effectiveness of enforcement institutions.

8.4 The design of organizations

The role of TCE in the design of organizations arises from the economizing role of a structure of interaction among economic actors built on a set of incentives and flows of information geared to achieve a defined set of of objectives.

A market is an organization with a specific set of features. It is interpreted (Furubotn and Richter, 2000) as a set of networks of relational contracts among individuals, economic entities or groups of individuals who are potential buyers and sellers. Market organization is deemed to be a creation to overcome information and TC problems (including those of co-ordination). The objective of the organization of a market is to facilitate market transactions, as in the case of any other organization; the distinction is in terms of control, authority and ownership. The main factors that distinguish markets and non-market organizations (including firms) include (Williamson, 1996, p. 170): adaptability differences, applications of different contract laws (both explicit and implicit contractual implications), incentive intensity differences, and bureaucratic cost differences (both the costs of organizing, and the inefficiency implications of different organizational structures). A combined approach of the law, economics and organization becomes very relevant in the context of the design of organizations.

Adaptation

Some of the early foundations of the roles of markets and other forms of organization may be stated briefly; Chapter 2 described some of the features emphasizing the crucial role of the adaptive efficiency in TCE. According to Hayek (1945) the economic problem of society is mainly one of rapid adaptation to changes in the economic environment at any given time, and over a period of time. The costs of adaptation are therefore critical determinants of economic progress. Price systems, when allowed to function properly, were given the key role in this adjustment and adaptation process. This position may not, however, explain such phenomena as 'price stickiness' or other collusive aspects of market conduct observed in modern markets. The factors that provide explanations for these features are, in terms of TC, involved in rapid responses to changes in the market.

In the context of other economic organizations, Barnard (1938) suggested that the survival of an organization depends on the maintenance of an equilibrium with the readjustment of processes internal to the organization and the process by which adaptation is accomplished. Thus adaptation, in the sense either of spontaneous market responses or of the hierarchical co-ordination of actions, remains critical for the required adjustment process for an economy or an economic organization. The costs of achieving these adjustments and adaptations need to be considered in a TC minimizing sense.

In a multi-lateral and hierarchical interactive sense, adaptation has been defined broadly as the adjustment of economic agents or the interaction of economic agents with the broader system of which a specific economic entity is a part. Nelson and Winter (1982, p. 25) observed: 'Positing adaptive (rather than maximizing) responses to unforeseen shocks is partially an implicit or explicit concession to the existence of some adjustment costs or "friction" in economic adjustment'; friction is not usually considered in the rational maximizing behaviour of traditional economic models. The role of friction in rapid adaptation to changes remains the key to efficient governance.

If the central problem of economic organization is that of adaptation, then the object of economic organization may be expressed as follows (Williamson, 1996, p. 162): 'adapt to disturbances (of both autonomous and bilateral kinds) in ways that economize on bounded rationality while simultaneously safeguarding the transactions in question against the hazards of opportunism'. This assertion is based on the recognition that bounded rationality contributes to inevitable incompleteness of all complex contracts, and *ex post* opportunism characterizes contracts as being founded on moral hazard.

The issue of spontaneous and sequential adaptation is a matter of practical arrangement, since the imperatives of change do not wait for an entity's convenience. Thus both types of adaptation are relevant simultaneously; the choice of the mix is to be guided by the overall efficiency criteria, taking into account the interdependencies of both streams of adaptation. The features of bounded rationality and system uncertainties suggest the need for the application of adaptive efficiency criteria. The dynamics of adaptation is a subject for considerable further investigation, in both analytical and empirical terms.

Theories of economic design

In the NE literature, the theory of the design of economic mechanisms comprises primarily the integration of the information and incentive aspects of resource allocative processes. Rao (1978) suggested that the aggregate economic efficiency levels of both the command economy system and the free market price system (with common resource constraints) can be equal provided the relative intensities of incentives and disincentives are 'properly' assigned. This conclusion was based on the following steps:

(i) Incentives and/or disincentives can be augmented as factors in the objective function of the economic system (such as social welfare maximization);

(ii) For linear system economic models, the well-known results of optimization theory suggest that the optimal values of both primal and dual formulations are equal; and

(iii) The centralized command economy has its dual as a decentralized free market economy, and vice versa.

The above description does not always extend to general non-linear models, however. In certain cases of non-linearities involving assumptions of convex structures, the equivalence of the primal and dual optimal values holds; see the 'duality theorem' 30.5 in Rockefeller (1970, p. 318).

Let us introduce a definition from NE (a modified version of the definition given in Chapter 3, using game theoretic structures):

> *Incentive compatibility*: a configuration of behavioural features constituting a Nash equilibrium, implying that no participant finds it advantageous to depart from his or her behavioural pattern so long as others do not.

In the framework of NE, the superiority of an economic organization or economic system could possibly be viewed in terms of the following important criteria:

(i)   Pareto-optimality of equilibria;
(ii)   Incentive compatibility; and
(iii)   Informational decentralization.

Hurwicz (1972, 1979) observed that uniformly superior solutions in terms of all three criteria may not exist in any system. Also, for economic systems with the existence of externalities, there are no informationally decentralized mechanisms that achieve Pareto-optimality.

An optimality criterion for an economic system which presupposes a type of organizational mechanism and institutional structure cannot serve as a useful criterion because this forgoes the role of dynamic flexibility and endogenous responsiveness to changes over time. Accordingly, organizational features must be treated as variables, along with other economic parameters. Such an approach enables the reaping of the benefits arising from the recognition of the interdependencies of economic efficiency and organizational efficiency.

The design of regulatory institutions requires particular attention as weak functioning can both cost the system directly in terms of running the infructuous organization, and in terms of the social cost of suboptimal regulation. It is therefore very important that the objectives of the regulatory agents conform to the objectives of the regulatory institution. The usual problems of informational asymmetry apart, the motivational aspects of the regulators are thus very important. Non-benevolent bureaucrats and associated political powers pursue private agendas that diminish potential social welfare. The degree of specificity of a regulatory body is sometimes an influencing parameter in the design of appropriate organizations. When the impact of the influence groups is specified exogenously, it usually loses sight of the effect of different institutional configurations on the interest groups. Laffont and Martimort (1998) suggested the role of these interrelationships, and indicated that decentralized governance may be useful only if it can separate the communication and influence functions of the local pressure groups from those of the local authorities. This may pose several contradictory postulations of decentralized governance, however. It is not the apparent compromise potential of the local authorities but the role of efficient legal institutions that generally restricts the collusive behaviour of pressure groups and the discretionary powers of local authorities.

Many of the theoretical and operational aspects of the design of organizations are dealt with in traditional organization theory. Some of the features of common focus between organizations theory (categorized under management science and/or behavioural science) and TCE are (Williamson, 1996):

(i)   Behavioural assumptions: the roles of opportunism and bounded rationality;
(ii) The role of adaptation;
(iii) The role of property rights in the design of organizational structure;
(iv) Transaction as a unit of analysis; and
(v)   Comparative economic organization.

The analysis of comparative organization is primarily that of choices among 'feasible forms' of organization. One of the prescriptions for the selection of organizational forms for economic governance states: 'because hypothetical forms of economic organization are operationally irrelevant and because all forms of organization are flawed, assess alternative feasible forms in a comparative institutional way' (Williamson, 1996, p. 346). This does not clarify the ingredients necessary for the design of an efficient organization for realistically complex environment.

Dynamic capabilities and TC

An organization's survival depends critically on its ability to achieve maximum performance per unit of resources in the short run while being able to adapt rapidly with optimal speed of adjustment and with minimum TC of adjustment. These are among the desired features of an 'efficient organization', of both market and non-market categories. The definition of organizational capability has to include these imperatives of economic success and sustainability; definitions that do not consider sustainability features may admit potential failures of organizations. Winter (2000, p. 983) defined organizational capability as 'a high-level routine (or collection of routines)' when combined with its implementing input flows, enables a decision set of options for an organization's management in 'producing significant outputs of a particular type'. Interpreted strictly, this offers a static definition, which is often less useful in a rapidly changing market environment.

In the context of firms, the resource-based view of the firm (RBVF) is one of the approaches to the analysis of firm capabilities to sustain it over time and adapt to the changes in market characteristics as well as other institutional factors. Teece *et al.* (1997) extended RBVF (see Chapter 2 for additional details) to dynamic markets involving rapid and unpredictable changes. The concept of dynamic capabilities was defined in a context where the competitive landscape is shifting. Dynamic capabilities involved features by which firm managers 'integrate, build, and reconfigure internal and external competencies to address rapidly changing environments' (Teece *et al.*, 1997, p. 516).

One of the key issues underlying these desired features is that of information flows and the costs of access to relevant information as economy of information. Other costs such as search, monitoring and implementation (typical elements of TC), are to be economized component-wise and jointly in any specific application of TCE in the design of organizations. An illustration of the survival and success of a rural bank is summarized below.

The rural credit co-operatives

One of the important explanations for the success of credit co-operatives is their ability to capitalize on superior information and to impose effective sanctions on loan defaulters with low costs of enforcement. Guinnane (2001) found this feature, empirically, in the German Rural Credit Co-operatives in their successful operation years (before the First World War). Unlike commercial banks, which do not have sufficient information advantage or low-cost enforcement mechanisms, the rural co-operatives have the advantage of these features and thus have the potential to operate efficiently. The case of the Bangladesh Grameen Bank (BGB) is an outstanding example of a rural bank operating at low

TC and maintaining stability. There have been attempts to float similar institutions in several regions of the world, but many of them did not succeed in replicating the features essential for their success.

The salient features for the sustainability and success of the BGB include: economizing information flows and TC by decentralization (selection of loan applicants and their monitoring, enforcement of loan recovery); internalization of externalities (denial of loans to defaulters on an individual or a collective basis at local group level), the avoidance of bureaucratic delays and procedures, and the provision of adaptive mechanisms at decentralized levels (tuning loan eligibility to the demands of the market for specific products and services).

Replicability of the successful case elsewhere in other socioeconomic settings requires complementarity or proper alignment of anthropological and political factors. The selection of loans based on arbitrary criteria lays the foundation of failure.

8.5 Conclusions

In the design of organizations, substituting one form of inefficiency for another is not uncommon, and is perhaps rooted in the feature of bounded rationality. The challenge is to expand the bounds to enable a larger set of pragmatic choices. Adaptation and adaptive efficiency remain the most significant criteria for organizational sustainability and efficiency, respectively. Excessive bureaucracy as a form of governance is an example of maladaptation with significant costs.

It is useful to view various forms of inefficiency in terms of contractual gaps of relevant explicit and implicit contracts of activities. These contractual factors require a focus for reform if the identified efficiencies are to be remedied. Such an approach integrated the approaches under the standard classification of firm, market, state or other institutional configuration. The dynamic capability of organizations, expressed in terms of adaptive efficiency, is one of the primary requirements of efficient organizations.

An optimality criterion for an economic system which presupposes a type of organizational mechanism and institutional structure cannot serve as a useful criterion because this forgoes the role of dynamic flexibility and endogenous responsiveness to changes over time. Organizational features must be treated as variables along with other economic parameters.

9
Environmental Economics

9.1 Introduction

The focus of environmental economics and governance varies from local to global environmental issues, and from preventive measures to mitigating aspects. In all cases, the design of policies involves the roles of various elements of behavioural, economic and scientific factors. Environmental governance requires the wider use of transaction cost economics (TCE), as this chapter demonstrates.

In the study of global commons, Ostrom (1990) and Rao (2001) observed that most studies on the governance issue for global commons do not take into account the role of transaction costs (TC), including the role of transformation costs. Transformation costs include the costs of resources devoted to the process of considering a change in the rules of governance. These costs may be related positively to the number of individuals or decision-making entities involved in making institutional choices, the heterogeneity of interests at stake, and the critical mass required to effect a rule change. It was also stated (Ostrom, 1990, p. 198): 'Because transformation costs are up-front costs, they are less likely to be affected by the discount rates used by participants.' For the purpose of this chapter and elsewhere in this context, TC include transformation costs as well.

This chapter addresses a few important aspects of environmental economics and management. The role of market-based instruments and regulatory instruments (which may or may not be entirely market-based) are examined with due recognition of the role of TC. Governance of global commons is of special relevance in the international arena. The economics of global environmental phenomena such as climate change require a much broader comprehension and assessment of costs that are generally not considered in traditional economic literature. Some of the relevant features are discussed in this chapter, along with those of sustainable development. Emissions trading and other instruments of environmental policy are also examined in terms of the relevance of TCE in the design and management of policies and institutions for environmental governance.

9.2 Markets and environmental regulation

If markets can solve all problems there is little need for a regulatory role by the state. The prevalence of environmental (as well as economic) externalities is the most significant aspect of the failure of environmental and economic markets. Since this does not happen, we need to examine alternative forms of environmental governance. The existence of TC means that a market-based property rights (PR) approach is not a universal solution for environmental problems (Nalebuff, 1997).

The role of PR is rather common when regulating economic resources, especially when they are perceived as being relatively scarce. Most environmental resources are perceived to be relatively abundant in supply, and generally do not seem to attract the specification of PR. In the extreme form of allocation of PR, it could lead to some form of privatization or state control that may not be conducive to resource allocative efficiency or equity. The role of specifying PR is not to render exclusive control or ownership, but rather to identify the stakeholders, and their rights and duties, in the sustainable use of specific resources.

Global commons broadly fit into two classes of environmental resources: *res communis* and *res nullius*, defined below:

res communis: assets of global common interest but not amenable to state sovereign control; these are also referred to as common property resources.

res nullius: an asset amenable to control/acquisition/ownership or use but not yet in the possession of any entity of legal existence; these are also referred to as open-access resources.

PR as well as liability rules (LR) apply to the resources in the *res communis* category. However, by definition, PR do not apply to the resources under the *res nullius* category. Global environmental resources, both under *res nullius* and *res communis* categorizations are, in effect, not governed if there are no well-defined and enforceable rights and duties on the resource exploiter nations (or other entities). In the absence of any legally valid methods of global environmental accounting and sharing of responsibilities, even the features of *res communis* degenerate into those of *res nullius*. In such a system, global environmental externalities remain the norm rather than the exception, thus leading to externalities affecting identifiable or unknown victims. Thus the role of well-defined PR complemented by enforceable LR is often a prerequisite for a meaningful design of sharing of responsibilities in the governance of the global environment. The economics of PR and LR are beset with the role of TC, as explained in Chapter 6.

Commons and anticommons

In the classical 'tragedy of the commons' (Hardin, 1968), the hypothesis suggests that lack of assignment of property rights can lead to overuse of environmental resources from the global common pool, to the detriment of all. In contrast to this proposition, Heller (1998) postulated the 'anticommons tragedy' hypothesis, where under-usage of resources from potential exclusion rights can lead to unrealized economic potential, and the under-usage remains a function of the number of firms assigned simultaneous usage rights or other property rights in the context of resource use. The loss of economic use or 'option value' in this case is a special type of TC. Heller's motivation for the postulation was the observation that in cities such as Moscow many buildings remained unoccupied in the 1990s while there were people living on the pavements, and the buildings remain empty because potential dwellers must obtain several permissions, each of which possesses certain powers of exclusion. The inefficiencies introduced by overlapping bureaucracies bring in special TC. Buchanan and Yoon (2000, p. 12) suggested: 'Economists and environmentalists have perhaps concentrated too much attention on the commons side of the ledger to the relative neglect of the anticommons side.' Perhaps this is valid.

Either way, TC thus play an important role in affecting economic behaviour, and influence the specifications of different economic instruments to govern environmental resources. Apart from TC, any number of ideal solutions exist, but the existence of TC constrains the choices for solving real-world problems. However, due recognition of the role of TC enables the design and implementation of 'efficient' systems.

Race to the bottom

Do the environmental regulatory regimes lead to the location of polluting industries in the places that have the fewest environmental regulations – that is, to the 'safe havens'? This is the 'race to the bottom' proposition. This is largely untenable in the international context, because country-risk assessment and corresponding cost implications are often more important than savings on the avoidance of environmental regulations. Several logistics and business linkage assessments are important for an industrial enterprise to make an industry-locating decision, apart from being environmental 'safe havens' for dumping pollution. The direct costs of environmental compliance are usually estimated as being relatively low: at less than about 3 per cent of the total costs of the operation (Low, 1993). A vector of the elements of transaction costs is the real determinant affecting investment decisions, and environmental costs are just a minor part of such a basket of costs (Rao, 2000a).

Institutional transaction costs (ITC)

ITC consist of four broad components (Thompson, 1999): legislative or regulatory enactment costs; implementation costs; monitoring costs; and enforcement costs. It may not always be necessary to assess total TC, and may be feasible to ignore some components of costs – if these are common to alternative policies or regulations – and assess only the other required elements. This approach is especially useful when we are focusing on cost-effectiveness analysis rather than on cost–benefit analysis of specific actions.

Environmental policies are usually complex in their incidence of costs and benefits. Policies are affected by rather uncertain structural specifications of the cause–effect relationships in the physical systems, incomplete information, and economic uncertainties about the effects of alternative policy specifications. It is often useful to consider ITC for a better appreciation of associated costs of different policy alternatives. This is particularly relevant when the institutional configurations of the policies and their operationalization differ significantly.

Variations in the formulation and implementation of PR lead to different magnitudes of TC. More specifically, these imply varying costs in terms of the component levels of ITC. The role of the state in the governance of common pools of environmental resources at local, regional and global levels is to be examined in terms of the relative cost-effectiveness of alternative modes of intervention. Enlarging the set of economic actors or stakeholders in the governance of the commons is often considered to be a viable alternative to state regulation; the participation of resource users in accordance with an assigned set of rights is often a useful approach. This does not alleviate the usual problems of incomplete contracts, monitoring and enforcement, however. To the extent that some of these costs can be internalized at the group or user association level, the approach can be TC minimizing and thus cost-effective.

9.3 Industrial emissions trading

Since bureaucratic regulation can often imply lack of cost effectiveness and delinking with incentives for innovation, a few market-related instruments of regulation and adoption of market-like trading of a new set of property rights have been considered in the context of environmental governance.

The choice of policy instruments for controlling environmental externalities, trading pollution rights, is one of the alternatives that has been theorized and implemented in some of the countries in the industrial world since about the 1970s. Assignment of property rights or entitlements, thereby allowing the rights holders to trade, is one such mechanism. The costs of developing an efficient market, based on a few polluters or buyer participants in the market, and devising various rules, monitoring and enforcement – all major components of TC – could be significant. This was envisaged by, among others, Just *et al.* (1982, p. 281), who suggested that TC may be high or impose substantial costs on other parties in the economy because competitive market forces do not operate effectively in such thin markets.

Dales (1968) first proposed the concept of marketable permits to allocate pollution reduction among private entities as a mechanism for cost-effective implementation. The legal origins of the air pollution market in the USA arose from the Clean Air Act of 1970. The US Environmental Protection Agency (USEPA) proposed in 1976 to offset pollution reduction targets for firms, with some conditions. These included, for example: offsets had to be for the same specific pollutant; and only new emission sources could enter the market as buyers. The 'bubble policy' was also devised. This policy allowed pollution-producing units to develop alternative emission control strategies: sources can belong to a 'bubble' and utilize cost-effective alternatives in meeting pollution reduction targets.

The cost minimizing potential of tradable pollution permits was first explored analytically by Montgomery (1972). Emissions trading was initiated in the 1970s as a cost-effective alternative to direct regulation by the government. Various applications of the pollution trading schemes in the USA include: the Lead Permits Program; the Acid Rain

Program to reduce sulphur dioxide emissions; and the USEPA's Emissions Trading Program for Industrial Pollutants. The role of TC as inhibiting determinants of the efficiency or success of the Tradeable Emission Permits (TEP) was noted in a few case studies in the USA; see, for example, Hahn and Hester, 1989, for a study of the Fox River Water-Pollutant Trading Program in Wisconsin that involved cumbersome permit issue procedures.

Tradable permits for emissions trading remains a high priority in both national and institutional settings. This is because of the promise of market-based implementation. It is not entirely clear, however, whether these mechanisms can be cost-effective when we consider all the relevant transaction costs and uncertainties in attaining environmental goals via market mechanisms. Using the market institutions to correct market failures or externalities is not inconsistent with effective institutional management of the environment. The problem is one of ensuring efficient implementation in a quasi-market framework of trading public goods. The complementarity of government institutions and market institutions in this activity is an essential prerequisite to the achievement of cost-effective implementation. There exists a positive correlation between the quality of the governmental institutions and of the private market institutions, since the governance of the latter is not independent of the quality of governance of the former. This combined operation is not a common feature in most countries, where the general quality of these institutions is still lagging far behind those of some of the developed economies.

Let us recall that TC in the present context (Rao, 2000c; Dudek and Wiener, 1996) include, but are not limited to, adaptation costs, search costs, information costs, negotiation costs, approval costs, monitoring costs, enforcement costs, costs of externalities arising out of specific transactions, insurance or related costs, and opportunity costs of time or other resources. When adaptation costs involve or eventually lead to higher efficiency (with or without technical innovation), these costs tend to become negative in some of the scenarios, thus becoming net benefits. In other words, what are considered to be costs in the short term may essentially be viewed as investments for a return in the long run.

Can the trading of industrial emission rights lead to efficiency? As is well known, the applicability of the Coase theorem, which suggests that the assignment of private property rights could lead to an efficient outcome, is founded on the assumption of zero transaction costs. This theorem (see Chapter 3 for detailed interpretations) is founded on the assumption, among others, of common knowledge among participants in the environmental damage resolution or compensation negotiation. While the absence of well-defined enforceable property rights poses a set of externalities, the application of these PR regimes does not automatically ensure efficient environmental solutions. High TC pose a major hurdle in the emissions trading markets. The existence of high TC and the degree of uncertainty (for details, see Montero, 1997) in regulatory approval of some of the trading permits, even in developed systems like those in the USA, suggests that the principle of market-based emission trading may have a long way to go before being effective in any sense. Earlier, the UNCTAD (1994) study emphasized the significance of TC (especially monitoring and enforcement costs) in the potential market efficiency of the proposed market for greenhouse gas emissions.

Using a simple analytical optimization model, Gangadharan (2000) noted that the presence of TC makes the difference between participation and non-participation by eligible firms in the trading scheme. First-order conditions of optimality suggest that the trading price adjusted by the TC is the determining factor for selling, buying, or no trade at all. It was suggested that the state can contribute to a reduction in some of the components of TC applicable at the firm level, especially information costs and market co-ordination costs. Since new starts and initial years of trading are the most complex for the evolution of the relevant market, the state has a greater responsibility at that stage to ensure that firm-level TC are minimized to enable their effective participation in the relatively thin market. Lack of incentives for firm participation can negate the objectives of the trading scheme as the market thinness vitiates principles of competitiveness and efficiency.

In policy applications, the Economic Report 1998 of the US President (1998) argued in the context of domestic (rather than international) emissions trading and the role of tradable emission permits (TEP): 'Any firm that can reduce its emissions for less than the going price of permit has the incentive to do so and then sell its unused permits to other firms for which emissions reduction is more costly...the firms can meet environmental standards at lower cost than under traditional regulation'. The problems of the market concentration in permits, lack of competitive features with thin markets, manipulated market price variations and TC are some of the considerations in the evolution of an efficiently functioning market for TEP. Although some of the market-based regulatory instruments involving emissions trading met with some effectiveness and 'success', there are a number of issues to be resolved for further expansion of these policies, especially at the global level (as proposed under the provisions of some of the agreements of the Climate Change Convention or its Protocols).

A number of characteristics of TEPs affect their role in the efficient governance of environmental systems. Stavins (1995) stated a few factors that could have an adverse effect on the efficiency properties of TEPs: the concentration or iniquitous distribution in the permit market and/or output market; the role of non-proft-maximizing behaviour (for example, as in some state enterprises); the role of effective monitoring and enforcement; and interactions with pre-existing regulatory provisions affecting other aspects of environmental governance or profitability, and various other forms of transaction costs. Rather than seeking equalization of marginal costs across sources in traditional cost minimization models, the presence of TC leads to the result that the costs include source/technology/institution-specific TC as well as the cost components. These features are relevant in both domestic and international market settings.

9.4   Adaptation, sustainability and climate change

The governance of the environment at the global level requires a variety of measures, some of which may not be related to any of the existing institutions. Besides, some of the approaches (as in the case of curbing greenhouse gases and minimizing climate change) require multisectoral international co-ordination. Clearly, such widespread activities can draw upon the market institutions (with generally low TC) only to a very limited extent, and much of the intervention requires several types of information and co-ordination, in addition to monitoring, drawing up international agreements, and their enforcement (under sovereign rights regimes, posing significant informational and enforcement problems). As a result, several aspects of ITC are involved in this effort of global environmental governance. Rao (2001) deals with some of the issues, including those of international environmental treaty formation, *ex post* opportunism, and various related TC. Among other issues of significance is the adoption of widely accepted environmental sustainability and sustainable development.

Sustainability and TC

The concept of sustainability in its weaker forms allows limited substitutability within allowable limits between different forms of capital. This is subject to the requirement that each component of the ecological capital vector be equipped with certain critical threshold levels, dictated by the requirements of avoiding stresses and maintaining system resilience (Rao, 2000a). A number of components of natural capital and other forms of capital are allowed to be substituted, subject to preserving these critical levels.

The concept of economic sustainability advanced by Solow (1994) states that a society that invests aggregate resource rents in reproducible capital is preserving its capacity to sustain a constant level of consumption. Solow argued that the concept implies a bias towards investment with a general interpretation: just enough investment to maintain the broad stock of capital intact and not every stock of every single thing. Substitution of resources is essential for continued economic progress. This statement does imply the need for continued technical progress, and continued improvements in resource use efficiencies.

The usefulness of a 'wealth-like magnitude', such as the present discounted value of future consumption, if it bears a meaningful relationship to economic welfare in a dynamic economy, was indicated by Samuelson (1961). This concept was explored in detail by Weitzman (1976), who argued that the welfare justification of the NNP, defined as the gross national product adjusted by depreciation, is 'just the idea that in theory it is a proxy for the present discounted value of future consumption'. This reasoning was based on a few important assumptions, including (i) all sources of economic growth have been identified and attributed to one or other form of capital; (ii) future felicity can be discounted at a constant rate for ever, based on currently available information; and (iii) there is no positive TC to have an adverse effect on the potential to gain rental from time to time.

Weitzman's (1976) methodology relied on the current value Hamiltonian interpretation of NNP, based on an optimal control-theoretic modelling of the economy (see also Chapter 1). The approach was extended by Solow (1986) to include natural and exhaustible resources that generate income and/or deplete it over various time intervals. Solow's extension was based partly on the validity of Hartwick's rule (Hartwick, 1977) for exhaustible resources: a society that invests aggregate resource rents in reproducible capital is preserving its capacity to sustain a constant level of consumption (for ever). However, Hartwick derived this proposition using a simplified growth model (with Cobb–Douglas technology, using constant rates of substitution and time preferences, for a closed economy) with no recognition of the role of TC and based on autonomous dynamics models that do not involve a 'time' dimension explicitly. Solow (1994) proved the following.

Propositions:

(a) NNP measures the maximum current level of consumer satisfaction that can be sustained for ever; it is therefore a measure of sustainable income given the state of the economy at that very instant; and

(b) Investment and depletion decisions determine the real wealth of the economy, and each year's NNP appears as the return to society on the wealth it has accumulated in all forms.

The propositions are built on the assumption of perfect foresightedness and on the availability of time profiles of relevant accounting prices of resources. The TCE approach may question some of these assumptions. The limitations that apply to the validity of the Hartwick rule apply here as well. None the less, the following argument advanced by Solow holds: the same calculation that is required to construct an adjusted NNP for current economic evaluation of economic benefit is also essential for the construction of a strategy aimed at sustainability.

These propositions assume the substitutability of various forms of capital and hence are relevant under the 'weak sustainability' criterion that allows the aggregation of capital vector components with weighted valuations of each of the components. These rely on competitive market prices for valuation and expect markets to govern the factors involved, including an exogenous discounting factor of the future values of resources. If any of these assumptions are relaxed, we arrive at a wealth-like magnitude, but the NNP interpretation is then subject to several modifications.

The NNP measure advocated by Weitzman (1976) as 'the stationary equivalent of future consumption (or utility), and this is its primary welfare interpretation' is valid when the economy is described by constant time-discounting. The corresponding results for the variable time-discounting case were obtained by Sefton and Weale (1996). However, this improvement is inadequate to take into account endogenous preferences and relevant externalities. If the pure effect of 'time' alone is caused solely by identified exogenous factors (expressed in terms of a fraction of income) such as new resource discoveries, progress in technology, changes in consumer tastes, or population growth, the expression for the NNP admits a straightforward generalization, suggested by Sefton and Weale (1996). If any of these are treated endogenously, we need further investigations. Since the relative price of human-produced capital in terms of natural capital depends on the entire future equilibrium path, the concept of NNP as an indicator of sustainability may not be tenable in the conventional form, as argued in Asheim (1994). This is what would be predicted from the TCE viewpoint. Information limitations and bounded rationality problems suggest that an adaptive framework be considered rather than one that is predicated on infinite foresightedness. Besides, endogenous discount factors (see below) or time-varying preferences and corresponding discount factors, habit formation or other factors affecting discount factors will be relevant in this context. Thus there is a far greater role for the influences of TC to be reflected in these analyses of economic and environmental sustainability.

Explicit time factor

Explicit time-dependence must be recognized in all the formal formulations of models of sustainable development. Analytically, the role of the 'time' element in formal models need not be that of real time alone. An explicit time argument leads to a non-autonomous Hamiltonian formulation of the NNP. This representation arises naturally whenever positive or negative externalities or TC exist. In such a world (that is, the real world) there is no static equivalent of the expression for wealth (Rao, 2000a). The usual Hamiltonian representation of the economic welfare measure requires substantial modifications for any real-world structure. When the economic system is fundamentally non-autonomous as a consequence of TC, externalities and/or technical progress are not reflected in the production functions or other constraints, and the shadow prices in Weitzman's framework do not reflect the true accounting prices for the purpose of cost–benefit analysis (Aronsson and Lofgren, 1995). This is because the latter are to be corrected for future information, which is reflected in the non-autonomous parameters. Let us cite a result from Rao (2000a):

> *Theorem*: Hartwick's rule and Weitzman's interpretation of the expression for the NNP do not apply when we deal with non-autonomous systems which arise with factors such as changes in technical progress, in tastes and preferences, and in externalities.

The Hamiltonian measure of income ceases to function as a measure of return on wealth (even with any variations in terms of 'generalized wealth') whenever economic growth cannot be attributed directly to capital formation, holds good only when the Hamiltonian is autonomous. It is necessary to formulate the optimizing problem as a non-autonomous problem and interpret the Hamiltonian in terms of relevant contributing factors and parameters.

The roles of environmental externalities, technological externalities, TC and changing preferences, as well as non-constant discount rates in an infinite horizon decision framework, cast serious doubts on the standard methods that advocate the NNP as an indicator of sustainability. The suggested role of the NNP in traditional NE literature is founded on major assumptions. In general, it is not an indicator of economic sustainability. This measure, when adjusted for technological progress in the future, and taste premium or discount, could be a better indicator of sustainability; this relies on the continuous revision of the indicator in an adaptive efficiency-maximizing sense, and has implications for paths of sustainable development in that these should be more flexible towards adopting changes. These considerations tend to bring greater flexibility and pragmatism to policies dictated by the requirements of sustainable development, than when viewed conventionally, as argued in Rao (2000a).

The choice of discount rates or future time-discounting is a critical area of valuation of resources and the future. A non-constant rate of discounting is especially important when the rate or trade-off involved in current and future time periods is based on unsustainable features, namely, based on current information or historical considerations, an area of focus in TCE. One of the important conclusions that emerged during the discussions and analyses is: non-constant and endogenous discounting is the only relevant form of discounting for environmental decision-making.

Dynamics of conservation

A basis of investigations into conserving wealth begins with two conservation laws offered by Samuelson (1990). These were based on three assumptions: (i) autonomous Hamiltonian; (ii) constant returns to scale in the production function; and (iii) time-additive preferences. The first conservation law stated that the value of net output (NNP) expressed in terms of any selected good as the numeraire accumulates over time as the (numeraire-good's own) rate of interest, just as the value of capital does. The second law stated that, along any optimal path, the ratio between the value of income and the value of capital wealth is a constant. These laws lend support to Weitzman's (1976) NNP interpretation, but they require extensions to include time-varying and endogenized discounts reflective of TC, as well as preferences. The equivalence of the Hamiltonian with total 'energy' (argued by Samuelson, 1990) – that is, kinetic energy plus potential energy – is a sufficient but not necessary condition for the law of conservation of energy (see, for example, Marion and Thornton, 1995, p. 266).

When the utility function is subject to changes in taste and through technical progress, or reflects the role of TC, the modified conservation law under constant time-discounting states that (see also Sato, 1990):

Income (NNP) + Current worth of taste/technical change/TC = Discount rate × Wealth

This result suggests that there is a 'cost', 'penalty' or gain associated with TC, taste and technical factors. However, the valuation of these factors is rather simplistic and requires further strengthening. This is because the valuation was only a result of the effect of change in utility (over time) for the entire remaining time horizon, using a constant discount rate. Further work using an endogenous discount function in these formulations will be relevant.

Climate change and economic assessment

Most of the existing literature on this issue is based on conventional NE models and corresponding economic assessment of the potential costs and benefits of global climate change. These studies are far from realistic in their accounting for relevant ingredients of economic analysis. Traditional methods of assessing costs of climate change or of its control are rather narrow; these have generally neglected various important ingredients such as transaction and adaptation costs, or the effects of feedback mechanisms; a comprehensive concept of costs and benefits is necessary to derive an operationally meaningful policy framework. In addition, the following observations based on Rao (2000c) are relevant:

(i) the critical issue of time discounting or valuation over time for long horizons requires variable discounting with requisite endogenization of the discount function; and

(ii) considering the marginal value of information in reducing climatic unknowns and their uncertainties, it remains a cost-effective priority to invest in the understanding of the phenomena for the prevention and control of anthropogenic influences which have adverse effects on climate, the environment and the economy.

Transient costs and equilibrium costs

In a relatively long-term (ten or more years) framework, it is important to recognize that the equilibrium is not expected to remain invariant to the continued disturbances to the systems involved and the significant possibilities of mechanisms of adaptation. Thus it is not only the common forms of uncertainty that alter the equilibria, but also the systematic feedback mechanisms and adaptation responses of the components of the system which lead to transient equilibria. The effects of such changes on relevant costs and benefits are to be examined from the perspective of TCE. This would enable the assessment of these factors under an adaptive framework, since none of the economic parameters will remain unresponsive to changes. The requisite level of adaptive efficiency may not exist in some sectors, but that does not mean that the role of adaptation is unimportant.

Comprehensive cost assessment

There are hardly any economic studies that are comprehensive enough to accommodate all relevant costs. In general, the following cost assessment criteria will be relevant (Rao, 2000b):

$$\text{General cost} \quad G_1 = T_1 + T_3 + T_5$$
$$\text{Shadow/true cost} \; G_2 = T_2 + T_4 + T_6$$

where T_1 represents transaction costs, T_2 their shadow value, T_3 transition/adaptation costs, T_4 their shadow value, T_5 market value or non-market value of resource costs, and T_6 their shadow value.

Some of the elements in each of the odd numbered Ts may be illustrated here. T_1 includes the costs of information, enforcement of regulations, and of institutional mechanisms for internalizing externalities; T_2 includes the costs of compliance, hedging and uncertainty in future regulations and of changing technological implications, adjustment costs in forgoing consumption or other benefits, reduction in profits because of possible higher costs of production, price–income–consumption effects on consumers, and cost–price–profit effects on producers; and T_5 includes the costs of resource inputs, costs of usage of sources and sink capacities, and other ecological costs of consumption and production.

The focus of issues in the field of environmental economics has been largely in terms of environmental or other externalities caused by the economic activities. Such an approach leads to finding methods to mitigate the effects of externalities such as the provisions of taxes, and environmental regulations. These approaches continue to be relevant, but they form only a part of the larger set of instruments relevant to ecological and economic governance.

The elements involved in assessing costs must reflect the concerns of sustainability and thus cover implications of ecological and economic dimensions in a comprehensive manner. The costs of transition and transaction are very significant and should be incorporated in any cost–benefit analysis.

9.5   Environmental conflicts and mediation

A considerable amount of literature in the area of environmental economics sought to suggest a significant role of the Coase theorem in resolving environmental management problems using the property rights approach, including market-based instruments such as emissions trading. There are two major limitations to most of these approaches (Rao, 2001): (i) the role of significant TC, which invalidates the applicability of the theorem; and (ii) a lack of distinction between local environmental externalities (where presumably there are a small number of identifiable contributors to pollution or the problems of its victims) and global environmental externalities (where the atomistic contributors to environmental problems and diffused sets of their actual and potential victims, numbering to millions of scattered victims). In an analytical investigation, DeSerpa (1994) asserted that, if anything, the Coase theorem may be valid only in some of the situations governing local externalities (the types of railway and farm crop damage examples considered by Coase, 1960). It was also suggested that global environmental externality differs from the local one in that individual victims are affected adversely not by the activity of individual culprits, but by the 'collective action of a large number of culprits'.

When there are multiple and often unidentified parties causing environmental problems or related externalities, there is little possibility of bargaining or the application of the Coase theorem. At the global level there is no single co-ordinating entity that could meaningfully assign PR (including seeking the attainment of global welfare maximization) regarding various environmental assets, and their stocks and flows.

The existence of well-defined, transparent and enforceable LR tends to send the right signals to decision-making entities. Often, some of the important elements of such factors are missing in practice, or the corresponding TC are very high. The result is the achievement of limited efficiency in regulating externalities or undesirable environmental consequences. In addition, LR may not suffice to preserve global environmental features. Such provisions, if credibly enforceable, are likely to supplement the roles of various rules/standards or other preventive measures developed under international law (Rao, 2001). LR are unlikely to restore the *status quo ante* resources, as in the case of problems of loss of biodiversity or genetic resources.

Thus, in environmental resources that are potentially irreversible in their quality/existence, the role of LR remains rather limited. Besides, the existence of significant magnitudes of TC implies that the role of LR will be even more restricted; the practicality of the rules of liability should act as a guiding principle for the substitution rules in relation to negotiated solutions (Demsetz, 1972).

TCE plays a major role in environmental conflict resolution, with or without third-party mediation. Let us recall that the origins and applications of TCE are based mainly on Coase (1960), in which the problem was one of resolving a local environmental damage problem, that of crop damage caused by rail company activity involving sparks from railway engines. The most efficient form of resolution relied on efficient bargaining in a TC-free scenario. However, the use of the Coase theorem in relation to the problems of environmental management is confined largely to local environmental issues, as explained in Rao (2001). Yet the role of TCE is not confined only to local environmental governance; it is also well suited to global environmental governance. The formation of treaties and mechanisms for dispute resolution rely on the role of TCE (Rao, 2001).

Environmental conflicts depict complex problems of measurement and the establishment of cause-and-effect relationships (including various inherent uncertainties), in addition to the need to devise preventive measures that do not necessarily fit into an existing framework of rules. Unlike traded goods and services, environmental resources and ecosystem services do not usually constitute markets at the present time. Thus missing or non-existent markets pose special problems of valuation and provision of fair compensation for damages. This requires a set of forward-looking norms and applications of the law. In global environmental measures, the roles of diffused and distant phenomena also require particular attention. State sovereignty poses problems of centralized or co-ordinated enforcement, and monitoring of non-compliance of agreements is also very difficult or involves high TC. All these special features of the environment necessitate the recognition of problems of incomplete information, imperfect and/or missing markets, and imperfect monitoring and measurement.

An agreement on how to resolve environmental disputes as and when they arise is an important aspect of common information among parties affecting one or more aspects of environmental assets. A common agreement for a broad mediation measure is itself an achievement.

Bringing parties together to do this is a complex task, and significant TC arise in the process. The methods of dispute resolution are varied and have been evolving over the years in the global arena.

Blackburn and Bruce (1995) compiled a set of relevant issues in the theory and implementation of environmental mediation by third parties. They stated (pp. 42–3) that: 'Regulatory agencies and the court may intervene to increase certainty and reduce risk, thereby creating incentives for dispute resolution...When risk and uncertainty are reduced and the parties are free to negotiate a resolution of their conflict, an optimal situation occurs.'

Among some of the relevant practical measures that are not dependent on judicial measures, the USEPA developed during the 1980s a set of criteria for 'regulatory negotiation' (Reg-Neg) as an alternative dispute resolution process which brings together representatives of various stakeholders potentially affected by a proposed rule, and interactions with the apex federal agency are geared towards reaching a consensus on the specifications of a proposed rule. Among the criteria for participants in the negotiation are (for more details see, Blackburn and Bruce, 1995, pp. 210–11): (i) participants interested in or affected by the outcome of the proposed rule should be readily identifiable and relatively few in number, representing the interests of their constituencies; and (ii) the parties should view themselves in terms of an ongoing relationship with the EPA beyond the specific item under consideration for negotiation.

In international interactions, TC primarily include the costs of information, contracting and monitoring at the interface level; the elements differ in their intensity and require the addition of a few more factors at national and lower levels. As Boadu (1998) pointed out in connection with an international water transfer treaty between Lesotho and the Republic of South Africa, parties to an agreement incur costs of contracting, negotiation and of related aspects in order to reduce their risks of *ex post* opportunism, and thus maximize their relative benefits. Accordingly, there exists a limited trade-off between *ex ante* and *ex post* costs. This observation is typical of most cases of contracts, and these highlight the role of TC at different stages. The environmental negotiation context of different countries also depicts some similarities.

Whereas the Coase theorem typically addresses potential negotiating solutions involving identifiable local (or other) environmental problems, a similar approach, whenever relevant, does not extend to situations in the global environment (Rao, 2001) because of the diffused accountability of polluter–victim relationships as well as cause–effect relationships. When the 'collective action of a large number of culprits' is involved, Coasean bargaining solutions may not exist, even when the TC are near zero (DeSerpa, 1994).

As a result of these observations, it is prudent to devise methods of wider consultation with stakeholders in an attempt to minimize the demand for potential litigation. Once dispute arises, arbitration and other third-party mediation may be cost-effective. Finally, both the design of regulatory provisions and other contractual specifications as well as their compliance/enforcement aspects must include the role of TC.

9.6 Conclusions

The roles of environmental externalities, technological externalities, TC and changing preferences as well as non-constant discount rates in decision frameworks pose limitations on the standard methods of NE which advocate the NNP as an indicator of sustainability. The suggested role of the NNP in traditional NE literature is founded on major assumptions. In general, it is not an indicator of economic sustainability. This measure requires revisions using endogenous preferences in an adaptive efficiency-maximizing sense, the focus of TCE. Since the relative price of capital depends on the entire future equilibrium path, the concept of NNP as an indicator of sustainability may not be tenable in the conventional form. Non-constant and endogenous discounting is the only relevant form of discounting for environmental decision-making.

The economics of global environmental phenomena, such as climate change, require a much broader comprehension and assessment of costs, which are generally not considered in traditional economic literature. AE is required for any institutions that are devised for global environmental governance.

TC may be high or impose substantial costs on other parties in the economy because competitive market forces do not operate effectively in such thin markets. This poses problems for the use of TEP and the efficiency of pollution markets. A mix of market and non-market methods of intervention remains relevant in this context. The role of contestable markets also needs to be explored further.

10
Perspectives

10.1 New approaches and applications

Transaction costs represent resource losses, not necessarily because of the lack of information alone. TC also arise where economic decision-makers face uncertainties about the activities of other actors in the economic system. The ITCE framework suggested in Chapter 1 needs to be advanced further. Similarly, there is a need to move forward from the accounting approaches of assessing TC in terms of the costs of information, monitoring and enforcement (and related aspects) to include opportunity costs and loss of efficiency relative to a feasible alternative organization of activities. Some parts of the TCE literature suggest that TC are near zero if there exists perfect information; this is not tenable, as the definition of TC in this instance is very narrowly interpreted.

TCE should address both partial and general economic settings for potential reform and thus arrive at a pragmatic governance of economic institutions. Williamson (1998) suggested the doctrine that TCE should subscribe to explanations organized around partial mechanisms rather than general theories. This may not be an entirely tenable position.

Among the illustrations of the applications of TCE for economic governance and choice of institutions, the issue of 'privatization' may be considered. The fashionable economic reform involving privatization during the 1990s was founded only partly on sound logic but largely on fallacy. The adverse implications of the process of privatization was either not thought through or deliberately ill-designed, or a combination of the two. The multi-billion dollar scams in the processes from countries across the globe surfaced after the processes got through. It is useful to recall a forewarning of Frydman and Rapacynski (1993, p. 13):

The meaning of 'privatization' in Eastern Europe has turned out to be complex and ambiguous. Instead of the clarification of property rights and the introduction of incentives characteristic of a capitalist society, the privatization process has so far often led to a maze of complicated economic and legal relations that may even impede a speedy transition to a system in which the rights of capital are clearly defined and protected.

One problem is that conflicts broke out 'between the interests of insiders, intent on retaining authority over their enterprises, and the right of outside investors to acquire control'. The main problem is one of getting the institutions right. ITCE is more relevant for this purpose.

Allocative efficiency and adaptive efficiency may not always be compatible. Much of economics (and law and economics) literature deals with the former to the detriment of the latter, and seeks to maximize efficiency (allocative efficiency); in this process, TC maximization over time cannot be ruled out. This possibility exists whenever drastic failures of the market or governmental institutions occur.

Traditional economics

Much of what most economists believed for over a century turns out to be far from robust in the prescriptions of economics. This is the result of the implicit assumption of the non-existence or near-negligible level of TC. The simultaneous emergence and development of the economics of information complemented the contributions of TCE to facilitate a more advanced standing and appreciation of TCE as an essential ingredient of most aspects of economic analysis. Just as the neglect of the role of varying informational characteristics led to the irrelevance of some of the findings of traditional economics (for an update and review, see Stiglitz, 2000), recognition of the role of transaction costs (which include information costs as a sub-set) casts a shadow on the validity of most standard results of economic analyses.

It is not claimed here that the approach of TCE constitutes a panacea for all shortcomings of economic theory and practice, but it does reduce the extent of lacunae. Some of the important results of 'economics as usual' do not hold the moment the role of TC (and of information economics, as argued by Stiglitz, 2000) is recognized in the analysis of economic transactions. Some of these are illustrated below:

1. The issues of income distribution and economic efficiency are not separable in assessing the performance of economic systems, since

the interactions of the two features are iterative functions of TC. The latter may be influenced by information costs or other economic behavioural attributes. Ironically, 'Coase's theorem' itself stands invalid in light of these features. The endogeneity of TC relative to a given configuration of income distribution determines a set of efficiency measures (in the sense of wealth maximization) that differ from another variation of income distribution and attendant TC).

2. Market clearing equilibria may not exist in the sense of equating demand and supply at any price if we recognize that the role of TC leads to excess demand or excess supply, depending on the relative distribution of elements of TC (including search and information costs) among buyers and sellers in the market system.

3. The pervasive non-convexities of production functions and cost functions lead to the phenomenon of the existence of multiple equilibria. Fundamental non-convexities of the information cost functions (and of the value of information functions) are part of the contributing factors.

4. The phenomenon of equilibrium price dispersion and the existence of multiple prices in a given market in its equilibrium is best explained by invoking the role of TC. Information and search costs alone do not explain the existence of spatial (or other) price dispersion; only TC explain such equilibria. As a result of these findings, it is apt to describe some of the markets typically described as 'perfect competition' models in terms of 'monopolistic competition' models, and equilibrium results thus deflect from the former to the latter in the presence of TC. As a consequence, marginal cost does not equal price in most scenarios involving TC, even when the traditional marginal cost is augmented to reflect TC. Thus it is behavioural attributes and their effects on consumer demand functions that affect competition in equilibrium in relation to consumer attributes reflected in differential TC.

5. The notion of TC alone tends to change economic behavioural attributes of economic entities, and assumptions of negligible TC do not usually enable the convergence of economic results with traditional economic findings (for a similar observation on the role of information costs, see Stiglitz, 2000).

6. Non-market institutions are not always an automatic alternative to the failure or sub-optimal performance of market institutions. This is because the former could even exacerbate the adverse consequences of the latter because of the lack of internalization of relevant externalities and/or the incorporation of new externalities (see

also Arnott and Stiglitz, 1991). The robust prescription here is: comprehend the relevant TC and assess alternatives along a feasible continuum of institutional arrangements.

10.2 Directions for research

Several specific research issues have been identified and stated in the context of relevant analysis in various parts of this book, and it is not proposed to reiterate them here. A few additional or supplementary directions are provided below for possible further use by interested researchers.

Although TCE makes some claims regarding its recognition of adaptation factors, it is better handled with an effective integration of NE and Institutional Economics (IE). The relative significance of analytical methods and quantified approaches should not be lost sight of when institutional issues are considered as in much of IE. On the other hand, many NE studies deal with institutional issues as an appendage, and do not pay sufficient attention to the intricacies of the issues as they relate to initial conditions and dynamics of evolution underlying the explicit specifications of similar parameters as they concern economic models under NE formulations. In other words, for each integrated formulation that is desirable in a given situation, two sets of initial conditions and two sets of dynamics need to be spelt out formally, and analytical solutions (or their closest approximations) need to be derived. The first set will clarify the institutional factors at the specific point in time, and the second will specify the conditions relevant to each of the variables considered under the NE formulation; similar clarifications hold for the dynamics of institutions and economic variables as well.

The theme for further research then centres around the development of analytical methods and data/information systems integrating the two streams of inputs in a multi-period setting, recognizing the roles of incomplete information and uncertainties of different types. It is entirely feasible that a computable fuzzy-set theoretic optimization model might possess the capability to handle most of these desired features, but the economic interpretations may not be as precise as the ones that the NE solutions tend to offer; however, the latter obtain, often at the expense of insensitivity to institutional assumptions, and thus seeking to obtain, for example, 'prices right' without getting the 'institutions right'. One of the key improvements required of the quantitatively and analytically motivated NE models (optimizing or otherwise) and their solutions, is to incorporate a 'sensitivity analysis' with respect to plausible variations in the specifications in the models, and also to seek relatively robust prescriptions of solutions to problems (thus avoiding hypersensitive solutions that could play havoc with even minor changes in the specifications in either stream (NE and/or IE). One of the relevant approaches for further analysis is that of fuzzy mathematics.

Fuzzy systems

A number of potentially useful enrichments of the economics of transaction costs deserve further attention. Some of these start with refinements of the definition of transaction costs, and greater formalization of the same with a broad analytical basis. A combination of behavioural and positive economics juxtaposed with methods of decision-making under uncertainty with a 'fuzzy information' base could lead to improved solutions; the role of fuzzy mathematics is expected to be significant in its comprehensive strength in dealing with systems of bounded and unknown rationality features, incomplete and unknown information constraints and risk, and uncertain characteristics. It is not likely that fuzzy optimization methods are a panacea for all the limitations of current analyses, but a more robust method of analysis is perhaps preferable to methods that are hypersensitive to the simplest of assumptions, and the latter are not verifiable as part of a priori information. There is scope for enhancing the harmonious amalgamation of neoclassical economics with institutional economics, and a starting point for this purpose is to ensure that students of economics are trained in both streams of economics as well as retaining a focus on analytical methods. Such an integration advances the development of economic analysis with greater awareness of the role of transaction costs in the conditioning of economic performance at all levels of economic activity.

When the TC concept does not permit the ranking of different economic equilibria in terms of corresponding implications for the performance of the relevant economic system (that is, the profit or revenue maximization for an enterprise, and social welfare maximization for a national economy, and so on), the costs of switching from one equilibrium to another should be recognized and incorporated in the assessment of total costs of the specific transactions. Warneryd (1994) explored a few illustrative examples using static game models; substantial additional work is required in this direction.

The limited use of mathematical models in TCE and greater descriptiveness are not to be construed as leading to a sub-optimal mode of analysis; the question of optimality arises only after articulation of the alternatives, and TCE provides the right direction for that purpose. The role of TCE continues to be recognized in almost all sectors of economic activity, market-oriented or otherwise. Progress in the theory and application of TCE is expected to bridge the gap between NE and TCE, with the simultaneous enhancement of the strengths of both streams of exploration.

References

1 Background

Arrow, K. J. (1969) The Organization of Economic Activity: Issues Pertinent to the Choice of Market versus Nonmarket Allocation, in *The Analysis and Evaluation of Public Expenditure: The PPB System 1*, US Joint Economic Committee, 91st Congress (Washington, DC: US Government Printing Office), pp. 59–73.

Arrow, K. J. (1979) The Property Rights Doctrine and Demand Revelation under Incomplete Information, in M. J. Boskin (ed.), *Economics and Human Welfare: Essays in Honor of Tibor Scitovsky* (New York: Academic Press), pp. 23–39.

Benham, A. and Benham, L. (2000) Measuring the Costs of Exchange, in Menard C. (ed.), *Institutions, Contracts and Organizations*, (Cheltenham: Edward Elgar), pp. 367–75.

Broome, J. (1990) Bolker–Jeffrey Expected Utility Theory and Axiomatic Utilitarianism, *Review of Economic Studies*, 57, pp. 477–502.

Caplan, B. (2001) Rational Ignorance versus Rational Irrationality, *Kyklos*, 54, pp. 3–26.

Coase, R. H. (1937) The Nature of the Firm, *Economica*, 4, pp. 386–405.

Coase, R. H. (1988) *The Firm, the Market and the Law*, (Chicago: University of Chicago Press).

Dahlman, C. (1979) The Problem of Externality, *Journal of Law and Economics*, 22, pp. 141–62.

Dietrich, M. (1994) *Transaction Cost Economics and Beyond* (London: Routledge).

Dorward, A. (1999) A Risk Programming Approach for Analysing Contractual Choice in the Presence of Transaction Costs, *European Review of Agricultural Economics*, 26, pp. 479–92.

Fischer, S. (1977) Long-term Contracting, Sticky Prices, and Monetary Policy: Comment, *Journal of Monetary Economics*, 3, pp. 317–322.

Furubotn, E. G. and Richter, R. (2000) *Institutions and Economic Theory* (Ann Arbor, Mich.: University of Michigan Press).

Groenewegan, J. (1996) Transaction Cost Economics and Beyond: Why and How in Groenewegan, J. (ed.), *Transaction Cost Economics and Beyond* (Dordrecht: Kluwer), pp. 1–9.

Hurwicz, L. and Majumdar, M. (1988) Optimal Intertemporal Allocation Mechanisms and Decentralization of Decisions, *Journal of Economic Theory*, 45, pp. 228–61.

Jones, R. A. (1976) The Origin and Development of Media of Exchange, *Journal of Political Economy*, 84, pp. 757–75.

Joskow, P. L. (1988) Asset Specificity and the Structure of Vertical Relationships: Empirical Evidence, *Journal of Law, Economics, and Organization*, 4, pp. 95–118.

Klein, P. and Shelanski, H. (1995) Empirical Research in Transaction Cost Economics: A Review, *Journal of Law, Economics and Organization*, 11, pp. 335–62.

Krickx, G. A. (1995) Vertical Integration in the Computer Mainframe Industry: A Transaction Cost Interpretation, *Journal of Economic Behavior and Organization*, 26, pp. 75–91.

Laffont, J. (1985) On the Welfare Analysis of Rational Expectations Equilibria with Asymmetric Information, *Econometrica*, 53, pp. 1–29.

Masten, S. E. (1996) Empirical Research in Transaction Cost Economics: Challenges, Progress, Directions, in J. Groenewegan (ed.), *Transaction Cost Economics and Beyond* (Boston: Kluwer), pp. 43–64.

Milgrom, P. and Roberts, J. (1992) *Economics, Organization, and Management* (Englewood Cliffs, NJ: Prentice-Hall).

Monteverde, K. and Teece, D. J. (1982) Supplier Switching Costs and Vertical Integration in the Automobile Industry, *Bell Journal of Economics*, 13, pp. 206–13.

Niehans, J. (1969) Money in a Static Theory of Optimal Payment Arrangements, *Journal of Money, Credit and Banking*, 1, pp. 796–826.

North, D. C. (1990) *Institutions, Institutional Change, and Economic Performance* (New York: Cambridge University Press).

North, D. C. (1995) Constraints on Institutional Innovation – Transaction Costs: Incentive Compatibility and Historical Considerations, in V. W. Ruttan (ed.), *Agriculture, Environment, and Health – Sustainable Development in the 21st Century*, (Minneapolis, Minn.: University of Minnesota Press), pp. 48–70.

Rindfleisch, A. and Heide, J. B. (1997) Transaction Cost Analysis: Past, Present, and Future Applications, *Journal of Marketing*, 61, pp. 30–54.

Samuelson, P. (1948) *Foundations of Economic Analysis* (Cambridge, Mass.: Harvard University Press).

Samuelson, P. (1995) Some Uneasiness with Coase Theorem, *Japan and the World Economy*, 7, pp. 1–7.

Seierstat, S. and Sydsaeter, K. (1987) *Optimal Control Theory with Economic Applications* (Amsterdam: North-Holland).

Simon, H. A. (1957) *Models of Man: Social and Rational* (New York: Wiley).

Simon, H. A. (2000) Barriers and Bounds to Rationality, *Structural Change and Economic Dynamics*, 11, pp. 243–53.

Slater, G. and Spencer, D. A. (2000) The Uncertain Foundations of Transaction Cost Economics, *Journal of Economic Issues*, 34, pp. 61–87.

Takayama, A. (1993) *Analytical Methods in Economics* (Ann Arbor, Mich.: University of Michigan Press).

Warneryd, K. (1994) Transaction Cost, Institutions, and Evolution, *Journal of Economic Behavior and Organization*, 25, pp. 219–39.

Williamson, O. E. (1985) *The Economic Institutions of Capitalism* (New York: Free Press).

Williamson, O. E. (1989) Transaction Cost Economics, in Schmalensee, R. and Willig, R. D. (eds), *Handbook of Industrial Organization* (New York: Elsevier Science), pp. 136–82.

Williamson, O. E. (1996) *The Mechanisms of Governance* (Oxford University Press).

2   Elements of Industrial Organization

Barnard, C. (1938) *The Functions of the Executive* (Cambridge, Mass.: Harvard University Press).

Coase, R. H. (1937), The Nature of the Firm, *Economica*, pp. 386–405.

Cohen, W. M. and Klepper, S. (1996) A Reprise of Size and R&D, *The Economic Journal*, 106, pp. 925–51.

Cohen, W. M. and Levin, R. C. (1989) Empirical Studies of Innovation and Market Structure, in Schmalensee, R. and Willig, R. D. (eds), *Handbook of Industrial Organization* (Amsterdam: North-Holland), pp. 1059–107.

Day, R. H. and Groves, T. (eds) (1975) *Adaptive Economic Models* (New York: Academic Press).

Day, R. H. and Singh, T. J. (1977) *Economic Development as an Adaptive Process* (New York: Cambridge University Press).

Eisenhardt, K. M. and Martin, J. A. (2000) Dynamic Capabilities: What Are They?, *Strategic Management Journal*, 21, pp. 1105–21.

Faure-Grimaud, A., Laffont, J. J. and Martimort, D. (1999) The Endogenous Transaction Costs of Delegated Auditing, *European Economic Review*, 43, pp. 1039–48.

Hart, O. (1989) An Economist's Perspective on the Theory of the Firm, *Columbia Law Review*, 89, pp. 1757–74.

Hayek, F. (1945) The Use of Knowledge in Society, *American Economic Review*, 35, pp. 519–30.

Jensen, M. C. and Meckling, W. H. (1976) Theory of the Firm: Managerial Behavior, Agency Costs and Ownership Structure, *Journal of Financial Economics*, 3, pp. 305–60.

Joskow, P. (1991) The Role of Transaction Cost Economics in Antitrust and Public Utility Regulatory Policies, *Journal of Law, Economics and Organization*, 7, pp. 53–83.

Klein, P. and Shelanski, H. (1995) Empirical Research in Transaction Cost Economics: A Review, *Journal of Law, Economics and Organization*, 11, pp. 335–62.

Machlup, F. (1978) *Methodology of Economics and Other Social Sciences* (New York: Academic Press).

Milgrom, P. and Roberts, J. (1988) Economic Theories of the Firm: Past, Present and Future, *Canadian Journal of Economics*, 21, pp. 444–58.

Panzar, J. and Willig, R. (1981) Economies of Scope, *American Economic Review Papers and Proceedings*, 71, pp. 268–72.

Penrose, E. T. (1959) *The Theory of the Growth of the Firm* (New York: Wiley).

Phillips, A. and Stevenson, R. E. (1974) The Historical Development of Industrial Organization, *History of Political Economy*, 6, pp. 323–45.

Pitelis, C. N. (1998) Transaction Costs and the Historical Evolution of the Capitalist Firm, *Journal of Economic Issues*, 32, pp. 999–1017.

Powell, W. W., Koput, K. W. and Smith-Doerr, L. (1996) Interorganizational Collaboration and the Locus of Innovation: Networks of Learning in Biotechnology, *Administrative Science Quarterly*, 41, pp. 116–45.

Raider, H. J. (1998) Market Structure and Innovation, *Social Science Research*, 27, pp. 1–21.

Robertson, P. L. and Langlois, R. N. (1995) Innovation, Networks, and Vertical Integration, *Research Policy*, 24, pp. 543–62.

Silverman, B. S. (1999) Technological Resources and the Direction of Corporate Diversification: Toward an Integration of the Resource-Based View and Transaction Cost Economics, *Management Science*, 45, pp. 1109–24.

Spulber, D. F. (1999) *Market Microstructure: Intermediaries and the Theory of the Firm* (New York: Cambridge University Press).

Stigler, G. (1968) *The Organization of Industry* (Homewood, Ill.: Richard D. Irwin).

Teece, D. (1980) Economics of Scope and the Scope of the Enterprise, *Journal of Economic Behavior and Organization*, 1, pp. 223–47.

Teece, D. (1982) Towards an Economic Theory of the Multiproduct Firm, *Journal of Economic Behaviour and Organization*, 3, pp. 39–64.

Teece, D. J., Pisano, G. and Shuen, A. (1997) Dynamic Capabilities and Strategic Management, *Strategic Management Journal*, 18, pp. 509–34.

Tirole, J. (1988) *The Theory of Industrial Organization* (Cambridge, Mass.: MIT Press).

Vilasuso, J. and Minkler, A. (2001) Agency Costs, Asset Specificity, and the Capital Structure of the Firm, *Journal of Economic Behaviour and Organization*, 44, pp. 55–69.

Wernerfelt, B. (1984) A Resource-based View of the Firm, *Strategic Management Journal*, 5, pp. 171–80.

Wiggins, S. N. (1991) The Economics of the Firm and Contracts: A Selective Survey, *Journal of Institutional and Theoretical Economics*, 147, pp. 603–61.

Williamson, O. E. (1996) *The Mechanisms of Governance* (New York: Oxford University Press).

Winter, S. G. (2000) The Satisficing Principle in Capability Learning, *Strategic Management Journal*, 21, pp. 981–96.

3 Economic Externalities

Aidt, T. (1998) Political Internalization of Economic Externalities and Environmental Policy, *Journal of Public Economics*, 69, pp. 1–16.

Aivazian, V. A. and Callen, J. L. (1981) The Coase Theorem and the Empty Core, *Journal of Law and Economics*, 24, pp. 175–81.

Allen, D. (1991) What are Transaction Costs?, pp. 1–8, in Zerbe, R. O. Jr and Goldberg V. P. (eds), *Research in Law and Economics, Vol. 14* (Greenwich, Conn.: JAI Press).

Arrow, K. J. (1951) An Extension of the Basic Theorems of Classical Welfare Economics, in Neyman, J. (ed.), *Proceedings of the Second Berkeley Symposium on Mathematical Statistics and Probability* (Berkeley, Calif.: University of California Press).

Ascher, W. (1999) *Why Governments Waste Natural Resources: Policy Failures in Developing Countries* (Baltimore, Md: Johns Hopkins University Press).

Bernholz, P. (1999) The Generalized Coase Theorem and Separable Individual Preferences: An Extension, *European Journal of Political Economy*, 15, pp. 331–5.

Blankart, C. B. and Knieps, G. (1993) State and Standards, *Public Choice*, 77, pp. 39–52.

180   *References*

Bowles, S. (1998) Endogenous Preferences: The Cultural Consequences of Markets and other Economic Institutions, *Journal of Economic Literature*, 36, pp. 75–111.

Calabresi, G. (1968) Transaction Costs, Resource Allocation, and Liability Rules – A Comment, *Journal of Law and Economics*, 11, pp. 67–90.

Coase, R. H. (1937) The Nature of the Firm, *Economica*, 4, pp. 386–405.

Coase, R. H. (1960) The Problem of Social Cost, *Journal of Law and Economics*, 3, pp. 1–44.

Coase, R. H. (1988) *The Firm, the Market and the Law* (Chicago: University of Chicago Press).

Cooter, R. (1982) The Cost of Coase, *Journal of Legal Studies*, 11, pp. 1–33.

Cooter, R., Marks, S. and Mnookin, R. (1982) Bargaining in the Shadow of the Law – a Testable Model of Strategic Behavior, *Journal of Legal Studies*, 11, pp. 225–51.

Dahlman, C. (1979) The Problem of Externalities, *Journal of Law and Economics*, 22, pp. 141–62.

Cooter, R. D. (1989) The Coase Theorem, in Eatwell, J., Milgate, M. and Newman, P. (eds), *Allocation, Information, and Markets* (London: Macmillan), pp. 64–70.

Demsetz, H. (1967) Toward a Theory of Property Rights, *American Economic Review*, 57, pp. 347–69.

Demsetz, H. (1996) The Core Disagreement between Pigou, the Profession, and Coase in the Analysis of the Externality Question, *European Journal of Political Economy*, 12, pp. 565–79.

Dixit, A. and Olson, M. (2000) Does Voluntary Participation Undermine the Coase Theorem?, *Journal of Public Economics*, 76, pp. 309–35.

Easterbrook, F. H. and Fischel, D. R. (1991) *The Economic Structure of Corporate Law*, Executive Order of the US President 12866, 1993, Regulatory planning and review, Weekly Compilation of Presidential Documents, 39 (Washington: USGPO), pp. 1925–1933.

Farber, D. A. (1997) Parody Lost/Pragmatism Regained – the Ironic History of the Coase Theorem, *Virginia Law Review*, 83, pp. 397–428.

Greenwood, P. and Ingene, C. (1978) Uncertain Externalities, Liability Rules, and Resource Allocation, *American Economic Review*, 68, pp. 300–32.

Hoffman, E. and Spitzer, M. L. (1982) The Coase Theorem – Some Experimental Tests, *Journal of Law and Economics*, 25, pp. 73–96.

Hurwicz, L. (1995) What Is the Coase Theorem?, *Japan and the World Economy*, 7, pp. 49–74.

Inada, K. and Kuga, K. (1973) Limitations of the 'Coase Theorem' on Liability Rules, *Journal of Economic Theory*, 6, pp. 606–13.

Johnston, J. (1993) The Influence of *The Nature of the Firm* on the Theory of Corporate Law, *Journal of Corporate Law*, 18, pp. 213–42.

Katz, M. L. and Shapiro, C. (1985) Network Externalities, Competition, and Compatibility, *American Economic Review*, 75, p. 424.

Katz, M. L. and Shapiro, C. (1986) Technology Adoption in the Presence of Network Externalities, *Journal of Political Economy*, 94, pp. 822–47.

Klausner, M. (1995) Corporations, Corporate Law, and Networks of Contracts, *Virginia Law Review*, 81, pp. 757–852.

Leifer, E. M. and White, H. C. (1987) A Structural Approach to Markets, in Mizruchi, M. S. and Schwartz, M. (eds), *Intercorporate Relations: The Structural Analysis of Business* (New York: Cambridge University Press), pp. 85–108.

Milgrom, P. and Roberts, J. (1992) *Economics, Organization, and Management* (Englewood Cliffs, NJ: Prentice-Hall).

Nalebuff, B. (1997) On a Clear Day, You Can See the Coase Theorem, in Dasgupta, P. and Maler, K. G. (eds), *The Environment and Emerging Development Issues* (Oxford: Clarendon Press), pp. 35–47.

Olson, M. (1996) Big Bills Left on the Side Walk: Why Some Nations are Rich, and Others Poor, *Journal of Economic Perspectives*, 10, pp. 3–24.

Otani, Y. and Sicilian, J. (1977) Externalities and Problems of Nonconvexity and Overhead Costs in Welfare Economics, *Journal of Economic Theory*, 14, pp. 239–51.

Pigou, A. C. (1932) *The Economics of Welfare*, 4th edn (London: Macmillan).

Posner, R. (1993) Nobel Laureate: Ronald Coase and Methodology, *Journal of Economic Perspectives*, 7, pp. 193–9.

Rao, P. K. (2001) *International Environmental Law and Economics* (Oxford: Blackwell).

Samuels, W. J. (1992) *Essays on the Economic Role of Government* (New York: New York University Press).

Shapley, L. S. and Shubik, M. (1969) On the Core of an Economic System with Externalities, *American Economic Review*, 59, pp. 678–90.

Simpson, A. W. B. (1996) Coase v. Pigou Reexamined, *Journal of Legal Studies*, 25, pp. 53–101.

Starrett, D. (1972) Fundamental nonconvexities in the theory of externalities, *Journal of Economic Theory*, 4, pp. 180–99.

Stigler, G. (1966) *The Theory of Price* (New York: Macmillan).

Sunstein, C. (1999) Behavioral Law and Economics: A Progress Report, *American Law and Economics Review*, 1, pp. 115–57.

Thaler, R. (1991) *Quasi-Rational Economics* (New York: Sage).

Thaler, R. (1992) *The Winner's Curse* (Princeton, NJ: Princeton University Press).

Usher, D. (1998) The Coase Theorem is Tautological, Incoherent or Wrong, *Economics Letters*, 61, pp. 3–11.

White, B. (1987) Coase and the Courts: Economics for the Common Man, *Iowa Law Review*, 72, pp. 577–636.

Williamson, O. E. (2000) Ronald Harry Coase: Institutional Economist / Institution Builder, in C. Menard (ed.), *Institutions, Contracts and Organizations* (Cheltenham: Edward Elgar), pp. 48–53.

Wolf, C. Jr (1979) A Theory of Nonmarket Failure: Framework for Implementation Analysis, *Journal of Law and Economics*, 22, pp. 107–39.

Zerbe, R. O. Jr and McCurdy, H. E. (1999) The Failure of Market Failure, *Journal of Policy Analysis and Management*, 18, pp. 558–78.

4 New Neoclassical Economics

Amelung, T. (1991) The Impact of Transaction Costs on the Direction of Trade: Empirical Evidence for Asia Pacific, *Journal of Institutional and Theoretical Economics*, 147, pp. 603–61.

Arnott, R. and Stiglitz, J. (1991) Moral Hazard and Nonmarket Institutions: Dysfunctional Crowding Out after Monitoring, *American Economic Review*, 81, pp. 179–90.

Barro, R. J. (1997) *Determinants of Economic Growth: A Cross-Country Empirical Study* (Cambridge, Mass.: MIT Press).

Bowles, S. (1998) Endogenous Preferences: The Cultural Consequences of Markets and other Economic Institutions, *Journal of Economic Literature*, 36, pp. 75–111.

Coase, R. H. (1960) The Problem of Social Cost, *Journal of Law and Economics*, 3, pp. 1–44.

Coase, R. H. (1964) The Regulated Industries: Discussion, *American Economic Review*, 54, pp. 194–7.

Colombatto, E. and Macey, J. (1999) Information and Transaction Costs as the Determinants of Tolerable Growth Levels, *Journal of Institutional and Theoretical Economics*, 155, pp. 617–42.

De Alessi, L. (1983) Property Rights, Transaction Costs, and X-Efficiency: An Essay in Economic Theory, *American Economic Review*, 73, pp. 64–81.

Easterly, W. (2001) *The Elusive Quest for Growth: Economists' Adventures and Misadventures in the Tropics* (Cambridge, Mass.: MIT Press).

Ehrlich, I. and Lui, F. T. (1999) Bureaucratic Corruption and Economic Growth, *Journal of Political Economy*, 107, pp. S270–S293.

Food and Agriculture Organization (FAO) (1989) *Aspects of Stabilization and Structural Adjustment Programmes on Food Security*, Rome: FAO Economic and Social Development Paper 89, p.12.

Franke, G. (1991) Avenues for Reduction of LDC Debt – An Institutional Analysis, *Journal of Institutional and Theoretical Economics*, 147, pp. 274–95.

Frooth, K. A. (1988) Credibility, Real Interest Rates, and the Optimal Speed of Trade Liberalization, *Journal of International Economics*, 25, pp. 71–93.

Furubotn, E. G. (1991) General Equilibrium Models, Transaction Costs, and the Concept of Efficient Allocation in a Capitalist Economy, *Journal of Institutional and Theoretical Economics*, 147, pp. 662–86.

Furusawa, T. and Lai, E. L. (1999) Adjustment Costs and Gradual Trade Liberalization, *Journal of International Economics*, 49, pp. 333–61.

Granovetter, M. (1985) Economic Action and Social Structure: The Problem of Embeddedness, *American Journal of Sociology*, 91, pp. 481–510.

Greif, A. (1992) Institutions and International Trade – Lessons from the Commercial Revolution, *American Economic Review*, 82, pp. 128–33.

Heckscher, E. (1919) The Effect of Foreign Trade on the Distribution of Income, Economisk Tidskrift, 21, trans. and ed. by Flam, H. and Flanders, M. J. *Heckscher–Ohlin Trade Theory* (Cambridge, Mass.: MIT Press), pp. 497–512.

Helliwell, J. F. (1998) *How Much Do National Borders Matter?* (Washington, DC: Brookings Institution Press).

Hurwicz, L. (1973) The Design of Mechanisms for Resource Allocation, *American Economic Review*, 63, pp. 1–30.

Klein, B. and Leffler, K. (1981) The Role of Market Forces in Assuring Contractual Performance, *Journal of Political Economy*, 89, pp. 615–41.

Kogiku, K. C. (1971) *Microeconomic Models* (New York: Harper & Row).

Kormendi, R. C. and Meguire, P. G. (1986) Macroeconomic Determinants of Economic Growth: Cross-Country Evidence, *Journal of Monetary Economics*, 16, pp. 141–63.

Kuznets, S. (1973) Modern Economic Growth: Findings and Reflections, *American Economic Review*, 63, pp. 247–58.

Layard, R. and Glaister, S. (1994) *Cost–Benefit Analysis* (New York: Cambridge University Press).

Mehlum, H. (2001) Speed of Adjustment and Self-fulfilling Failure of Economic Reform, *Journal of International Economics*, 53, pp. 149–67.

Mill, J. S. (1848) *Principles of Political Economy* (London: J. W. Parker).

Mosley, P. (1994) Decomposing the Effects of Structural Adjustment – the Case of Sub-Saharan Africa, in Van der Hoeven, R. and Van der Kraaji, F. (eds), *Structural Adjustment and Beyond in Sub-Saharan Africa* (London: James Currey).

Mussa, M. (1986) The Adjustment Process and the Timing of Trade Liberalization, in Choksi, A. M. and Papageorgiou, D. (eds), *Economic Liberalization in Developing Countries* (Oxford: Basil Blackwell).

Nelson, R. R. and Sampath, B. N. (2001) Making Sense of Institutions as a Factor Shaping Economic Performance, *Journal of Economic Behavior and Organization*, 44, pp. 31–54.

North, D. C. (1990) *Institutions, Institutional Change and Economic Performance* (New York: Cambridge University Press).

Ohlin, B. (1924) The Theory of Trade, reprinted in Flam H. and Flanders, M. J. (eds), *Heckscher–Ohlin Trade Theory* (Cambridge, MA: MIT Press).

Olson, M. (1963) Rapid Growth as a Destabilizing Force, *Journal of Economic History*, 23, pp. 529–52.

Pigou, A. C. (1932) *The Economics of Welfare*, 4th edn (London: Macmillan).

Pryor, F. L. (1994) Growth Deceleration and Transaction Costs: A Note, *Journal of Economic Behavior and Organization*, 25, pp. 121–33.

Putnam, R. D. (1993) The Prosperous Community – Social Capital and Public Life, *The American Prospect*, 13, pp. 35–42.

Radner, R. and Stiglitz, J. (1983) A Nonconcavity in the Value of Information, in Boyer M. and Kihlstrom R. (eds), *Bayesian Models in Economic Theory* (Amsterdam: North-Holland).

Rao, P. K. (2000a) *Sustainable Development: Economics and Policy* (Oxford: Blackwell).

Rao, P. K. (2000b) *The World Trade Organization and the Environment* (London: Macmillan).

Rao, P. K. (2001) *International Environmental Law and Economics* (Oxford: Blackwell).

Rebelo, S. T. (1991) Long-run Policy Analysis and Long-run Growth, *Journal of Political Economy*, 99, pp. 500–21.

Reynolds, J. (1983) The Spread of Economic Growth to the Third World, 1850–1980, *Journal of Economic Literature*, 21, pp. 941–80.

Rockefeller, R. T. (1970) *Convex Analysis* (Princeton, NJ: Princeton University Press).

Rodrik, D. (1990) How Should Structural Adjustment Programs be Designed?, *World Development*, 18, pp. 933–47.

Rodrik, D. (1996) Understanding Economic Policy Reform, *Journal of Economic Literature*, 34, pp. 9–41.

Rodrik, D. (1999) *The New Global Economy and Developing Countries: Making Openness Work* (Washington, DC: Overseas Development Council).

Santilli, R. M. (1983) *Foundations of Theoretical Mechanics II: Birkhoffian Generalization of Hamiltonian Mechanics* (New York: Springer-Verlag).

Shultz, G. P. and Dam, K. W. (1997) *Economic Policy Beyond the Headlines* (Chicago; Ill.: University of Chicago Press).

Stewart, F. (1995) *Adjustment and Poverty* (New York: Routledge).

Stern, N. (1991) Public Policy and the Economics of Development, *European Economic Review*, 35, pp. 241–71.

Stiglitz, J. (2000) The Contributions of the Economics of Information to the Twentieth Century Economics, *Quarterly Journal of Economics*, 115, pp. 1441–78.

Stiglitz, J. and Weiss, A. (1981) Credit Rationing in Markets with Imperfect Information, *American Economic Review*, 71, pp. 393–410.

Tarp, F. (1993) *Stabilization and Structural Adjustment* (New York: Routledge).

Trefler, D. (1995) The Case of Missing Trade and Other Mysteries, *American Economic Review*, 85, pp. 1029–46.

UN (1997) *International Cooperation to Accelerate Sustainable Development in Developing Countries and Related Domestic Policies*, New York: UN Document E/CN.17/1997/12/Add.1, made available from the UN website.

UNICEF (1992) *State of the World's Children* (New York: Oxford University Press).

Webb, D. C. (1991) Long-term Financial Contracts Can Mitigate Adverse Selection Problems in Project Financing, *International Economic Review*, 32, pp. 305–20.

Williamson, S. D. (1987) Costly Monitoring, Loan Contracts, and Equilibrium Credit Rationing, *Quarterly Journal of Economics*, 102, pp. 135–46.

Wolinsky, A. (1983) Prices as Signals of Product Quality, *Review of Economic Studies*, 50, pp. 647–58.

World Bank (1990) *World Development Report*, (Washington, DC: World Bank).

World Bank (1994) *Adjustment in Africa – Reforms, Results, and the Road Ahead* (New York: Oxford University Press), p. 171.

Zak, P. J. and Knack, S. (2001) Trust and Growth, *Economic Journal*, 111, pp. 295–321.

Zerbe, R. O. Jr and Mc Curdy, H. E. (1999) The Failure of Market Failure, *Journal of Policy Analysis and Management*, 18, pp. 558–78.

5   New Institutional Economics

Aceves, W. J. (1996) An Economic Analysis of International Law – Transaction Cost Economics and the Concept of State Practice, *University of Pennsylvania Journal of International Economic Law*, 17, pp. 995–1068.

Arrow, K. J. (1971) Political and Economic Evaluation of Social Effects and Externalities, in Intrilligator M. D. (ed.), *Frontiers of Quantitative Economics* (Amsterdam: North-Holland), pp. 3–24.

Barzel, Y. (1982) Measurement Costs and the Organization of Markets, *Journal of Law and Economics*, 25, pp. 27–48.

Baumol, W. Panzar J. and Willig R. (1982) *Contestable Markets* (New York: Harcourt Brace Jovanovich).

Bergson, A. (1948) Socialist Economics, in Ellis, H. (ed.), *Survey of Contemporary Economies* (Philadelphia, Pa.: Blakiston) pp. 430–58.

Blankart, C. B. and Knieps, G. (1993) State and Standards, *Public Choice*, 77, pp. 39–52.

Braithwaite, V. and Levi, M. (ed.), (1998) *Trust and Governance* (New York: Russell Sage Foundation).

Buchanan, J. M. (1987) *Economics – Between Predictive Science and Moral Philosophy* (College Station, Texas: Texas A & M University Press).

Cairns, R. D. and Long, N. V. (1991) Rent Seeking with Uncertain Opposition, *European Economic Review*, 35, pp. 1223–35.

Coase, R. H. (1937) The Nature of the Firm, *Economica*, 4, pp. 386–405.

Coase, R. H. (1988) *The Firm, the Market and the Law* (Chicago, Ill.: University of Chicago Press).

Davis, L. and North, D. (1971) *Institutional Change and American Economic Growth* (Cambridge University Press).

De Alessi, L. (1983) Property Rights, Transaction Costs, and X-Efficiency: An Essay in Economic Theory, *American Economic Review*, 73, pp. 64–81.

Demsetz, H. (1968) Why Regulate Utilities?, *Journal of Law and Economics*, 11, pp. 55–65.

Dixit, A. (1998) *The Making of Economic Policy: A Transaction-Cost Politics Perspective* (Cambridge, Mass.: MIT Press).

Dunoff, J. L. and Trachtman, J. P. (1999) Economic Analysis of International Law, *The Yale Journal of International Law*, 24, pp. 1–59.

Eggertsson, T. (1989) *Economic Behavior and Institutions* (Cambridge University Press).

Eggertsson, T. (1990) The Role of Transaction Costs and Property Rights in Economic Analysis, *European Economic Review*, 34, pp. 450–7.

Feige, E. L. (1990) Defining and Estimating Underground and Informal Economies: The New Institutional Economics Approach, *World Development*, 18, pp. 989–1002.

Fleming, M. H., Roman, J. and Farrell, G. (2000) The Shadow Economy, *Journal of International Affairs*, 53, pp. 387–412.

Fukuyama, F. (1995) *Trust: Social Virtues and Creation of Prosperity* (New York: Free Press).

Hart, H. L. A. (1961) *The Concept of Law* (Oxford: Clarendon Press).

Hodgson, G. M. (1998) The Approach of Institutional Economics, *Journal of Economic Literature*, 36, pp. 166–92.

Hurwicz, L. (1972) On Informationally Decentralized Systems, in McGuire, C. and Radner, R. (eds), *Decision and Organization* (Amsterdam: North-Holland), pp. 297–336.

Keohane, R. O. (1988) International Institutions: Two Approaches, *International Studies Quarterly*, 32, pp. 379–98.

Knack, S. and Keefer, P. (1997) Does Social Capital have an Economic Payoff? A Country Investigation, *Quarterly Journal of Economics*, 112, pp. 1251–88.

Krueger, A. (1974) The Political Economy of Rent-Seeking Society, *American Economic Review*, 64, pp. 292–303.

Lahno, B. (1995) Trust, Reputation and Exit in Exchange Relationships, *Journal of Conflict Resolution*, 39, pp. 495–510.

Lange, O. (1938) On the Theory of Economic Socialism, pp. 55–143, in Lippincott, B., *On the Economic Theory of Socialism* (Minneapolis, Minn.: University of Minnesota Press).

Leibenstein, H. (1966) Allocative Efficiency vs. 'X-Efficiency', *American Economic Review*, 56, pp. 392–415.

Leibenstein, H. (1978) On the Basic Proposition of X-Efficiency Theory, *American Economic Review Papers and Proceedings*, 68, pp. 328–34.

Lerner, A. (1934) Economic Theory and Socialist Economy, *Review of Economic Studies*, 1, pp. 51–61.

Majone, G. (2001) Nonmajoritarian Institutions and the Limits of Democratic Governance: A Political Transaction-Cost Approach, *Journal of Institutional and Theoretical Economics*, 157, pp. 57–78.

Milgrom, P. and Roberts, J. (1988) Economic Theories of the Firm: Past, Present, and Future, *Canadian Journal of Economics*, 11, pp. 444–58.

North, D. (1990) A Transaction-Cost Theory of Politics, *Journal of Theoretical Politics*, 2, pp. 355–67.

North, D. (1993) Institutions and Credible Commitment, *Journal of Institutional and Theoretical Economics*, 149, pp. 11–23.

North, D. (1999) Dealing with a Non-Ergodic World: Institutional Economics, Property Rights, and the Global Environment, *Duke Environmental Law and Policy Forum*, 10, pp. 1–12.

Posner, R. (1993) New Institutional Economics meets Law and Economics, *Journal of Institutional and Theoretical Economics*, 149, pp. 73–87.

Postema, G. J. (1982) Coordination and Convention at the Foundations of Law, *Journal of Legal Studies*, 11, pp. 165–203.

Rao, P. K. (2001) *International Environmental Law and Economics* (Oxford: Blackwell).

Rodrik, D. (1990) How Should Structural Adjustment Programs be Designed?, *World Development*, 18, pp. 933–47.

Ruttan, V. W. (1988) Cultural Endowments and Economic Development: What Can We Learn from Anthropology?, *Economic Development and Cultural Change*, 36, pp. S247–S271.

Schaffer, M. E. (1989) Are Profit Maximizers the Best Survivors? A Darwinian Model of Economic Natural Selection, *Journal of Economic Behavior and Organization*, 12, pp. 29–45.

Schneider, F. and Enste, D. H. (2000) Shadow Economies: Size, Causes, and Consequences, *Journal of Economic Literature*, 38, pp. 77–114.

Schumpeter, J. (1942) *Capitalism, Socialism, and Democracy* (New York: Harper & Row).

Seligman, A. B. (1997) *The Problem of Trust* (Princeton, NJ: Princeton University Press).

Shapiro, K. and Muller, J. (1977) Sources of Technical Efficiency: The Role of Modernization and Information, *Economic Development and Cultural Change*, 25, pp. 293–310.

Snidal, D. (1996) Political Economy and International Institutions, *International Review of Law and Economics*, 16, pp. 121–38.

Stigler, G. J. (1976) The Xistence of X-Efficiency, *American Economic Review*, 66, pp. 213–16.

Tullock, G. (1967) The Welfare Cost of Tariffs, Monopolies, and Theft, *Western Economic Journal*, 5, pp. 224–32.

Wiggins, S. N. (1991) The Economics of the Firm and Contracts: A Selective Survey, *Journal of Institutional and Theoretical Economics*, 147, pp. 603–61.

Williamson, O. E. (1996) *The Mechanisms of Governance* (New York: Oxford University Press).

Williamson, O. E. (1998) Transaction Cost Economics: How It Works, Where It Is Headed, *De Economist*, 146, pp. 23–58.

Williamson, O. E. (2000) The New Institutional Economics: Taking Stock, Looking Ahead, *Journal of Economic Literature*, 38, pp. 595–613.

Witt, U. (1986) Evolution and Stability of Cooperation without Enforceable Contracts, *Kyklos*, 39, pp. 245–66.

Wolf, C. Jr (1988) *Markets or Governments – Choosing Between Imperfect Alternatives*, (Cambridge, Mass.: MIT Press).

Yarbrough, B. V. and Yarbrough, R. M. (1990) International Institutions and the New Economics of Organization, *International Organization*, 44, pp. 235–259.

6 Law and Economics

Anderlini, L., and Felli, L. (1994) Incomplete Written Contracts: Undescribable States of Nature, *Quarterly Journal of Economics*, 109, pp. 1085–124.

Bercovitz, J. E. L. (1999) An Analysis of the Contract Provisions in Business-Format Franchise Agreements, in Stanworth, J. and Purdy, D. (eds), *Franchising Beyond the Millennium: Learning Lessons from the Past. Proceedings of the 13th Conference of the Society of Franchising*, cited in Masten, S. E. and Saussier, S. (2000).

Calabresi, G. and Melamed, A. D. (1972) Property Rules, Liability Rules, and Inalienability: One view of the Cathedral, *Harvard Law Review*, 85, pp. 1089–120.

Chen, Y. (2000) Promises, Trust, and Contracts, *Journal of Law, Economics and Organization*, 16, pp. 209–32.

Coase, R. H. (1937) The Nature of the Firm, *Economica*, 4, pp. 386–405.

Coase, R. H. (1960) The Problem of Social Cost, *Journal of Law and Economics*, 3, pp. 1–44.

Cordato, R. E. (1998) Time Passage and the Economics of Coming to the Nuisance – Reassessing the Coasean Perspective, *Campbell Law Review*, 20, pp. 273–92.

Crocker, K. J. and Masten, S. E. (1988) Mitigating Contractual Hazard: Unilateral Options and Contract Length, *Rand Journal of Economics*, 19, pp. 327–43.

Demsetz, H. (1966) Some Aspects of Property Rights, *Journal of Law and Economics*, 9, pp. 61–71; also reprinted in Manne, G. (ed.), (1975), pp. 184–93.

Demsetz, H. (1967) Towards a Theory of Property Rights, *American Economic Review*, 57, pp. 347–60; reprinted also in Manne, G. (ed.), (1975), pp. 23–36.

Demsetz, H. (1972) When Does the Rule of Liability Matter?, *Journal of Legal Studies*, 1, pp. 13–28; also reprinted in Manne, G. (ed.), (1975), pp. 168–83.

Dunoff, J. L. and Trachtman, J. P. (1999) Economic Analysis of International Law, *Yale Journal of International Law*, 24, pp. 1–59.

Eggertsson, T. (1989) *Economic Behavior and Institutions* (Cambridge University Press).

Fournier, G. M. and Zuehlke, T. W. (1989) Litigation and Settlement – An Empirical Approach, *Review of Economics and Statistics*, 71(2), pp. 189–95.

Furubotn, E. G. and Pejovich, S. (1972) Property Rights and Economic Theory: A Survey of Recent Literature, *Journal of Economic Literature*, 10, pp. 1138–1170.

Goetz, C. and Scott, R. (1981) Principles of Relational Contracts, *Virginia Law Review*, 67, pp. 1089–150.

Haas, P. (1980) Why Collaborate? Issue Linkage and International Regimes, *World Politics*, 32, pp. 355–67.

Hardin, G. H. (1968) The Tragedy of the Commons, *Science*, 162, pp. 1243–8.

Heller, M. A. (1998) The Tragedy of Anticommons, *Harvard Law Review*, 111, pp. 621–88.

Hovenkamp, H. (1990) Marginal Utility and the Coase Theorem, *Cornell Law Review*, 75, pp. 783–810.

Hylton, K. N. (1996) A Missing Markets Theory of Tort Law, *Northwestern University Law Review*, 90, pp. 977–1008.

Jensen, M. C. and Meckling, W. H. (1976) Theory of the Firm: Managerial Behavior, Agency Costs and Ownership Structure, *Journal of Financial Economics*, 3, pp. 305–60.

Joskow (1985) Vertical Integration in Long term Contracts: The Case of Coal Burning Electric Generating Plants, *Journal of Law, Economics and Organization*, 33, pp. 33–80.

Klausner, M. (1995) Corporations, Corporate Law, and Networks of Contracts, *Virginia Law Review*, 81, pp. 757–852.

Landes, W. M. and Posner, R. A. (1987) *The Economic Structure of Tort Law* (Cambridge, Mass.: Harvard University Press).

Lyons, B. (1996) Empirical Relevance of Efficient Contract Theory: Inter-firm Contracts, *Oxford Review of Economic Policy*, 12, pp. 27–52.

Macneil, I. (1981) Economic Analysis of Contractual Relations: Its Shortfalls and the need for a 'Rich' Classificatory Apparatus, *Northwestern University Law Review*, 75, pp. 1018–63.

Mahoney, P. G. (2001) The Common Law and Economic Growth: Hayek Might Be Right, *Journal of Legal Studies*, 30, pp. 503–20.

Manne, H. G (ed.) (1975) *The Economics of Legal Relationships: Readings in the Theory of Property Rights* (New York: West Publishing).

Maskin, E. and Tirole, J. (1999) Two Remarks on the Property Rights Literature, *Review of Economic Studies*, 66, pp. 139–49.

Masten, S. E. (1984) The Organization of Production: Evidence from the Aerospace Industry, *Journal of Law and Economics*, 27, pp. 403–17.

Masten, S. E. and Saussier, S. (2000) Econometrics of Contracts: An Assessment of Developments in the Empirical Literature on Contracting, *Revue D'Economie Industrielle*, 92, pp. 215–36.

Mattei, U. (1997) *Comparative Law and Economics* (Ann Arbor, Mich.: University of Michigan Press).

Milgrom, P. and Roberts, J. (1988) Economic Theories of the Firm: Past, Present, and Future, *Canadian Journal of Economics*, 11, pp. 444–58.

Milgrom, P. and Roberts, J. (1990) Bargaining Costs, Influence Costs, and the Organization of Economic Activity, in Alt, J. and Shepsle, K. (eds), *Perspectives on Positive Political Economy* (Cambridge University Press), pp. 57–89.

Monteverde, K. and Teece, D. J. (1982) Supplier Switching Costs and Vertical Integration in the Automobile Industry, *Bell Journal of Economics*, 13, pp. 206–13.

North, D. C. (1992) 'Institutions and Economic Theory', *The American Economist*, 36, pp. 3–6.

Polinsky, M. A. and Shavell, S. (1998) Punitive Damages: An Economic Analysis, *Harvard Law Review*, 111, pp. 870–962.

Rao, P. K. (2001) *International Environmental Law and Economics* (Oxford: Blackwell).

Samuels, W. J. (1992) *Essays on the Role of Government, Vol. 2* (New York: New York University Press).

Saussier, S. (1998) La durée des contrats interentreprises, *Economie et Prevision*, 137–46.

Saussier, S. (1999) Transaction Cost Economics and Contract Duration: An Empirical Analysis of EDF Coal Contracts, *Louvain Economic Review*, 65, pp. 3–21.

Saussier, S. (2000a) When Incomplete Contract Theory Meets Transaction Cost Economics: A Test, in Menard, C. (ed.), *Institutions, Contracts and Organizations* (Cheltenham: Edward Elgar), pp. 376–98.

Saussier, S. (2000b) Transaction Costs and Contractual Incompleteness: The Case of Electricite de France, *Journal of Economic Behavior and Organization*, 42, pp. 189–206.

Schwartz, A. (1992) Legal Contract Theories and Incomplete Contracts, in Werin, L. and Wijkander, H. (eds), *Contact Economics* (Oxford: Blackwell), pp. 76–108.

Shavell, S. (1982) Suit, Settlement, and Trial: A Theoretical Analysis under Alternative Methods for the Allocation of Legal Costs, *Journal of Legal Studies*, 11, pp. 55–81.

Stubblebine, W. C. (1975) On Property Rights and Institutions, in Manne (ed.), *op cit.*, pp. 11–22.

Sunstein, C. (1997) *Free Markets and Social Justice* (New York: Oxford University Press).

Tirole, J. (1999) Incomplete Contracts: Where Do We Stand?, *Econometrica*, 67, pp. 741–81.

Tirole, J. (1988) *The Theory of Industrial Organization* (Cambridge, Mass.: MIT Press).

Wiggins, S. N. (1991) The Economics of the Firm and Contracts: A Selective Survey, *Journal of Institutional and Theoretical Economics*, 147, pp. 603–61.

Wiggins, S. N. (1990) The Comparative Advantage of Long-term Contracts and Firms, *Journal of Law, Economics, and Organization*, 6, pp. 155–70.

Williamson, O. E. (1975) *Markets and Hierarchies* (New York: Free Press).

Williamson, O. E. (1985) *The Economic Institutions of Capitalism* (New York: Free Press).

Williamson, O. E. (1996) *The Mechanisms of Governance* (New York: Oxford University Press).

Wolf, C. Jr (1988) *Markets or Governments – Choosing Between Imperfect Alternatives* (Cambridge, Mass.: MIT Press).

7 Behavioural Economics

Amihud, Y. and Mendelson, H. (1986) Asset Pricing and the Bid–Ask Spread, *Journal of Financial Economics*, 17, pp. 223–49.

Bagehot, W. (1971) The Only Game in Town, *Financial Analysts Journal*, 27, pp. 31–53.

Blankart, C. B. and Knieps, G. (1993) State and Standards, *Public Choice*, 77, pp. 39–52.

Bowles, S. (1998) Endogenous Preferences: The Cultural Consequences of Markets and other Economic Institutions, *Journal of Economic Literature*, 36, pp. 75–111.

Buchanan, J. M. (1987) *Economics – Between Predictive Science and Moral Philosophy* (College Station, Texas: Texas A & M University Press).

Campbell, J. Y. (2000) Asset Pricing at the Millennium, *Journal of Finance*, 55, pp. 1515–67.

Cyert, R. M. and March, J. G. (1963) *A Behavioral Theory of the Firm* (Englewood Cliffs, NJ: Prentice-Hall).

Demsetz, H. (1968) The Cost of Transacting, *Quarterly Journal of Economics*, 82, pp. 33–53.

Fehr, E. and Gachter, S. (1998) Reciprocity and Economics: The Economic Implications of *Homo Reciprocans*, *European Economic Review*, 42, pp. 845–59.

Fehr, E., Gachter, S. and Kirchsteiger, S. (1997) Reciprocity as a Contract Enforcement Device, *Econometrica*, 65, pp. 833–60.

Glosten, L. R. and Milgrom, P. R. (1985) Bid, Ask and Transaction Prices in a Specialist Market with Heterogeneously Informed Traders, *Journal of Financial Economics*, 14, pp. 71–100.

Greif, A. (1997) Cultural Beliefs as a Common Resource in an Integrating World, in Dasgupta, P., Maler, K. G. and Vercelli, A. (eds), *The Economics of Transnational Commons* (Oxford: Clarendon Press), pp. 238–96.

Hahn, R. W. and Hird, J. A. (1991) The Costs and Benefits of Regulation: Review and Synthesis, *Yale Journal on Regulation*, 8, pp. 233–78.

Hirschman, A. O. (1985) Against Parsimony: Three Easy Ways of Complicating Some Categories of Economic Discourse, *Economics and Philosophy*, 1, pp. 7–21.

Holly, S. and Hallett, A. H. (1989) *Optimal Control, Expectations and Uncertainty* (Cambridge University Press).

Jorgenson, D. W. and Wilcoxen, W. (1990) Environmental Regulation and U.S. Economic Growth, *Rand Journal of Economics*, 21, pp. 314–350.

Kahneman, D. and Tverskey, A. (1979) Prospect Theory: An Analysis of Decision Under Risk, *Econometrica*, 47, pp. 263–92.

Kaplow, L. (1992) Rules versus Standards – An Economic Analysis, *Duke Law Journal*, 42, pp. 557–629.

Kydland, F. E. and Prescott, E. C. (1977) Rules Rather Than Discretion: The Inconsistency of Optimal Plans, *Journal of Political Economy*, 85, pp. 473–91.

Platteau, J.-P. (1994) Behind the Market Stage where Real Societies Exist – I & II, *Journal of Development Studies*, 30, pp. 533–77, 753–817.

Pollak, R. A. (1968) Consistent Planning, *Review of Economic Studies*, 35, pp. 201–8.

Rao, P. K. (2000) *Sustainable Development: Economics and Policy* (Oxford: Blackwell).

Rao, P. K. (2001) *International Environmental Law and Economics* (Oxford: Blackwell).

Roberds, W. (1987) Models of Policy under Stochastic Replanning, *International Economic Review*, 28, pp. 731–55.

Rubinstein, A. and Wolinsky, A. (1982) Renegotiation-proof Implementation and Time Preferences, *American Economic Review*, 82, pp. 600–14.

Schaeffer, M. E. (1989) Are Profit Maximizers the Best Survivors? A Darwinian Model of Economic Natural Selection, *Journal of Economic Behavior and Organization*, 12, pp. 29–45.

Stoll, H. R. (2000) Friction, *Journal of Finance*, 55, pp. 1479–1514.

Strotz, R. H. (1956) Myopia and Inconsistency in Dynamic Utility Maximization, *Review of Economic Studies*, 23, pp. 167–77.

Sunstein, C. (1993) Endogenous Preferences, Environmental Law, *Journal of Legal Studies*, 22, pp. 217–54.

Warneryd, K. (1994) Transaction Cost, Institutions, and Evolution, *Journal of Economic Behavior and Organization*, 25, pp. 219–39.

Williamson, O. E. (1985) *The Economic Institutions of Capitalism* (New York: Free Press).

Williamson, O. E. (1996) *The Mechanisms of Governance* (New York: Oxford University Press).

Young, H. P. (1995) The Economics of Convention, *Journal of Economic Perspectives*, 10, pp. 105–22.

Young, H. P. (1998) *Individual Strategy and Social Structure – An Evolutionary Theory of Institutions* (Princeton, NJ: Princeton University Press).

8 Organizations Theory

Barnard, C. (1938) *The Functions of the Executive* (Cambridge, Mass.: Harvard University Press).

Eisenhardt, K. M. and Martin, J. A. (2000) Dynamic Capabilities: What Are They?, *Strategic Management*, 21, pp. 1105–21.

Furubotn, E. G. and Richter, R. (2000) *Institutions and Economic Theory* (Ann Arbor, Mich.: University of Michigan Press).

Guinnane, T. W. (2001) Cooperatives as Information Machines: German Rural Credit Cooperatives 1883–1914, *Journal of Economic History*, 61, pp. 366–89.

Hayek, F. (1945) The Use of Knowledge in Society, *American Economic Review*, 35, pp. 519–30.

Hurwicz, L. (1972) On Informationally Decentralized Systems, in McGuire, C. and Radner, R. (eds), *Decision and Organization* (Amsterdam: North-Holland), pp. 297–336.

Hurwicz, L. (1979) The Design of Mechanisms for Resource Allocation, in Intrilligator, M. D. (ed.), *Frontiers in Quantitative Economics* (Amsterdam: North-Holland), pp. 3–42.

Laffont, J. J. and Martimort, D. (1998) Transaction Costs, Institutional Design and the Separation of Powers, *European Economic Review*, 42, pp. 673–84.

Milgrom, P. and Roberts, J. (1990) Bargaining Costs, Influence Costs, and the Organization of Economic Activity, in Alt, J. and Shepsle, K. (eds), *Perspectives on Positive Political Economy* (Cambridge University Press), pp. 57–89.

Nelson, R. R. and Winter, S. G. (1982) *An Evolutionary Theory of Economic Change* (Cambridge, Mass.: Belknap Press).

North, D. (1990) A Transaction-Cost Theory of Politics, *Journal of Theoretical Politics*, 2, pp. 355–67.

Pryor, F. L. (1994) Growth Deceleration and Transaction Costs: A Note, *Journal of Economic Behavior and Organization*, 25, pp. 121–33.

Rao, P. K. (1978) Hierarchical and Decentralised Planning and Decision-Making: A Synthesis of Analytical Models, in Titli, A. (ed.), *Control and Management of Integrated Industrial Complexes* (Oxford: Pergamon Press), pp. 237–48.

Rockefeller, R. T. (1970) *Convex Analysis* (Princeton, NJ: Princeton University Press).

Teece, D. J., Pisano, G. and Shuen, A. (1997) Dynamic Capabilities and Strategic Management, *Strategic Management Journal*, 18, pp. 509–34.

Varian, H. (1990) Monitoring Agents with Other Agents, *Journal of Institutional and Theoretical Economics*, 146, pp. 153–74.

Williamson, O. E. (1996) *The Mechanisms of Governance* (New York: Oxford University Press).

Winter, S. G. (2000) The Satisficing Principle in Capability Learning, *Strategic Management Journal*, 21, pp. 981–96.

Yarbrough, B. V. and Yarbrough, R. M. (1994) International Contracting and Territorial Control: The Boundary Question, *Journal of Institutional and Theoretical Economics*, 150, pp. 239–64.

9   Environmental Economics

Aidt, T. (1998) Political Internalization of Economic Externalities and Environmental Policy, *Journal of Public Economics*, 69, pp. 1–16.

Aronsson, T. and Lofgren, K. G. (1995) National Product Related Welfare Measures in the Presence of Technological Change, *Environmental and Resource Economics*, 5, pp. 321–32.

Asheim, G. B. (1994) Net National Product as an Indicator of Sustainability, *Scandinavian Journal of Economics*, 96, pp. 257–65.

Blackburn, J. W. and Bruce, W. M. (eds) (1995) *Mediating Environmental Conflicts: Theory and Practice* (Westport, Conn.: Quorum Books).

Boadu, F. O. (1998) Relational Characteristics of Transboundary Water Treaties: Lesotho's Water Transfer Treaty with the Republic of South Africa, *Natural Resources Journal*, 38, pp. 381–409.

Buchanan, J. M. and Yoon, Y. J. (2000) Symmetric Tragedies: Commons and Anticommons, *Journal of Law and Economics*, 43, pp. 1–13.

Coase, R. H. (1960) The Problem of Social Cost, *Journal of Law and Economics*, 3, pp. 1–44.

Dales, J. (1968) *Pollution, Property, Prices* (Toronto: University Press of Toronto).

Demsetz, H. (1972) When Does the Rule of Liability Matter?, *Journal of Legal Studies*, 1, pp. 13–28.

DeSerpa, A. C. (1994) Pigou and Coase – A Mathematical Reconciliation, *Journal of Public Economics*, 54, pp. 267–86.

Dudek, D. J. and Wiener, J. B. (1996) *Joint Implementation, Transaction Costs, and Climate Change*, OECD Document OECD/GD (96) 173 (Paris: OECD Secretariat).

Gangadharan, L. (2000) Transaction Costs in Pollution Markets: An Empirical Study, *Land Economics*, 76, pp. 601–14.

Hahn, R. W. and Hester, G. L. (1989) Marketable Permits: Lessons for Theory and Practice, *Ecology Law Quarterly*, 16, pp. 361–406.

Hardin, G. (1968) The Tragedy of the Commons, *Science*, 162, pp. 124–48.

Hartwick, J. (1977) Intergenerational Equity and the Investing of Rents from Exhaustible Resources, *American Economic Review*, 67, pp. 972–74.

Heller, M. A. (1998) The Tragedy of the Anticommons: Property in the Transition from Marx to Markets, *Harvard Law Review*, 111, pp. 621–88.

Just, R. E., Hueth, D. L. and Schmitz, A. (1982) *Applied Welfare Economics and Public Policy* (Englewood Cliffs, NJ: Prentice-Hall).

Low, P. (1993) *Trading Free: The GATT and US Trade Policy* (New York: Twentieth Century Fund).

Marion, J. B. and Thornton, S. T. (1995) *Classical Dynamics of Particles and Systems* (New York: Harcourt Bruce).

Montero, J. P. (1997) Marketable Pollution Permits with Uncertainty and Transaction Costs, *Resource and Energy Economics*, 20, pp. 27–50.

Montgomery, W. D. (1972) Markets in Licenses Efficient Pollution Control Programs, *Journal of Economic Theory*, 5, pp. 395–418.

Nalebuff, B. (1997) On a Clear Day, You Can See the Coase Theorem, in Dasgupta, P. and Maler, K. G. (eds), *The Environment and Emerging Development Issues* (Oxford: Clarendon Press), pp. 35–47.

North, D. (1999) Dealing with a Non-Ergodic World: Institutional Economics, Property Rights, and the Global Environment, *Duke Environmental Law and Policy Forum*, 10, pp. 1–12.

Ostrom, E. (1990) *Governing the Commons: The Evolution of Institutions for Collective Action* (New York: Cambridge University Press).

Rao, P. K. (2000a) *Sustainable Development: Economics and Policy* (Oxford: Blackwell).

Rao, P. K. (2000b) *The World Trade Organization and the Environment* (London: Macmillan).

Rao, P. K. (2000c) *The Economics of Global Climatic Change* (Armonk, NY: M. E. Sharpe).

Rao, P. K. (2001) *International Environmental Law and Economics* (Oxford: Blackwell).

Samuelson, P. A. (1961) The Evaluation of 'Social Income' – Capital Formation and Wealth, in Lutz, F. and Hague, D. (eds), *The Theory of Capital* (New York: St Martin's Press).

Samuelson, P. A. (1990) Two Conservation Laws in Theoretical Economics, in Sato, R. and Ramachandran, R. (eds), *Conservation Laws and Symmetry – Applications to Economics and Finance* (Boston, Mass.: Kluwer), pp. 57–70.

Sato, R. (1990) The Invariance Principle and Income–Wealth Conservation Laws, in Sato and Ramachandran (eds), *Conservation Laws and Symmetry*, pp. 71–106.

Sefton, J. A. and Weale, M. R. (1996) The Net National Product and Exhaustible Resources – the Effects of Foreign Trade, *Journal of Public Economics*, 61, pp. 21–47.

Solow, R. M. (1986) On the Intergenerational Allocation of Natural Resources, *Scandinavian Journal of Economics*, 88, pp. 141–9.

Solow, R. M. (1994) An Almost Practical Step Towards Sustainability, in *Assigning Economic Values to Natural Resources* (Washington, DC: National Acdamey Press).

Stavins, R. N. (1995) Transaction Costs and Tradeable Permits, *Journal of Environmental Economics and Management*, 29, pp. 133–48.

Thompson, D. B. (1999) Beyond Benefit–Cost Analysis: Institutional Transaction Costs and Regulation of Water Quality, *Natural Resources Journal*, 39, pp. 517–41.

UNCTAD (1994) *Combating Global Warming: Possible Rules, Regulations and Administrative Arrangements for a Global Market in* CO_2 *Emission Entitlement,* UNCTAD Report GID/8 (Geneva: UNCTAD).

US President, (1998) *Economic Report of the US President 1998* (Washington, DC: US GPO).

Weitzman, M. L. (1976) On the Welfare Significance of National Product in a Dynamic Economy, *Quarterly Journal of Economics,* 90, pp. 156–62.

10   Perspectives

Arnott, R. and Stiglitz, J. E. (1991) Moral Hazard and Nonmarket Institutions: Dysfunctional Crowding Out After Monitoring, *American Economic Review,* 81, pp. 179–90.

Dahlman, C. (1979) The Problem of Externality, *Journal of Law and Economics,* 22, pp. 141–62.

Frydman, R. and Rapacynski, A. (1993) Privatization in Eastern Europe, *Finance and Development,* 6, pp. 10–13.

Stiglitz, J. E. (2000) The Contributions of the Economics of Information to the Twentieth Century Economics, *Quarterly Journal of Economics,* 115, pp. 1441–78.

Warneryd, K. (1994) Transaction Cost, Institutions, and Evolution, *Journal of Economic Behavior and Organization,* 25, pp. 219–39.

Williamson, O. E. (1998) Transaction Cost Economics: How it Works; Where It Is Headed, *De Economist,* 146, pp. 23–58.

Index

157, 158, 164, 165, 168, 170, 173, 174

Vertical integration   7, 14, 28, 30, 31, 121

Wealth effect   47, 51, 56

X-efficiency   89, 99, 100